ORNAMENTALISM

Clarkson N. Potter, Inc./Publishers
DISTRIBUTED BY CROWN PUBLISHERS, INC.
NEW YORK

THE NEW DECORATIVENESS IN ARCHITECTURE & DESIGN

ORNAMENTALISM

BY ROBERT JENSEN & PATRICIA CONWAY

FOREWORD BY PAUL GOLDBERGER

DESIGN BY HERMANN STROHBACH

The photographs on pages 14 (top right), 206, 207, and 208 are from *The Art of Decorative Stenciling* by Adele Bishop and Cile Lord. Copyright © 1976 and in all countries of the International Copyright Union by Adele Bishop and Cile Lord. Reprinted by permission of Viking Penguin Inc.

Back jacket photo credits, from top, left to right: (no credit), Peter Aaron (ESTO), Wayne Berg; Kenneth M. Hay, (no credit), (no credit); Stan Ries, (no credit), D. James Dee

Endpapers after Valerie Jaudon, "Canton," 1979, oil on canvas, 72 × 72 in. See also page 247.

Title page: Albert Paley, portal gates, 1974, forged, fabricated and inlaid mild steel, brass, bronze and copper, 90½ × 72½ in. Installed in the Smithsonian Institution's Renwick Gallery, Washington, D.C.

Published by Clarkson N. Potter, Inc., One Park Avenue, New York, New York 10016, and simultaneously in Canada by General Publishing Company Limited

Manufactured in Japan by Toppan Printing Company, Inc.

Library of Congress Cataloging in Publication Data

Jensen, Robert, 1938-
Ornamentalism: the new decorativeness in architecture & design

1. Decoration and ornament, Architectural. 2. Decoration and ornament—History—20th century. 3. Architecture, Postmodern. I. Conway, Patricia. II. Title.
NA3485.J46 1982 729'.09'04 82-7508
ISBN: 0-517-54383-4 AACR2

10 9 8 7 6 5 4 3 2 1

First Edition

To Jane West

Contents

Public Buildings & Spaces

THE DECORATIVE CRAFTS

Glasswork

Wrought-Ironwork

FURNISHINGS & LIGHTING 211

PATTERNING, DECORATION & USABLE ART 239

All dimensions are given in order of height x width x depth

Acknowledgments

To describe a subject so unsettled as the current state of Modern design—even when that description is based in an admittedly selective point of view—is not an easy task. Fortunately we have had the benefit of moral support and inspiration from many friends and colleagues whose ideas have been invaluable to us in compiling this book. To name them all would be impractical, but there are a few whose contributions it would be remiss not to acknowledge with a special thanks.

We are grateful to Max Kozloff, William Pedersen, and Arthur May for sharing with us thoughts that enriched our perceptions as the book progressed. The comments of Nory Miller and Brian Percival, who took time to read early drafts of the text, were also helpful in this regard, as was the historical research of Linda Yankoschuk, Maryann Alheidt and Paul Rotstein. Current investigation was aided by Naomi Leff, who made available extensive files; Marie-Monique Steckel, whose sleuthing in galleries around the country turned up work we might otherwise have missed; and Judy Coady, whose knowledge of contemporary craft furniture has been enormously helpful.

Without the cooperation of many fine photographers, the breadth of the Ornamental Movement could never have been adequately documented. The generosity of these photographers in making available material over what must have seemed an interminable review period deserves special mention beyond the alphabetical listing of their names in the index of Photography Sources. We are similarly in debt to the hundreds of architects, designers, craftspeople, and artists who responded to our letters and phone calls over the past two years and who, in some cases, interrupted busy schedules for interviews. Although space has not permitted the work of all these people to be shown here, it is their efforts and creative impulses that lie at the heart of this book.

For technical assistance in putting all this material together we wish to thank Ilona Rider, who handled much of the graphic reproduction; Muriel Cuttrell, who redrew numerous plans; Lisa Negri and Natalie Hlavna, who produced the manuscripts; and Betsy Hobby and Donna Rayner, who organized our research mailings. Most especially we are indebted to our art director, Hermann Strohbach, whose involvement has helped to shape this book from its inception and whose unflagging attention to detail has maintained order where chaos continually threatened.

We must admit that none of this could have succeeded but for the indulgence of Patricia Conway's husband, Roger Milgrim, and her sons, Justin and Alexander, who more or less cheerfully endured 104 consecutive weekends of leftovers. To them we offer the prospect of resumed household normalcy and the sincere hope that they will find their sacrifice to have been worthwhile.

One last word on the origins of this book, which predate the coauthor's collaboration. Robert Jensen, who began investigations of the subject at the American Academy in Rome in 1975, first approached *Art Forum* in December 1976 with a proposed article on the ornamental impulse in Modern architecture. Some of his thoughts were summarized in a statement that he later published in the mid-May 1978 issue of the *AIA Journal* as part of a survey entitled "Design Directions: Other Voices." Concurrently but independently, Patricia Conway and Jane West, then publisher of Clarkson N. Potter, Inc., began discussions about a book on the subject. With Jane's strong encouragement and through an introduction by Joyce Kozloff, a mutual friend and artist whose work at that time placed her in the forefront of the Patterning and Decoration Movement, we began our collaboration in late 1979. Jane's boundless enthusiasm for the project and her forceful ideas about the direction it should take guided our efforts through the first draft and until her untimely death in September 1981. Our gratitude to her and our sorrow in her loss are beyond measure. We have been indeed fortunate to find in our editors, Carol Southern and Kathy Powell, the continuity, undiminished support, and ability to realize Jane's vision that have made this book possible.

Robert Jensen and Patricia Conway
New York, May 1982

Foreword

There are a lot of words to describe what is going on right now in architecture and design; Robert Jensen and Patricia Conway have chosen *Ornamentalism*. It is a good word and far more descriptive than the ambiguous "postmodern" that has become so firm a part of the architectural language in the last few years. What Jensen and Conway are telling us is that the urge to decorate, to elaborate, to seek a kind of visual delight, is the central impulse behind most of the architecture and design work laying claim to our attention today, and that the presence of this impulse is what unifies art, architecture, and design at this moment.

So this book is far more than a catalogue of ornament, or of works that use ornament; it is an attempt to shed some light on the state of the art of architecture. It does so, however, without pretense—it does not propose to give us the final word but rather to offer a broad survey, a sense of an increasingly potent and promising direction.

It is too early to say whether this book's basic thesis—that Ornamentalism is the essential characteristic of current architecture and design—will be borne out by history. There are too many streams right now, flowing in too many directions. But there is no question that the new generation of ornamentalists is producing impressive work—work that seems to speak to some very basic yearnings in our culture. These yearnings are not at all as simple as an urge to turn back the clock, to make architecture that looks as if it could have been built in 1880 or 1920; there is some of that, but such pure revivalism is not the essence of the contemporary phenomenon of Ornamentalism. Jensen and Conway correctly understand that there are qualities in the best of this new work that indicate the presence of, and a respect for, the modern experience. We are struggling now to go beyond the puritanical and harsh limits of orthodox Modernism, but we do not do so by pretending it is the nineteenth century.

The best work shown in these pages, such as the three projects in Vienna by Hans Hollein, the Portland Public Service Building by Michael Graves, the Poolhouse by Robert Stern, the Piazza D'Italia by Charles Moore, or the work for Best Products by Hardy Holzman Pfeiffer and Venturi, Rauch and Scott Brown, integrates elements of Modernism with elements of the classical architectural vocabulary, and it does so out of a genuinely pluralistic sensibility. I think there is a sense right now, far more than there was in the years of the International Style's reign, that the sensual aspects of buildings are important, and that buildings are emotional presences as well as intellectual ones. The drive to decorate is an attempt to respond to this recognition as much as it is an urge to tie our new architecture into the larger stream of historical continuity.

Indeed, history itself is not the point—the pluralistic sensibility of this moment comes out of a belief that there are things far more important than stylistic dogma. We are at a time when there is no clear right way and no clear wrong way; the skill of the designer means far more than stylistic choice or adherence to rules. We believe again that the pure visual pleasure of embellishment is no sin—and while that belief alone is no guarantee of quality, it is a welcome beginning.

Paul Goldberger

Ornamentalism: An Introduction

The world is still deceiv'd with ornament.

—*The Merchant of Venice,* William Shakespeare, 1600

Buildings can be made much more noble if one refrains altogether . . . from decorating them.

—*Thoughts on the Origins, Growth and Decline of Decoration in the Fine Arts,* Friedrich August Krubsacius, 1759

It would be greatly for our aesthetic good if we should refrain entirely from the use of ornament for a period of years, in order that our thought might concentrate acutely upon the production of buildings well formed and comely in the nude.

—*Ornament in Architecture,* Louis Sullivan, 1892

Not only is ornament produced by criminals but also a crime is committed through the fact that ornament inflicts serious injury on people's health, on the national budget and hence on cultural evolution.

—*Ornament and Crime,* Adolf Loos, 1908

Less is more.

—Attributed to Ludwig Mies van der Rohe, ca. 1923

Less is a bore.

—*Complexity and Contradiction in Architecture,* Robert Venturi, 1966

Ornament—anathema to Modernist design—is back in style. Long banished as aesthetically retarded, morally reprehensible, or simply the affliction of people who don't know better, ornament is suddenly reappearing in some of the most challenging new architecture, interior design, furniture, crafts, and even the fine arts. After more than a generation of glass boxes, white walls, and functional design, the validity of decorativeness as an *idea* is being reaffirmed. A growing number of architects, designers, and artists are consciously breaking one of the rules in which they themselves have been trained; they are violating the Modernist proscription against ornament. To ornament or decorate today is a radical act, quite the opposite of the conservative act that it has been for most of this century.

It is this renewed interest in patterning and decoration, in applying ornament to the surface of things in a manner not necessarily related to structure or function, that we call Ornamentalism. Evidence of Ornamentalism in architecture, which first appeared in the mid-1960s in the work of then relatively obscure practitioners like Robert Venturi

PHOTO STEVEN ZANE

OPPOSITE: Gargoyle, Chrysler Building, New York City, William Van Alen, architect, completed 1929.

Rendering of the AT&T Corporate Headquarters, New York City. Johnson/Burgee Architects with Simmons Architects. Scheduled to be completed late 1982. Ornamental moldings around entry arch and at top serve no functional purpose, nor does the "Chippendale" top, a controversial departure from unadorned Modern high-rise architecture.

CERVIN ROBINSON

FOREGROUND: The Marine Midland Bank, New York City. Skidmore, Owings & Merrill, architects, completed 1962. BACKGROUND: Woolworth Building. Cass Gilbert, architect, completed 1913. Absence of ornament is a distinguishing feature of Modernist skyscrapers.

and Charles Moore, can now be found on the drawing boards of established commercial firms. Even the high-rise office building—that unadorned inheritor of the modern Bauhaus style in America—is being transformed by polychrome surfaces, decorative patterning, or ornamental masonry as in Philip Johnson and John Burgee's AT&T Headquarters now under construction in New York City.

So serious is the challenge presented by this movement that late in 1980, Skidmore, Owings & Merrill, a giant architectural firm whose glass-and-steel boxes have dominated corporate architecture for the last thirty years, asked the editors of the *Harvard Architecture Review* to chair a private meeting between SOM's top designers and architects Michael Graves, Robert A. M. Stern, Jorge Silvetti, and Steven Peterson whose work rejects the austerity of Modernism in favor of a more ornamented style. While this encounter may not have inspired anything more adventurous than oblique angles in SOM's most recent buildings, and while distinguished senior architects like I. M. Pei may continue to design highly refined examples of pure, unembellished Modernism, the meeting was nonetheless historic. It signaled an acknowledgment in establishment circles of some of the most radical ideas about Modern design since the Bauhaus, and the ascendance of a movement that, beginning fifteen years ago with a few interior renovations, is now making itself felt even in the corporate boardroom.

At the heart of the Ornamental movement is an awakening of the long-suppressed decorative impulse and a desire to reassert the legitimate pleasures that flow from that impulse. Ornamentalism is characterized by a fascination with the surface of things as opposed to their essence; elaboration as opposed to simplicity; borrowing as opposed to originating; sensory stimulation as opposed to intellectual discipline. Sometimes it attempts to fool the eye, favoring humor and illusion over the honest expression of structure and function upon which Modernism has so long insisted. Yet, despite the fact that Ornamentalism rejects the Modernist proscription against ornament, it is not "postmodern" or even antimodern at all. There are other, more fundamental ideals that have sponsored twentieth-century architecture and art, and many of the people whose work is shown in this book are rejecting the proscription against ornament in order to keep these other Modern ideals alive, if possible to lend them new force. How they are doing this, why they are doing this, and the controversy it is causing is an interesting story.

The Ornamental Impulse

The urge to embellish and the love of ornamental effect are basic to human nature. In all ages and cultures the human race has demonstrated a persistent impulse to decorate, whether by appeasing the gods with magical signs or by using false shutters and columns to personalize tract houses. By ornamenting or decorating, people of every society have tried to transform the merely useful into the beautiful, giving meaning and importance to an often drab reality. The universal appeal of ornament is precisely its "uselessness" in the strict functionalist sense of that word. Because ornament is not there to hold things up or make things work, it is not bound by all the utilitarian constraints that threaten, at times, to suffocate us. Ornament is essentially free: free to move the eye, to intrigue the mind, to rest the soul; free simply to delight us.

Though the essence of ornament is its freedom from function, there are a number of practical necessities that ornament is uniquely able to satisfy. The most obvious is the need for identification: telling people what an object or building is, for what purpose it is intended. Ornament can be a wordless sign like a red-and-white striped pole signifying "barber shop." Or it can speak indirectly through sociohistorical associations: for example, broad, monumental steps with high colonnaded porch and pediment have come to signify "important public building." Conversely, because it is stripped of all ornamental clues, a modern bank might easily pass for a dry cleaning establishment or auto parts store, possibly a boon to future recycling but not much help to present users.

In a town- or cityscape, ornament makes places legible, helping people to sort out pathways, districts, and reference points so that, as urbanist Kevin Lynch has explained, "the various parts of a place can be recognized and can be organized into a coherent pattern." Decorative roof treatments help people to pick out individual buildings at a distance. Ornamental moldings, lintels, cornices, and friezes help to distinguish the tops, midportions, and bases of buildings, giving them clear identity at the ground level. Ornamental surrounds emphasize doors and windows, letting people know where to enter a building and, by the modulation of these elements, what to expect inside. Ornament also helps to orient people, telling them which way is in or out, up or down, toward the center or away from the center. Denied the use of ornament, Modern design has had to rely on the

Sidewalk barber pole, Haxtun, Colorado, 1980. A wordless sign becomes ornament.

JOHN MARGOLIES, ESTO

Detroit Northern Savings and Loan Association, Hancock, Michigan. TMP Associates, Inc., architects, completed 1972. Without ornament, buildings must depend on shape alone to tell what they are, where to enter, how to move about.

BALTHAZAR KORAB

manipulation of space and shape alone to tell people what buildings are for and how to move about in them. Often this is a cumbersome task, requiring the invention of private codes that may communicate to other designers but leave most people baffled. Hence the common complaints about modern buildings: we can't tell what they are, how to get in them, or where to go once we're inside.

Another practical use of ornament in architecture is as a scale device: breaking down the overall mass of a building into smaller pieces that relate comfortably to the human observer. In 1952, at a time when it was not very fashionable to say so, critic Henry Hope Reed argued that "it is only with ornament we can obtain a sense of scale; it is only on ornament that the eye can rest; it is only with ornament that the eye can measure." One reason that we enjoy older sections of towns and cities is that their scale "feels right" to us. Even the biggest buildings meant to awe us at a distance—like a late-nineteenth-century courthouse or skyscraper—reveal layers of ornament that become more and more intimate the closer we approach. While twentieth-century construction technology has permitted buildings to achieve greater height and bulk than the world has ever before seen, Modern design theory has, until recently, failed to acknowledge the serious scale problems that such height and bulk create. The renewed interest in architectural ornament is, in part, an attempt to restore human scale to the built environment, to give people some visual reference against which they can measure themselves and not feel overpowered.

There is also the symbolic force of ornament: the ability of ornament to impart to an object or building some meaning beyond its actual time, place, or purpose. For most people, a house is much more than shelter. It is a statement, like clothing or furniture, of self-image; of desired social status, lifestyle, or private fantasy. The roof may keep out the rain, but it is the elaborate lamppost at the front of the drive, the eagle over the door, or the intricate carving on the heirloom table with which people seem to identify.

Yet this simple impulse—the urge to embellish—has been subjected to some amazingly complicated theories over the last two hundred years. Since the Industrial Revolution, the use of ornament has been considered not only a matter of aesthetics and taste, but of moral propriety. Such moral theorizing helped to pave the way for the Modern Movement and, in turn, for the reaction to that movement which is now occurring. To put this in perspective we must go back, if not to our ancestors' cave paintings, at least to the Renaissance.

A Historical Perspective

The monuments of Renaissance and Baroque Europe are covered with ornament, but architects of that period, from about 1400 to 1750, did not think of ornament in the same way we do today. For instance, in his ten books on architecture (*De Re Aedificatoria*, ca. 1450), the Italian architect Leon Battista Alberti defined the "propriety" or essential principle of a building's organization as one of its ornaments. "The chief and first Ornament of any Thing," he said, "is to be free from all Improprieties." Alberti also spoke of a city's plan as one of its most important ornaments. Now, today, we think of "freedom from improprieties" as essential to good design, perhaps, but not as ornament, and certainly we do not consider a city's plan to be an ornament. Even though Alberti also used the word "ornament" to refer to parts of buildings that we do recognize as being ornamental (frescoes, sculpture, painting, furniture), it is clear that his understanding of ornament was substantially different from our own.

To Alberti, it was as if ornament *was* architecture, and architecture *was* ornament. The two words are occasionally synonymous in his writing because his goal was not so much to discriminate between parts of a building as it was to describe that unity which should permeate every stone and act of design in good architecture. He wanted buildings to depict the integration of humanity with God and nature, which was the intellectual and moral ideal of Renaissance culture. Regarding ornament, the architects of the Renaissance thought of wholes, not parts. The whole building in its firmness, its commodity, and its delight was at issue in any design, and its ornament was not merely applied at the

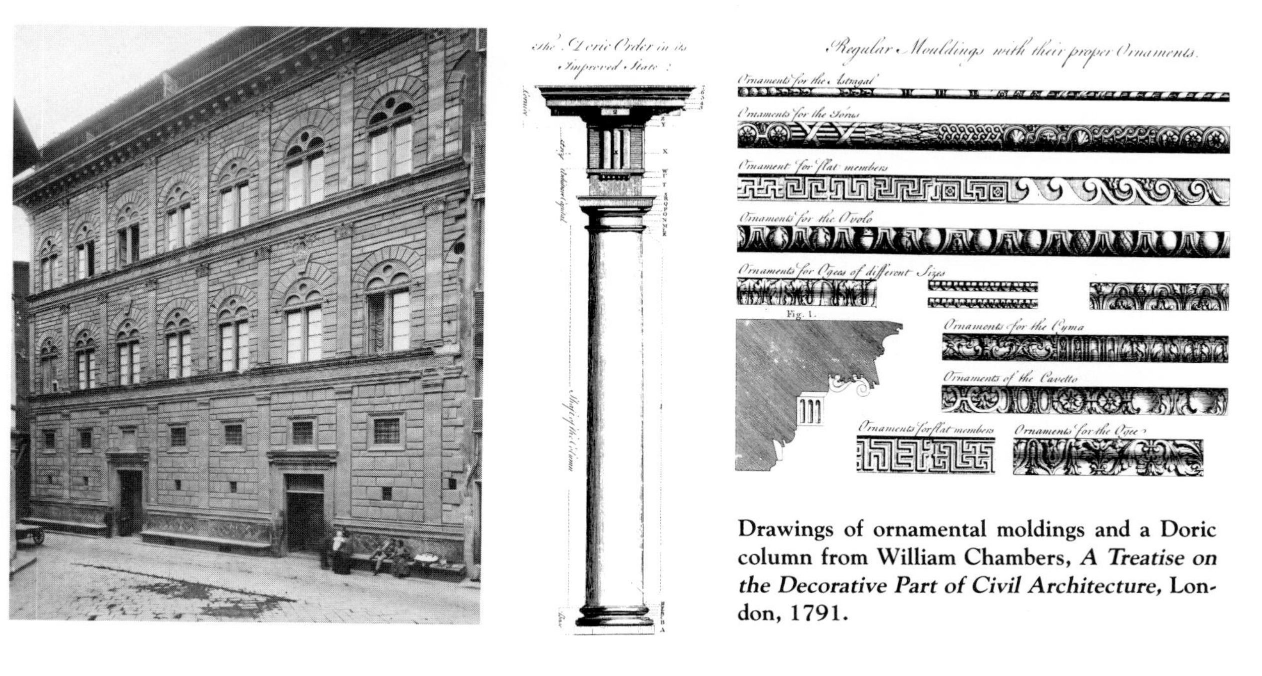

Palazzo Rucellai, Florence, Italy. Leon Battista Alberti, architect, completed 1451. The wall is the ornament and the ornament is the wall.

Drawings of ornamental moldings and a Doric column from William Chambers, *A Treatise on the Decorative Part of Civil Architecture,* London, 1791.

end. The wall *was* the ornament, and the ornament *was* the wall, at once: and the same was true of the column, the window, the doorway, or the ceiling.

Our contemporary understanding of what constitutes ornament or decoration began to develop in the late eighteenth century, long after the Renaissance was over and the Baroque period had declined. From about 1750, and accompanying the Industrial Revolution, there was an intellectual effort to describe and classify phenomena in all fields, and the previous unity of architecture, ornament, and art began to shatter. Archaeological studies of past architecture were undertaken, and the styles of previous historical periods were laboriously dissected and defined. Perhaps *definition* is too precise a term for the intellectual gymnastics that characterize late-eighteenth- and early-nineteenth-century discourses on ornament, but it is nonetheless illuminating to read about what was considered ornament on a building and what was not in this period.

In his influential *Treatise on the Decorative Part of Civil Architecture* (1791), the English architect Sir William Chambers distinguished two kinds of "principal constituent objects" in every architectural composition. The first are those which are basic to construction: columns, walls, beams, joists, rafters, roofs, and so forth.

> All of these are properly distinguished by the appellation of essential parts; and form the first class. The subservient members, contrived for the use and ornament of these, and intended either to support, to shelter, or to unite them gracefully together . . . constitute the second class.

Although Chambers used the word *ornament* in conjunction with what he considered the "second class" of forms, he implied elsewhere and by the title of his treatise that the ornamental parts of a building are much grander than just its decorative details. A building's ornament, according to Chambers, could also be the whole of the Doric, Ionic, or Corinthian order used to compose its façades and spaces. Whichever, Chambers's distinctions helped to establish the notion, still retained in our thinking today, that ornament is separate from and *subservient to* the more "essential" structural or functional forms. For Chambers, the purpose of ornament was to unite the essential forms more gracefully together. We see here the beginnings of our own understanding of what the "correct" use of ornament should be.

A little more than one hundred years later, the English botanist and pattern designer Christopher Dresser (*The Art of Decorative Design*, 1862) heightened this distinction between essential and ornamental forms. "Ornament," he said, "is that which, superadded to utility, renders the ob-

COURTESY NEW YORK PUBLIC LIBRARY

Catalogue illustration of terra-cotta architectural ornament manufactured by Wilcox & Co., Burmantofts, Leeds, 1882.

ARMEN, COURTESY NEWARK MUSEUM

Victoriana: dining room of the Ballantine House, Newark, New Jersey. George Edward Harney, architect, completed 1885. Restored by Rambusch Co., 1976.

ject more acceptable through bestowing upon it an amount of beauty which it would not otherwise possess." In linking ornament directly to "beauty," Dresser was also reinforcing an idea expressed by his better-known contemporary, the critic and social theorist John Ruskin who, in *The Stones of Venice* (1851–53), put it somewhat more gracefully:

> We have no more to do with heavy stones and hard lines; we are going to be happy: to look round in the world and discover what we like best in it, and to enjoy the same at our leisure: to gather it, examine it, fasten all we can of it into imperishable forms, and put it where we may see it forever.
>
> This is to decorate architecture.

Beauty, happiness, pleasure: these were the qualities associated with ornament in the nineteenth century. But, like most of us today, people then were also a bit suspicious of beauty and very much concerned about the propriety or decorum of its use. Ruskin himself criticized much of the ornament being designed in his day because it was misapplied to essential structure; or because he believed it did not spring from that hierarchy of natural sources (from abstract lines found in nature to images of "Mammalian animals and Man") of which he approved; or because it was used merely to display wealth. John Pollard Seddon, a follower of Ruskin, decried the situation in his book *Progress in Art and Architecture with Precedence for Ornament* (1852):

> . . . the modern idea of ornament consists in the simply cramming a certain amount of carved work upon the face of a building without reference to its meaning or propriety, the only aim being to attract the eye of the spectator by the general richness of the effect it produces, and to excite his astonishment at the wealth which can afford so lavish a display.

Seddon was pointing out the architectural consequences of current social changes that, at that time, were not yet fully understood. Under preindustrial conditions, ornament had been a more-or-less accurate proof of an owner's wealth, a correlation which applied in a hierarchy from gold leaf in a banquet hall to a bit of bright paint on a peasant's doorway. But with the Industrial Revolution, this clear correlation began to disintegrate. Ornament, like everything else, began to be made by machines rather than by hand, and it became relatively inexpensive. As the industrial middle class in England expanded, more and more "new rich" or "near rich" could afford to advertise their recently acquired wealth in a manner formerly reserved to people of recognized rank and status. The house of a newly successful mill owner, for example, might display more ornament than a ducal palace.

This distortion of traditional values and loss of aesthetic discrimination was profoundly disturbing to critics of the time, and they began to search for ideas through which the application of ornament might be ordered or regulated. Most of the "battle of the styles" that took place in the late nineteenth century centered around the meaning and propriety of various decorative systems: Gothic, Classic, Romanesque, Egyptian, Chinese. All were explained, studied, advocated, and denounced. But having been separated from the "essential" part of architecture, ornament was free to be whatever people wanted, and could no longer be controlled. The popular taste persisted: if it was ornament that made things *more* beautiful, then increasing all kinds of it everywhere would make things *most* beautiful. Or so the Victorians seemed to think.

By the early twentieth century, writers on the subject of ornament began to recoil from claims about the propriety or morality of ornament, from attempts to establish hierarchies of its goodness or badness. The American architectural historian A. D. F. Hamlin, in his encyclopedic *History of Ornament* (1916–23), offered, instead, this definition:

> By decoration is meant the adornment or embellishment of any object by purposed modifications of its form or color. . . . Pure ornament may be classified according to any of several principles:
>
> a. Its way of covering space
> b. The manner and means of its production
> c. The method or principle of its design
> d. The object to which it is applied
> e. Its relation to structure

At one point Hamlin concluded, "classification is not easy, and perhaps not important." He was right. But our contemporary understanding of the words *ornament* and *decoration* still echoes with the discriminations of the nineteenth century. We continue to define ornament as something *other than* structural, *other than* functional; as something *applied to* structure and function; something technically "useless" but nevertheless having a purpose in that it can make things beautiful. It is this separation of the ornamental from the essential that eventually resounded in some of the theories of the Modern Movement, that revolution in the arts and architecture that began in the last decades of the nineteenth century.

The Modernist Revolt against Ornament

Inspired in part by the revolutionary expression of structure and function in the late-nineteenth-century skyscrapers of American architect Louis Sullivan and the houses of Frank Lloyd Wright, the Modern Movement first took root in Europe where, from about 1910 on, its influence grew under the leadership of figures like Henry van de Velde, Peter Behrens, Walter Gropius, Lazlo Moholy-Nagy, Marcel Breuer, Ludwig Mies van der Rohe, and Le Corbusier. Although elaborate ornamentation and structural rationalism had been combined in early Modern buildings on both sides of the Atlantic (for example, Dankmar Adler and Louis Sullivan's Guaranty Building in Buffalo, completed in 1895, or the Majolica apartments in Vienna completed by Secessionist architect Otto Wagner in 1898), what was to become the mainstream of Modernist thinking in Europe grounded itself firmly in a rejection of ornament, particularly the traditional ornament of the revivalist styles so popular at the turn of the century. The tone of the Modernist argument against ornament was established in a most extraordinary tract written by the Austrian architect Adolf Loos in 1908.

> The child is amoral. To our eyes, the Papuan is too. The Papuan kills his enemies and eats them. He is not a criminal. But when modern man kills someone and eats him, he is either a criminal or a degenerate. The Papuan tattoos his skin, his boat, his paddles, in short everything he can lay hands on. He is not a criminal. The modern man who tattoos himself is either a criminal or a degenerate. . . . What is natural to the Papuan and the child is a symptom of degeneracy in the modern adult. I have made the following discovery and I pass it on to the world. *The evolution of culture is synonymous with the removal of ornament from utilitarian objects.*
>
> —*Ornament and Crime*

To understand why they were so passionate in their diatribes, we have to recognize that the early European Modernists were not just attacking ornament in their manifestos. Their real target was the continuing existence of unsanitary housing for the working classes, the overcrowding of cities, and outmoded building techniques. Rising expectations for social reordering and political reform were powerful forces within the European intellectual climate of that time, not a rhetorical invention of these architects. They wanted their buildings to serve these legitimate

COURTESY BUFFALO & ERIE COUNTY HISTORICAL SOCIETY

Guaranty Building, Buffalo, New York. Adler and Sullivan, architects, completed 1895.

ROBERT JENSEN

Art Nouveau: apartment house, Paris. Hector Guimard, architect, completed 1910.

Front façade of the Majolica Apartment House, Vienna. Otto Wagner, architect, completed 1899.

social expectations and become a symbol for them. By analogy, ornament and decoration came to represent the old order against which the Modernists were struggling, and the already-established notion of ornament being separate from essential structure led almost inevitably to the belief that ornament was inhibiting the new functions and concealing the new structures of the twentieth century. In 1914, the Italian Futurists Antonio Sant'Elia and Filippo Tommaso Marinetti declared:

> Since the eighteenth century there has been no more architecture. What is called modern architecture is a stupid mixture of the most varied stylistic elements used to mask the modern skeleton. The new beauty of concrete and iron is profaned by the superimposition of carnival decorative incrustations. . . . The constantly growing number of machines, the daily increase of needs imposed by the speed of communication, by the agglomeration of people, by the demands of hygiene and a hundred other phenomena of modern life, cause no concern to [young Italian architects]. . . . The decorative must be abolished.
>
> —*Manifesto of Futurist Architecture*

In 1919, the same year that he founded the Bauhaus at Weimar (an institute formed to combine the teaching of Modern architecture, arts, and crafts), the German-born architect Walter Gropius despaired of what he saw around him.

> We walk through our streets and do not howl with shame at such deserts of ugliness. Let us be quite clear: these grey, hollow, spiritless mockups, in which we live and work, will be shameful evidence for posterity of the spiritless decent into hell of our generation.
>
> —Statement, Exhibition for Unknown Architects

While it was possible for the early Modernists to be quite specific about what was wrong with society and its physical conditions (for the most part they had only to let the facts speak for themselves), it was considerably more difficult for them to translate prevailing aspirations for humanitarian reform into specific architectural concepts. The early Modernists tended to speak of "unknown, unconscious laws," of "a new plastic unity," of "the spirit of the age." But how does an architect put "the spirit of the age" into a building? How does a designer bridge the gap, artistically, between a deplorable present and an ideal future? That bridge was created in European intellectual circles during the 1920s and, by 1930, finally established as the principal artistic meta-

Villa Stein, Garches, France. Le Corbusier, architect, completed 1927.

COURTESY THE ARCHITECTS COLLABORATIVE

Apartment wing of the Bauhaus, Dessau, Germany. Walter Gropius, architect, completed 1926.

PETER PAIGE, COURTESY STENDIG INC.

Wassily chair, Marcel Breuer, designer, 1925. Breuer was on the faculty of the Bauhaus when he designed this classic Modern chair.

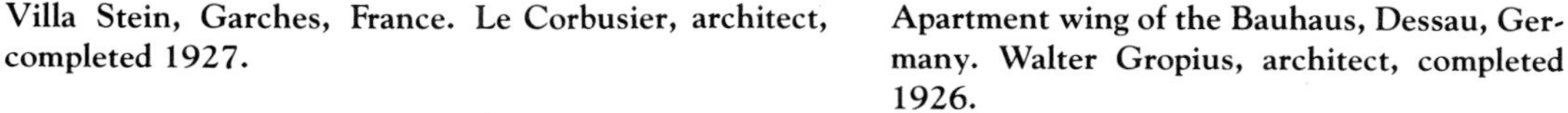

phor of Modernism. It was called the machine aesthetic or, occasionally, *Die Neue Sachlichkeit* (the new objectivity), or just functionalism. Its principal proselytizers were the Swiss-born Frenchman Le Corbusier practicing in Paris; the German-born Mies then working in Berlin; and Gerrit Rietveld, a member of De Stijl, the group of Dutch artists, architects, and poets whose influence paralleled, in many ways, that of the Bauhaus. From 1932 on, this new aesthetic was sometimes called the International Style, after the title of a book written in that year by Henry-Russell Hitchcock and Philip Johnson. This book accompanied an exhibition at the Museum of Modern Art in New York, an event which introduced to America the European Modernism of Gropius, Mies, Le Corbusier, and the Dutchman J. J. P. Oud, another member of De Stijl.

Whichever label was used, the full force of Modernist belief was henceforth gathered into one all-powerful image—the machine. In 1924, the Dutch painter and design theorist Theo van Doesburg had proclaimed:

> The machine is, *par excellence,* a phenomenon of spiritual discipline. Materialism as a way of life and art . . . reduced men to the level of machines: the proper tendency of the machine (in the sense of cultural development) is as the unique medium of the very opposite, social liberation.

That was the goal of the Modernists: social liberation. Their faith in the machine did not arise from some romanticizing of brainless technique; on the contrary, they deplored the chaos and dehumanization that had been brought on by the Industrial Revolution. To the Modernists, the machine aesthetic was an emblem for the spirit of scientific and technological progress underlying the machine. The contemporary historian Edward Shils has captured the social meaning of science and technology in the late-nineteenth and early-twentieth centuries:

> . . . political radicalism always regarded science as its great ally against the forces of clerical and worldly authority. Science and reason were at one in their implacable opposition to the traditional, the arbitrary, and the supernatural. Progressives and liberals regarded science as their ally in the campaign to erode the superstitions of traditional beliefs and hierarchical institutions.
> –*Daedalus*, Summer 1974

The machine aesthetic was as much a spiritual force as a stylistic inspiration, and the Modernist's reverence for it

ELLIOTT KAUFMAN

Art Deco: detail of elevator door, Chrysler Building, New York City. William Van Alen, architect, completed 1929.

ELLIOTT KAUFMAN

Women's lounge at Radio City Music Hall, Rockefeller Center, New York City. Donald Deskey, interior designer, completed 1932. Mural by Yasuo Kuniyoshi.

was based on the conviction, which they shared with society as a whole, that science and technology had a unique ability to transform the world; to resolve, finally, the contradiction between things as they are and things as they ought to be.

The institution most responsible for working out the forms and theories of this belief system was the Bauhaus in Germany. From 1925 until 1933 when it was closed by the Nazis, the Bauhaus focused its efforts on creating prototype designs for utilitarian objects that took advantage of modern machine techniques and industrial materials—objects strictly functional in appearance and devoid of any applied ornament. Both within the Bauhaus and among other European Modernists agreement had been reached: Modern design ought to expose to view nothing at all that could be described as traditional ornament. Far from enhancing a building, a room, or an object, the application of ornament was deemed to be the single act most likely to destroy its integrity. Where the nineteenth century had sought virtue in the proper or decorous use of ornament, the twentieth-century functionalists sought virtue in its absolute exclusion. Although little of what was designed at the Bauhaus ever was mass-produced, the style that emerged from that institution became the dominant influence on the following generation of architects and designers, both in Europe and the United States.

The Bauhaus style was not the only modern style to emerge in the first half of this century. There was Art Deco, which in America reached its zenith in the Chrysler Building completed in 1929, and the more streamlined Moderne style, some of the best examples of which were incorporated into Rockefeller Center completed in 1939. But the intellectual force of the machine aesthetic was so great that until quite recently these more decorative modern styles were dismissed by critics and historians as mere curiosities, despite the fact that they dominated commercial architecture and design in the United States right up to World War II.

The machine aesthetic was actually rather slow making its way to America. Although the Viennese architect Rudolph Schindler had come here to study and work under Frank Lloyd Wright as early as 1914, by 1930 he and another European-born Modernist, Richard Neutra, had built only a few houses in California. Walter Gropius and Marcel Breuer, a member of Gropius's faculty at the Bauhaus, did not arrive to teach at Harvard until 1937. Mies van der Rohe, who had become head of the Bauhaus in 1930, was made director of architecture at the Armour Institute, Chicago (now the Illinois Institute of Technology), in 1938. He designed twenty-one buildings for the school's new campus in 1940, but World War II delayed their construction.

Only after the war was over did the machine aesthetic really take hold in the United States and, somewhere in the course of its transatlantic journey, its social content had been jettisoned. What was embraced on these Western shores was simply a rational approach to design: a logical, deterministic means of addressing the economic and technological facts of mid-twentieth-century life. No messianic zeal, no utopian visions; just standardized machinelike forms, looking as if they could be mass-produced forever. For a young country that had rapidly become a major industrial power, the machine aesthetic was a perfect expression of belief in limitless technological progress: "better living through chemistry" and "building a better tomorrow today." Enthusiasm was (almost) unbounded.

By the 1950s, modern office buildings were providing more efficient, productive work space, even if much of it was without natural light (artificial lighting would take care of that). Modern heating and cooling systems ensured year-round temperature control, and no one seemed to mind that windows had to be inoperable, or that the cost of energy over the life of a building would eventually exceed the original cost of construction. Labor-saving appliances for the home bought on the installment plan freed American housewives to work in windowless offices so that they could keep up their payments on those appliances. Modern housing renounced rooms in favor of the "open plan" where various spaces could be distinguished only by the appliances placed in them (if there was a stove, the space was probably a "food preparation area," not to be confused with the "dining" or "family" area into which it "flowed"). Modern city planning eradicated pedestrian streets (everyone knew they were anachronisms doomed by the automobile anyway) and replaced them with more rational urban freeways, empty plazas, and isolated superblocks.

PHO-CO, INC.

Co-op City, New York City. Herman J. Jessor, architect, completed 1970. An example of bottom-line Modernism in subsidized housing, Co-op City houses 55,000 people in thirty-five 35-story apartment towers and 236 two-family houses.

"The house," Le Corbusier said in 1920, "is a machine for living in." By 1965 the office had come to look like a machine for working in; the street a machine for driving/parking in; the hospital a machine for recovering/dying in; the government building a machine for being taxed, regulated, and computerized in. The machine aesthetic fulfilled our destiny. Corporations loved it, bureaucrats felt naturally at home in it, real-estate developers were able to depreciate it almost before the welding cooled, and appliance manufacturers went nearly berserk with accelerated obsolescence. As for the increasingly affluent consumer, he or she was much too busy buying and disposing to have an opinion one way or the other. But by the 1960s there were also signs in this country that the future, in which Modernism had believed so passionately, does not always work.

The Machine Abandoned

It was when dead fish started washing up on our riverbanks and "killer" smogs began blanketing our cities that our faith in mere technology began to falter. Since 1960, we've been jolted repeatedly by revelations as apocalyptic in their import as any of the ills which the early Modernists sought to redress. Toxic wastes bubble up from their supposedly permanent burial grounds and deform our unborn children. We spray chemical defoliants so that we can bomb the enemy from the safety of high altitudes; then years later these chemicals kill us slowly and excruciatingly with mysterious illnesses. Such alarming events accompany less dramatic but even more pervasive characteristics of modern technological life. Hospitals and health care seem to be foundering in ever more elaborate laboratory testing, machine diagnosis, and drugs. Farming and food production based on genetic engineering bring us tasteless meats and inedible tomatoes whose only merit is that they can be shipped thousands of miles without rotting. Computer data banks now can be martialed—in an emergency, of course—to reveal the private life, economic history, and political actions of almost every citizen.

We have created a world relying on technology to solve immediate problems with no thought of future consequences. In this kind of world technology seems not to enhance but to threaten our human nature, as well as the nature around us. We are faced today with contradictions between what things are and what things ought to be—politically, socially, and economically—that are as great as when the moral energy of the Modern Movement was young. But the roles are now reversed. Technology and scientific rationality are what "is," no longer what "ought to be." To the degree that it is all-powerful and everywhere applied, the technical model of life, the mechanical utopia, has become the reality against which any liberating architectural or artistic expression must push. Though we cannot (and should not) abandon the convenience that modern science and technology have brought us, we can no longer believe in the machine as a "spiritual" force. We know now that there is no easy way to reconcile the contradictions between what things are and what things ought to be, that there is no well-marked path to future perfection.

Quite apart from the fact that the machine aesthetic is no longer a valid metaphor for our best hopes and dreams, we have also begun to question that a pure machine aesthetic, derived from the techniques of mass production, makes good design cheaply available to all. Nothing could be further from the truth. By insisting on an "honest" use of materials and the stripping away of all "irrational" elements such as ornament, Modernism focuses mercilessly on quality of materials and refinement of detailing (the way in which parts are joined together). But the seamless surfaces characteristic of Modern design require minute tolerances that only the most skilled labor can achieve. What the early Modernists could not foresee—and their disciples have been reluctant to admit—is that the machine aesthetic cannot be cheaply mass-produced.

Offices of C. F. Murphy Associates, Chicago. C. F. Murphy Associates, architects, completed 1962. The Modernist ideal of the seamless surface is manifest here.

HUBE HENRY, HEDRICH-BLESSING

Take, for example, the demountable wall system, a familiar feature of many office interiors since the 1950s. The wall is a series of prefabricated panels that, as needs change, can be moved from one configuration to another without any demolition or reconstruction. For years architects and interior designers have been searching for the virtually seamless system, pushing the fabrication process as far as it can go to make the vertical joints between these panels disappear. The result is the butt joint: two panels joined end to end with no post, hinge, overlap, or other visible means of connection or reinforcement. Very neat. Very clean. Very Modern. The only problem is that the butt joint requires skilled factory labor to align almost invisible hairlines within the most exacting tolerances.

One demountable wall system manufacturer estimates that about 40 percent of the butt-joint work on his assembly line has to be rejected. An architect hired recently to redesign that manufacturer's system suggested a radically different approach in which the panels would be jointed horizontally at chair-rail height with ornamental moldings applied in a manner recalling traditional wainscoting. Whatever his feeling about wainscoting, the manufacturer was overjoyed at the prospect of being able to conceal the system's joints with moldings, thus improving his productivity and cost competitiveness. Given today's labor and material costs, the use of ornament has once again become a very practical means of achieving design quality because the application of ornament works to "forgive" inferior materials and imperfect factory workmanship.

Relative to the total output of this century, examples of *good* Modern design are few and, for the most part, enjoyed only by the rich. By now it is common knowledge that in his landmark Seagram Building on Park Avenue in New York City, Mies van der Rohe applied custom-made bronze

I-section extrusions to every vertical window mullion. These extrusions were structurally and functionally superfluous, but aesthetically they were necessary and cost, as they say, a bit more. Mies was right: God *is* in the details, but He doesn't come cheap. Faced with the speculative developer's "sharp pencil," He doesn't even stand a chance. As fast as you can say "bottom line," the elegant formulations of Mies's Seagram Building are reduced to the "dumb box"—that pathetic legacy of Modernism that has visited blankness and sterility unto almost every corner of the earth. Given that the "dumb box" is all most people know of Modern architecture, it is not surprising that they have never much liked it.

Historically, one of the purposes of ornament has been to enhance the crudely made or poorer-quality objects affordable to ordinary people. It was because the craftsmanship of their joiners (chairmakers) had deteriorated and their supply of fine woods was becoming scarce that the seventeenth-century Italians began gessoing and gilding their furniture or painting it to look like marble (*faux marbre*). Similarly, marquetry (wood-veneer inlay) and *découpage* (gluing cut-out designs on furniture) were invented for the purpose of disguising inferior woods. Such "dishonesty" offended orthodox Modernists but, in practice, it is much more egalitarian than the severely reductionist machine aesthetic.

Restoring and Collecting the Past

Another impetus for the reevaluation of the machine aesthetic has come from the building preservation and restoration movement. Beginning in the late 1950s as a grass-roots protest against the demolition of homes to make way for urban renewal, the restoration movement has grown from a few isolated incidents where people lay in front of bulldozers to a multibillion-dollar industry. As the costs of real estate and new construction have skyrocketed, the recycling or rehabilitating of older buildings has become an economically feasible alternative to tearing down and starting over again. Years of grime and "modernization" are now being stripped away from these older buildings, revealing elaborate moldings, intricate paving patterns, polychrome surfaces, and a wealth of ornamental detail so conspicuously missing from our recent past. Suddenly, we are seeing the world with new eyes.

Preservation: Thomas Jefferson League Building in The Strand, Galveston, Texas. Constructed by local craftsmen in 1871–72 with a cast-iron façade and galvanized iron cornice. Restored and renovated, RIGHT, for use as a restaurant and upper floor offices by Ford, Powell & Carson, architects, 1979.

GALVESTON HISTORICAL FOUNDATION, INC.

GALVESTON HISTORICAL FOUNDATION, INC.

Restoration: galleria of the Biltmore tel, Los Angeles. Schultze and Weaver, architects, completed 1923. Restoration and renovation completed 1978 by Gene Summers and Phyllis Lambert.

HEDRICH-BLESSING

COURTESY DUFOUR GLASS STUDIOS, LTD.

Glass artist Samuel Corso at work on contemporary stained-glass panel.

WILLIAM ROWLEY

Fabrication and assembly of New York State Senate chamber gates in metalworker Albert Paley's studio, 1980.

Second stencil of tile pattern being positioned on wall with register marks to guide proper location.

JOCK POTTLE

Applying painted finish to chair in the Isabel O'Neil Studio, New York City.

JAN C. K. ANDERSON

A graduate of the New York City Municipal Arts Society RESTORE program demonstrating stone-dressing techniques at workshop session.

BOB HOLLINGSWORTH

Applying *faux-marbre* finish in the Security Pacific Bank, San Francisco. Built in 1918, the building was stripped of its original brass, marble, glass, column bases, and stair enclosures during a 1971 "modernization," then restored by Baldwin/Clarke Associates in 1978. Twenty-one plaster columns and twenty-seven pilasters were hand-sanded, given a coat of flesh-toned paint, streaked with six other colors, given "cracks" and "crevices," and finished with fine black lines brushed on with turkey feathers. Executed by Nat Weinstein of the John Seekamp Co.

The building restoration movement has been an important factor in rekindling our interest in ornament, and it is significant that this has happened not because of any intellectual argument, but because of popular reaction against the obliteration of buildings that embodied use and memories. The preservation and restoration movement, with its broad social base, has accomplished in the United States what the Modern Movement claimed to be trying to accomplish but never did: the projection of an architectural vision of new possibilities, of hope for our future. Preservation and restoration, without any theoretical base or grand social program, has become a carrier of that moral force which architecture needs if it is to have meaning beyond mere shelter. Responding to the force of preservation, and because ornament is such an important part of the buildings being preserved, architects have had to confront ornament again, to study its rules (omitted from their Modernist education), learn how it works, even to design it anew.

Restoration also has focused attention on many crafts supposed to have died out after World War II. Actually, these crafts never did die out; they were simply ignored and driven away from the building process (see "The Decorative Crafts," pages 159–63). Architect Philip Johnson, an early disciple of Modernism in America, now admits: "The fact that craftsmanship didn't exist was invented by people like me who didn't want to use it." Today stained glass, metalwork, stenciling, and mural painting are gradually being reassimilated into architecture, not just as afterthoughts but as integral parts of the design process.

In much the same way that the restoration and preservation movement has taught us new ways of seeing things, the current passion for "collecting" also has affected our aesthetic sensibilities. One out of every three Americans, according to the *New York Times,* has become a collector of something: antique furniture, comic books, Oriental rugs, political campaign buttons, pressed-glass salt shakers, Georgian silver. Whether motivated by nostalgia for the past, anxiety about the value of the dollar, or the simple pleasures of dilettantism, most people are collecting and investing in the heritage of more decorative pre-Modern periods. Living with the filigrees and finials and flutings trucked in from the auction house teaches us what has been missing from our recent past: the richness of ornament. This heightened appreciation of past decorative styles has aroused an appetite for idiosyncrasy and richness of detail in contemporary design. Suddenly we want more than plain white walls and clean surfaces; we want color and complexity and visual intrigue. The collecting of objects from the past, like building restoration, has moved us further away from the machine aesthetic, shifting our expectations about what kind of visual environment is possible in the late twentieth century and preparing the way for a totally new aesthetic—an aesthetic that transforms the decorative impulse into something quite different from anything before.

Fragments of decorative stone, wood, terra-cotta, and metalwork are salvaged from demolition sites and offered for sale at shops like Urban Archeology in New York City.

JOCK POTTLE

Salvaged architectural ornament, Urban Archeology, New York City.

JOCK POTTLE

JOCK POTTLE

The Ornamental Aesthetic

Ever since 1966, when American architect Robert Venturi observed that "less is a bore," the Modern attitude toward ornament and decoration has been undergoing a fundamental change. Venturi transformed the familiar maxim of architect Ludwig Mies van der Rohe to make the point that modern architecture had become too simplistic, had lost touch with life. His convictions, though smacking of heresy at the time, were shared by a small group of architects that included Charles Moore, then chairman of the Yale School of Architecture. Moore initially expressed his own rebellion by using graphics in a room to override and dismiss whatever was there for a functional or structural reason: "supergraphics" as critic C. Ray Smith labeled them in 1967. Students coming out of Yale under Moore in the late 1960s were painting the surfaces of their *de rigeur* boxes with a vengeance: purple diagonal stripes from floor to ceiling, big yellow dots in the corners—anything to loosen the grip of functionalist theory and its rules of design.

Probably the earliest use of supergraphics, although they weren't called that then, was in Venturi's 1962 renovation of Grand's Restaurant in Philadelphia. Four-foot-high stencil letters spelling out the name of the establishment were painted along one wall, then repeated in mirror image on the opposite wall. This superimposition of oversized letters on a small dining area dramatically expanded the apparent volume of that space. Intended more as spatial experiments than as decoration, exercises like this were followed by increasingly ornamental uses of paint and graphics such as artist William Tapley's intricately patterned rooms. Most of these supergraphics occurred in interior projects, but, by 1970, they were appearing on the outsides of buildings, too, in the form of huge wall murals painted to achieve "instant" urban renewal.

From these early adventures with paint, color, and out-of-scale-signs, a real movement has developed in architecture, the essence of which is ornament: ornament sometimes flat, sometimes fully three-dimensional and applied on both the outside and inside of buildings. Plain white walls are giving way to rich and complex color combinations; or sprouting pilasters, silhouettes, and other frankly tacked-on embellishments. Gigantic flowers or false columns completely out of scale and unrelated to structure

Interior of Grand's Restaurant, West Philadelphia. Venturi & Short, architects, completed 1962.

LAWRENCE S. WILLIAMS

"Supergraphics": interior of Athletic Club Number One, The Sea Ranch, Northern California. Moore, Lyndon, Turnbull, Whitaker, architects, with Barbara Stauffacher, graphic designer, completed 1966.

MORLEY BAER

Bedroom of the Perkel apartment, New York City. William Tapley, designer, completed 1971. Tapley combines graphics with decorative lighting and a bedspread of his own design.

LAURA ROSEN

LAURA ROSEN

"Instant" urban renewal: loft building in SoHo, New York City. The exposed lot-line wall, LEFT, was transformed in 1975 by artist Richard Haas to match the real cast-iron façade of this nineteenth-century structure.

are appearing on the outsides of buildings. Major public spaces are being designed almost as stage sets, evoking history or cultural antecedent with ornamental devices that are at once familiar and startling. The traditional columns and pediments are there, but fragmented, distorted, often ironically juxtaposed to other architectural elements; traditional wood and masonry forms surprise us in blatantly modern materials like stainless steel and neon.

The decorative crafts, particularly glasswork, wrought-ironwork and brushwork—which have long been excluded from the mainstream of building design—are receiving more significant architectural commissions. Stencil artists, the last traces of whose craft have been fading on the walls of forgotten farmhouses, are once again executing filigree borders or transforming whole rooms into dreamlike experiences. Furniture designers are creating pieces full of wit and allusion: chairs in the shape of butterflies or desks elaborately inlaid in a manner that recalls the eighteenth century. And a group of artists who constitute what is called the Patterning and Decorating Movement (see "Patterning, Decoration & Usable Art," pages 239–41) are leaving their canvases and covering entire walls with frankly decorative painting; or filling rooms with fanciful sculptured forms. Many of these artists are working in ceramic tile, dyed cloth, beads, sequins, even pheasant feathers—materials more often associated with the decorative crafts than the fine arts. Traditional distinctions between the two fields are further blurred by the fact that many Patterning and Decorating artists are also making screens, chairs, tables, beds, and lamps—pieces that freely evoke potential "usefulness" yet remain, at the same time, objects of contemplation.

This movement is changing the appearance of contemporary architecture in a way that is sometimes called *postmodern.* But the label *postmodern,* popularized by critic Charles Jencks in 1975 and quickly taken up by American architect Robert A. M. Stern, is a slippery term implying that the whole of the Modern Movement is now being abandoned and something entirely different is taking its place. This is simply not true. As critic Ada Louise Huxtable has so aptly put it,

> The high period of modernism is over; the Age of the Masters—Frank Lloyd Wright, Mies van der Rohe, Le Corbusier—is finished. We are clearly—or I should say, unclearly—moving on toward something else; in fact, we have been doing so for some time. But whatever comes next will be the product or inheritor of modernism, not the radical break that [postmodernism] is advertised to be. It will have at its heart the twentieth-century revolution that we call modern architecture.

It is obvious by looking at most of the work in this book

Ornamental embellishments: Best Products Showroom, Richmond, Virginia. SITE, architects, completed 1972. This wall, built to appear as if it were peeling away from the building, emphasizes the surface in a startling way.

Proposal for the Molino Stucky Mills, Venice, Italy. SITE, architects, 1975. This scheme to renovate an abandoned mill into a recreational facility reverses the familiar relationship between the Venetian canals and the buildings which line them. The façade of the mill becomes the horizontal plane, and a cascade of water flowing over a plate glass wall becomes the vertical plane.

that it could not have been designed prior to the Modern Movement and that the simple forms and technical means of Modernism are still there, just under the surface but still quite visible and useful. Ornamentalism is very much a reaction against the more obvious failures of Modernism, but it is not a wholesale rejection of Modernism. In response to the attempt to label him a *postmodernist,* Robert Venturi maintains that his firm (Venturi, Rauch and Scott Brown) is only practicing Modern architecture, and he's right.

One of the reasons that Ornamentalism is so clearly a Modern phenomenon is that it breaks the cardinal rule of ornament characteristic of all historical styles. Whereas ornament in the Gothic, Baroque, or Neoclassical styles usually reinforced or complemented the forms to which it was applied, in Ornamentalism it frequently contradicts or overrides them. Moreover, the embellishments of Ornamentalism are not applied in a manner subservient to structure as dictated by the theories of the eighteenth and nineteenth centuries. For example, the tile pattern on Venturi, Rauch and Scott Brown's ISI Building (pages 124, 125) creates a color and rhythm that ignore and try to override the window openings and the structural system. Michael Graves's addition to the Schulman house (pages 30, 31) purposely distorts the size of the new clapboard siding. Outside, the fireplace is depicted as a monumental column; inside it becomes a kind of giant keystone that one would expect to see thirty feet in the air rather than on the floor. The old two-story exterior is painted in contradiction to both its traditional gable and its symmetry.

Richard Fernau's fast food shop "Franks for the Memory" (pages 88, 89) contains "walls" that rise through two stories and are punched with cutouts in the shape of giant hot dogs. Though they define space in the interior, these walls are otherwise ornamental; they do not keep the weather out and they do not support anything. Most important, they contradict the real structure, ceiling, mechanical systems, and exterior walls of the space they occupy.

The new Ornamentalism also violates the well-known dictum of the nineteenth-century English architect Owen Jones: "Construction should be decorated. Decoration should never be purposely constructed" (*The Grammar of Ornament,* 1856). In Ornamentalism, decoration is very purposely constructed, and constructed in a manner to give it its own independent validity as in Hans Hollein's Austrian Travel Bureau (pages 102, 103). Here the palm trees neither imitate nature nor pretend to support the structure. Clad in polished metal, they stand free, symbolizing faraway places and, though purely decorative, become one of the most significant architectural elements of the space.

This purposeful construction of decoration, along with the tendency of Ornamentalism to contradict rather than reinforce essential structure and function, is important because it allows Ornamentalism to keep clear the distinctions between what is merely on the surface of things and what things really are. Thus we are never fooled by *faux bois* painting in the way that manufacturers of plastic woodgrain laminate would fool us. The two-dimensional columns appliquéd to the façade of Robert A. M. Stern's summer cottage do not try to be authentic in the way that the tract developer's "Southern Colonial" model does.

In this sense, Ornamentalism is quite the opposite of what we call kitsch. It is not an imitation or simulation of something that, by pretending to be real, programs a sentimental response. Ornamentalism may recall historical styles or evoke nature, it may refer to folk art or the human body; but it does so in a way that allows the audience to understand and participate in the process, to know what is genuine and what is not. The pleasures of the new Ornamentalism are all its own, not faked or hand-me-down, and they carry with them many of the aesthetic ideals of the last two hundred years. Ornamentalism, Modernism, and the numerous styles of the nineteenth century have in common the fact that all have expressed the aspirations of the societies for which they were created. Since the Industrial Revolution and its seeming mastery of the economic and technical means to transform the human condition, architecture has been required to depict society as it wishes to become, not, necessarily, as it is.

Thomas Jefferson's state capitol building at Richmond, Virginia (1789–98), was Roman in style because Jefferson and his contemporaries wished the newly created United States to be identified with the greatest working republic of them all, the old Roman republic. Their Federal style was an evocation of the country's ideal of republican government. Later, as the aspirations of the country shifted from republicanism to democracy, the Greek Revival style expressed those aspirations in buildings that evoked the democracy of ancient Greece: the old U. S. Custom House (designed 1834) in lower Manhattan was as nearly a replica of the Parthenon as its banking functions would allow. Similarly, at the time that the Houses of Parliament were built in London (1836–68), the English were in the throes of the Gothic Revival, a movement inspired by a rekindling of national and Christian ideals. Then, in the first half of this century, the goal of Modernism was to depict a social utopia based on science and technology. Although the image of that utopia—the machine—was radically different from previous Gothic and Classical images, the impulse to express the spirit of the age was exactly the same impulse that had informed architecture in the prior two centuries.

Entrance to the Stern House, East Hampton, Long Island. Robert A. M. Stern, architect, completed 1979. Applied columns are frankly two dimensional and out of scale.

University of Pennsylvania Science Department, Philadelphia. Inexpensive concrete-block construction, completed in 1963, has been transformed by an Ornamental renovation, RIGHT, that also uses low-cost materials. Voorsanger & Mills Associates, 1980. Resurfaced walls, false columns, and decorative paint provide a monumental setting for the statue of Benjamin Franklin at the end of a corridor.

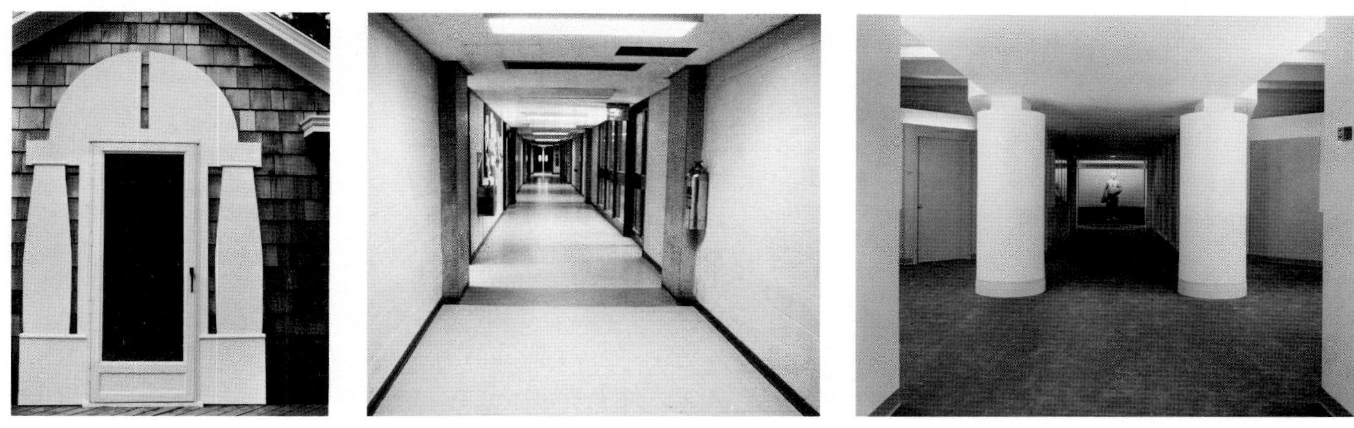

THEO WESTENBERGER

Now, because the depiction of the machine as a "spiritual" force is no longer plausible, contemporary architecture and art are faced with the challenge of discovering new and appropriate imagery for our society. What are the aspirations of the late twentieth century and how should they be depicted? The Ornamental aesthetic springs from a search for answers to these questions, from a search for new imagery to express the admittedly confused and shifting ideas of what our society ought to become. It begins by denying the old reverence for technology while taking full advantage of the light-switch/vacuum cleaner/toaster conveniences that technology has brought us. Ornamentalist forms are made with the most sophisticated factory processes and contemporary materials such as laminated plastics, anodized aluminum, stainless steel, and neon. The economic and practical benefits of machine production are enthusiastically embraced, but the awesome "spirit" of the machine is denied, and in its place, other kinds of imagery are projected.

One source of imagery in Ornamentalism is historical style, particularly Classicism. Although images from almost any period may be used (and sometimes combined with startling eclecticism), classicizing imagery abounds because the Classical language of architecture is the most universally recognized style of the past, touching Greece, Rome, the Renaissance, and nineteenth-century Neoclassicism simultaneously. But it is not Classicism itself that Ornamentalism seeks, so much as the connections between contemporary society and its cultural heritage, the linking of our present with our past.

For example, Piazza D'Italia by Charles Moore and August Perez (pages 154–57)—with its Doric, Ionic, and Corinthian columns, a pilastered arcade, grand arches, and a fountain—is an "almost" accurate evocation of some nineteenth-century Neoclassical building or public monument in Italy. The whole ensemble is vaguely symmetrical and placed on axis. Yet there is no attempt to be truly historical, for these classicizing forms are made from stainless steel and neon, the most contemporary of materials. The plan reveals that the fountain is actually a map of the Italian peninsula, culminating at the center with Sicily, the region from which most of New Orleans's Italian population originated. This pop reference is annoying or fun, take your pick, but it is also an attempt to touch people's memory, to reach for the past and tie it to the present without resorting to false nostalgia.

The abstraction from historical sources is what distinguishes Ornamentalist design from "Colonial" motels, "Edwardian" boardrooms, and "Old English" bars. Historical references in Ornamentalism tend to be dramatically out of scale or context, to be made from materials associated with today's technology, or to be presented as fragments from the past (a part of a cornice, one-half of a molding) rather than as wholes. Michael Graves's pediment fragments and moldings are always too large or too small, never in the "right" place, and usually depicted as fragments. The historical allusions are thus truncated, isolated as if in brackets, often with abrupt beginnings and ends.

Some of the most original Ornamentalist work is based on images of nature to which, historically, the primordial origins of all ornament can be traced. Tested, refined, and elaborated over thousands of years in successive styles, the natural origins of ornament continue to touch the subconscious of our species. Even elements of the Classical orders, such as the Corinthian capital with its acanthus leaves, can be seen as direct references to nature. The most full-blown use of nature in recent architecture is obviously Art Nouveau, that short-lived turn-of-the-century style in which an attempt was made to integrate natural form into the whole of building, even its structure and space.

In Ornamentalist architecture there is no such effort at integration. On the contrary, nature is kept clearly on the surface and it is the surface qualities of nature that are depicted: its colors, shapes, and rhythms rather than its organic structure. For example, the porcelain enamel flower panels on Venturi, Rauch and Scott Brown's Best Products Showroom (pages 97–99) seem to "paint" a giant garden over the entire building, but the building itself remains obviously a warehouse. Michael Graves, on the other hand, is more abstract in his use of natural imagery, developing associations with nature through color: browns for earth, blues for sky, greens for landscape. In the Patterning and Decorating Movement in painting and sculpture, the uses of nature may be more explicit: for example, "The Garden" of Ned Smyth and Brad Davis (pages 251–53), the paintings of Robert S. Zakanitch (pages 264–67), or the murals and screens of Arlene Slavin (pages 275–77). In the crafts, natural imagery has always been explicit—and the recent renaissance in glass, iron, and brushwork reemphasizes that fact. Traditional nature patterns are revived in the work of stencilers like Cile Lord and Adele Bishop (pages 206–8), while forms based in nature are being newly invented by people like metalworker Albert Paley (pages 182–85). The appeal of nature as a contemporary image for the expression of our best hopes and dreams lies in its diametric opposition to the machine and in its essentially life-affirming power.

Another source of power in Ornamentalism is its humor. Jim Tigerman makes a table supported by fat little ballerina legs (pages 74 and 235) that are the point of it all, like Walt Disney's ballerina elephants in *Fantasia*. Poetic License designs a small entry to the American Consulate in Paris (page 151) that is all red, white, and blue, a gentle parody of America as seen from abroad. Stanley Tigerman suspends a giant pencil from the ceiling of his own architectural office (page 118). Artist Thomas Lanigan-Schmidt combines garishness with black humor in works such as "Two Seconds Before the End of the World" (page 254), a deliberate manipulation of kitsch.

Ornamentalism permits us to laugh at ourselves, an honest and liberating act. It provides a means of dealing in imagination with our culture, of filtering the monsterously contradictory facts of our existence. Ornamentalism contains its own ideas about what things are and what things ought to be, about what is right and wrong with the twentieth century. But it does not insist on any correspondence between those ideas and some ultimate truth. Ornamentalism is, in part, a process of demystification, of retreat from Modernist claims to an exclusive means of salvation in a complicated world.

The force of Ornamentalism, its strength and originality, lie in its abandonment of the machine aesthetic and its simultaneous ability to keep contradictions alive and explicit in the forms created. It is the first serious attempt in fifty years to make Modernism keep its promise of projecting new possibilities, of showing us some release from the burdensome realities of the present. It is not the daily usefulness of technology that Ornamentalism questions, but our tendency to let technology tell us what to do, of our allowing technology to become an end in itself. Ornamentalism dances on the surface of technology, using it but denying its aura. Ornamentalism is a sign of life, not of compromise, and it promises a future that will look much different from what we have known for the better part of this century.

Salvaged architectural ornament, Urban Archeology, New York City.

Entrance to CBS Theatrical Film Division offices, New York City, completed by architects Voorsanger & Mills Associates, 1982. Opulent ornamental effect is achieved here on a minimum budget.

ARCHITECTURE & INTERIORS

PHOTO PETER AARON, ESTO

PHOTO PETER AARON, ESTO

Private Living

Residence and Poolhouse • Llewellyn Park, New Jersey

A new poolhouse with stainless-steel palm-tree columns, a curving skylight, and intricate tile patterning has been added to this 1929 mansion. Just as the mansion was designed to recall Georgian English architecture of the late eighteenth century, the poolhouse (below and opposite) recalls the Classical tradition, but with distortions of scale and ornamental flourishes that are decidedly late twentieth century. Robert A. M. Stern Architects hope the palm trees are pleasant reminders of sun-filled tropical islands; the tile is a sparkling blue that becomes darker at the base of the walls, like a lake or the ocean. The skylight captures solar heat in the winter and opens the pool to light and air. Stern's office has also designed extensive renovations to the living quarters of this mansion with the same energy that makes the poolhouse so powerful.

PHOTO PETER AARON, ESTO

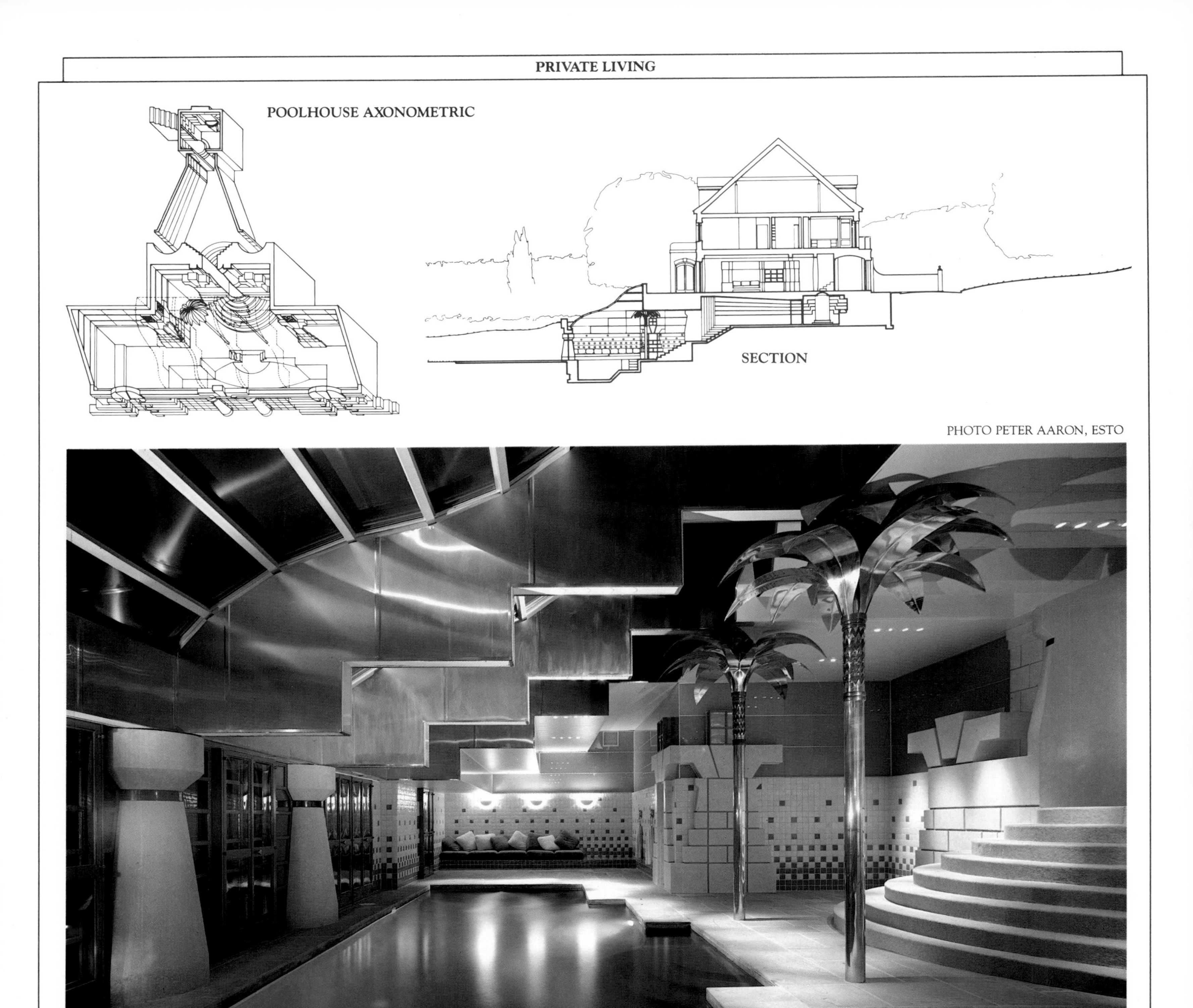

PHOTO PETER AARON, ESTO

PHOTOS PETER AARON, ESTO

OPPOSITE: Drawings show the new poolhouse in relation to the mansion. The stepped beams of the poolhouse interior, BOTTOM, are surfaced in stainless steel, and the palm-tree columns are polished brass and stainless steel. The exterior columns are load-bearing, of dolomitic limestone. ABOVE: Renovations to the living quarters feature custom-designed carpets, cabinetry, and built-in furnishings like the "Tuscan" writing table in the library, BOTTOM LEFT. The living room, TOP, and the poolhouse hall, BOTTOM RIGHT, are defined by new walls with moldings and classicized details. Assistants for design of the Llewellyn Park house were Ethelind Coblin, Anthony Cohn, Alan Gerber, and Gavin Macrae-Gibson. OVER: The poolhouse interior.

OVERLEAF: PHOTO PETER AARON, ESTO

PHOTO PETER AARON, ESTO

PHOTO PETER AARON, ESTO

PHOTO PETER AARON, ESTO

TOP: New garden façade with screening wall at left. BOTTOM, LEFT: Interior of the new living room looking at its fireplace and, RIGHT, the new entry foyer. OPPOSITE: Street façade of Schulman house, with new addition to the right.

Schulman House • Princeton, New Jersey

This small, quite ordinary 1940s house has been transformed by its addition, completed in 1978. Architect Michael Graves designed a new living room, fireplace, and garden wall extending across one side of the house in front of its garage. He then applied paint, new moldings, and some surprising half-round column forms to the existing exterior. The shift in scale, from modest to nearly monumental, achieved by these simple means is dramatic. The front door seems to rise through two stories; the clapboard siding on the new wall is twice the width of the old clapboard, then jumps to three times its width. The trellislike grids applied to the garden façade evoke summers and beaches. A sense of mystery, humor, and timelessness is present in the redesign of this modest house, accomplished on an equally modest budget.

PHOTO ROBERT JENSEN

Plocek House • Warren Township, New Jersey

Set high on a hill above the road, this large house by Michael Graves is approached on foot through a small entrance gate, then by a switchback path, reminiscent of the paths used by Greeks to approach a sacred acropolis. The Plocek house is frankly monumental and awesome. Graves calls it the Keystone house because the roof of the swimming pool changing room (see plan) is shaped like a distorted keystone from a Renaissance arcade. But there is a "void" at the front of the house, directly above the columns that mark the end of the footpath, where this same huge keystone seems to have been removed. The "real" keystone at the back of the pool could fit into the void at the front of the house, where it should be but isn't. The details and color used to achieve such illusions transform this simple rectangular house into a visual extravaganza.

PHOTO DOUGLAS PASCHALL, PROTO ACME PHOTO

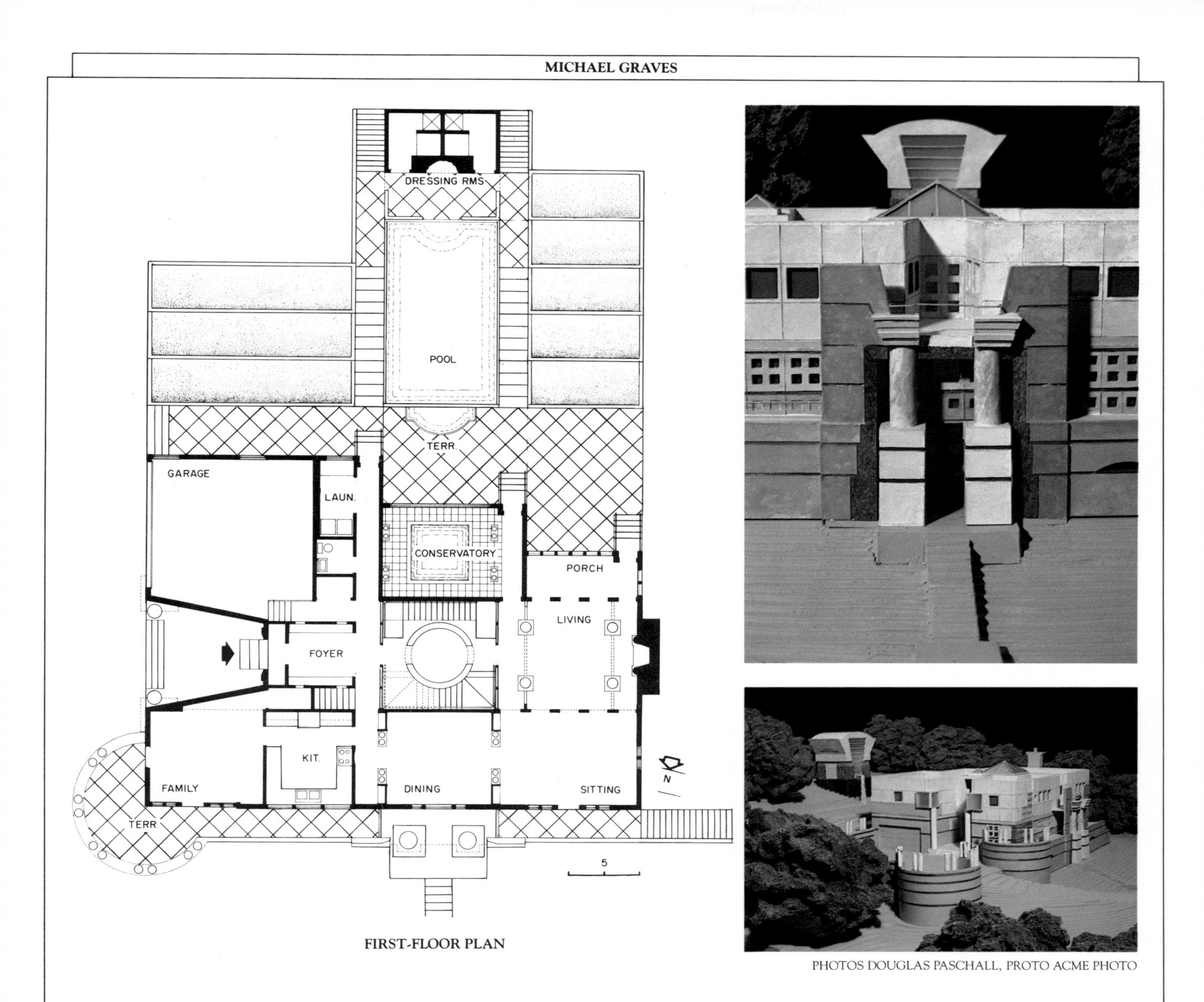

FIRST-FLOOR PLAN

PHOTOS DOUGLAS PASCHALL, PROTO ACME PHOTO

The Plocek house, shown here in model and plan, was designed in 1977, for completion in 1982. The exterior is tinted stucco. Inside, there are 3,500 square feet of living space on two floors.

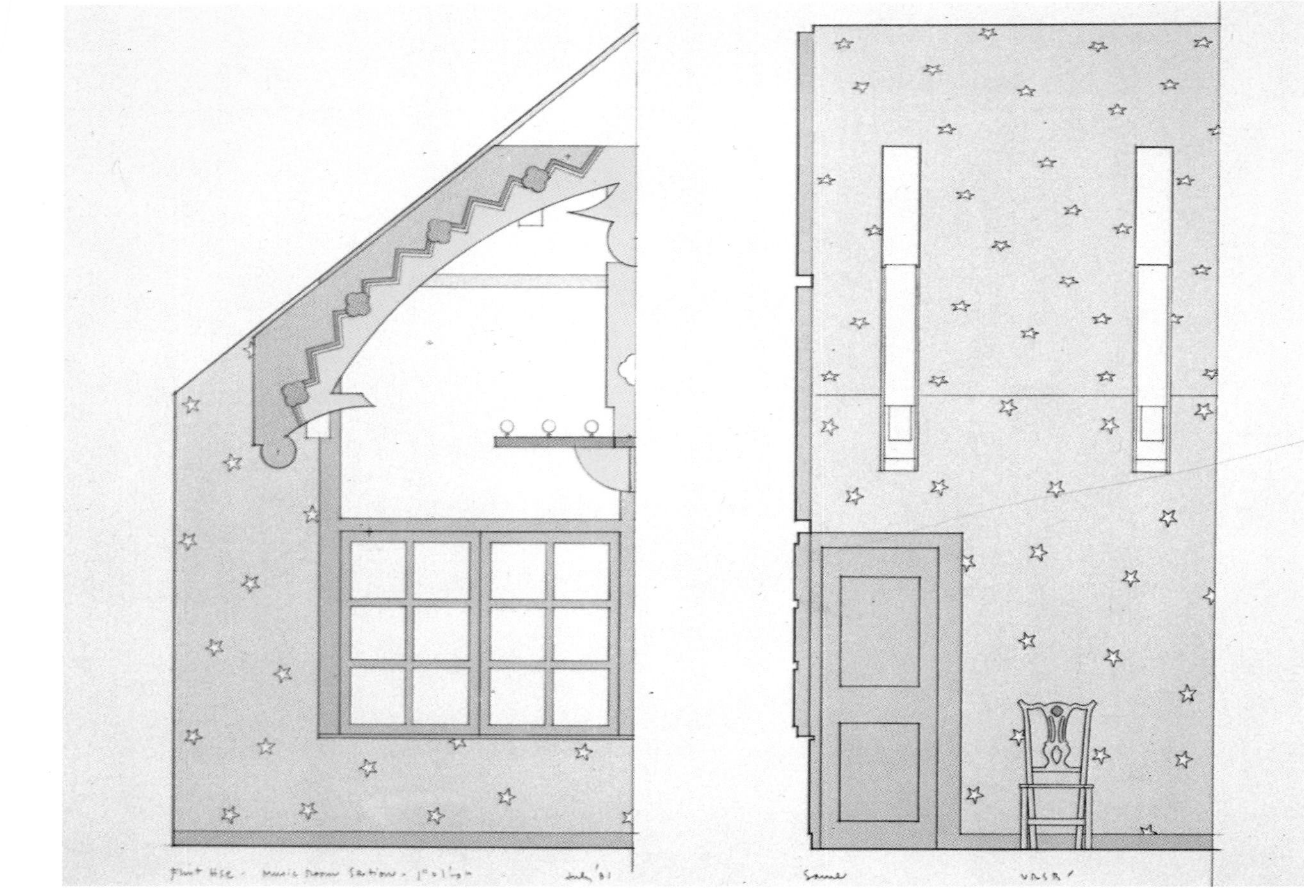
Same

Private Residence • New Castle County, Delaware

This wood-and-stucco house, completed in 1982, is described by architects Venturi, Rauch and Scott Brown as a cabinetmaker's dream. There are custom-made screens, storage cabinets, and ornamental details throughout, including the stencil patterns and exposed trusswork of the second-floor music room shown in drawings on the opposite page, bottom. The stars on the wall and ceiling are painted stencilwork, while the decorative painting on the trusses is achieved by masking. Outside, a huge arch fills the gables of both the east and west sides of the house, and thin, oversized columns made of wood help to define the back porch. Both the arch and the columns are actually 8-inch-thick screens, sitting about 4 feet in front of the real walls of the house. These screens are supported by steel brackets tied to concealed steel columns. Most of the major structural supports within this house are in fact steel: the interior spaces required spans greater than normal wood construction could achieve. At 8,000 square feet including garage and basement, this residence is larger than it appears.

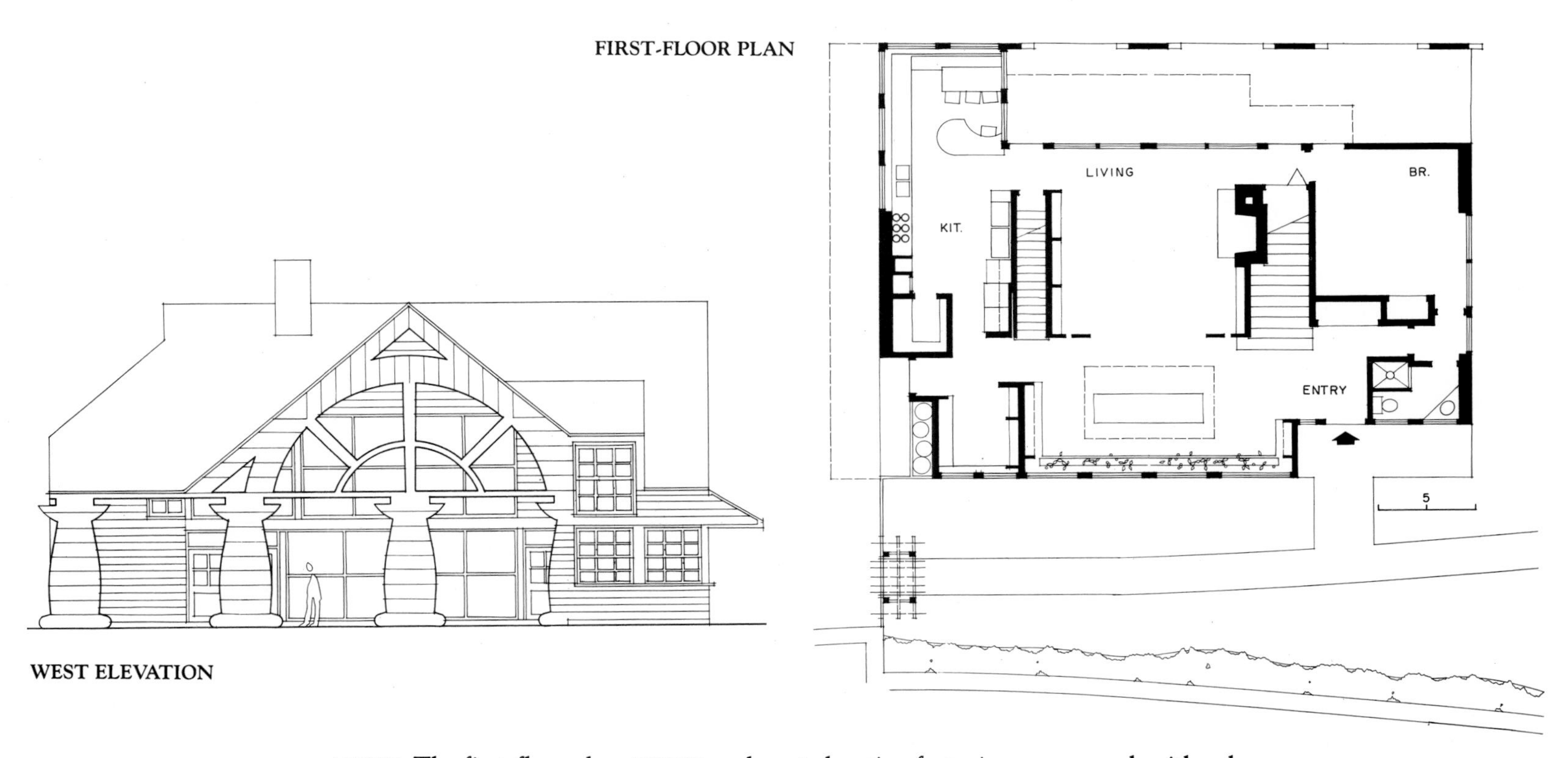

ABOVE: The first-floor plan, RIGHT, and west elevation featuring a rear porch with columns that are gigantic in profile but only about 10 inches thick. OPPOSITE: The east side of the house, TOP, and architect's drawings of the second-floor music room.

PHOTOS PETER AARON, ESTO

Peitzke House • Fire Island, New York

Surprises abound in this small summer home by the ocean. For instance, when you walk through the front door (opposite, top left) with its engaged columns and sunburst pediment, you are still outside. Nevertheless, you are in the "living room" of the house: an 18 × 35-foot symmetrical garden (below) that is the principal space for lounging and relaxing during the day. The garden is screened from the other nearby properties with a trellislike pavilion in wood (opposite, top right and below) that looks as if it were literally pulled off from the main body of the house and placed 18 feet away. By challenging our common expectations in this way, architect Peter Wilson has created a dramatic and original place.

PHOTO PETER AARON, ESTO

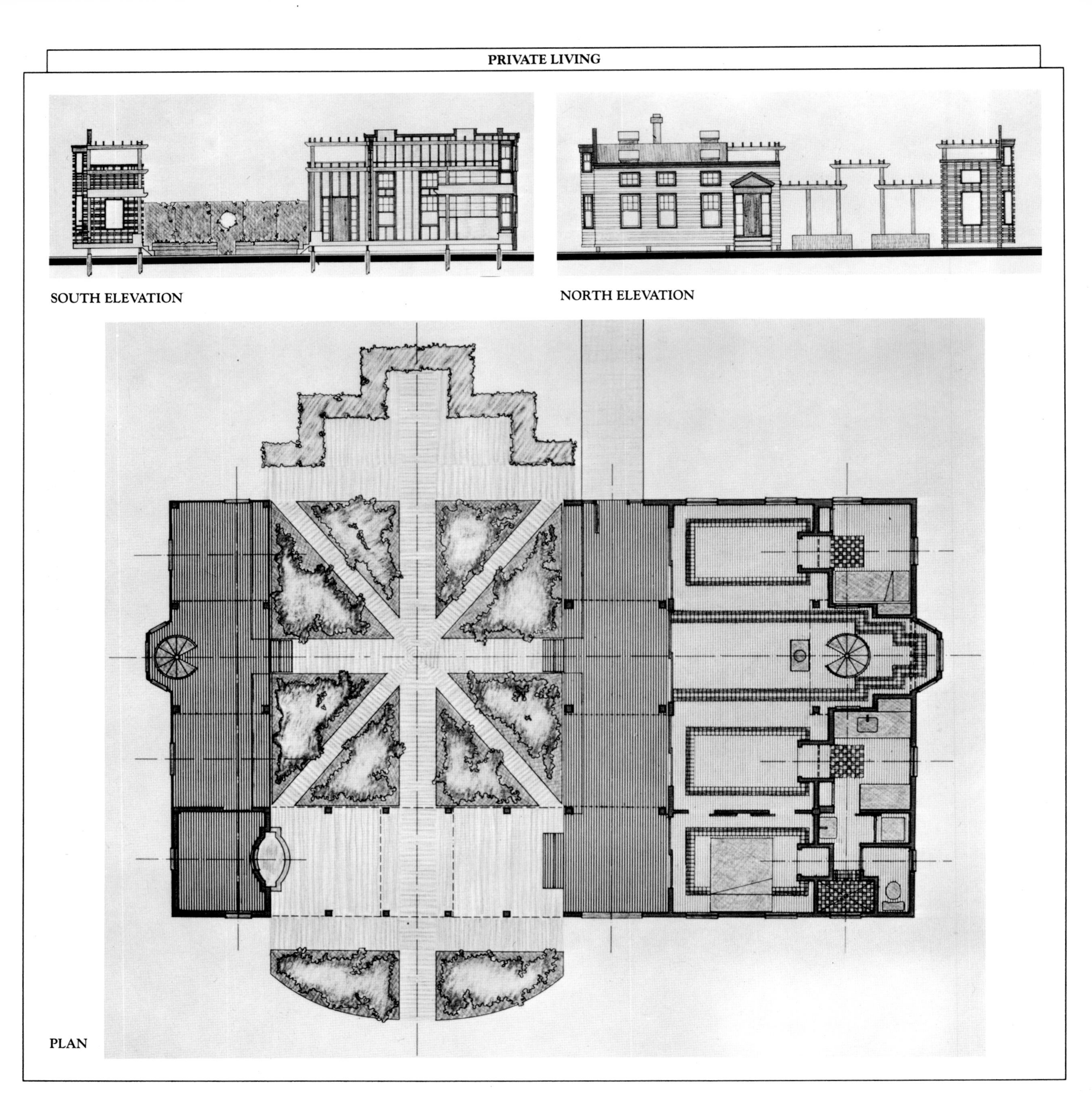
SOUTH ELEVATION
NORTH ELEVATION
PLAN

PHOTO PETER AARON, ESTO

The plan and elevations, OPPOSITE, show the care with which Peter Wilson has organized the decorative patterning of the Peitzke house on its walls, floors, and ceilings. Principal materials are wood and gypsum board, including the stonelike walls of the main living room, ABOVE. The 700 square feet of enclosed space are heated by the single woodburning stove. But it is the garden, OVER, that is the focus of the house. James Viles did the landscape design.

OVERLEAF: PHOTO PETER AARON, ESTO

Beasley House • Monroe, Wisconsin

This might appear to be an old farmhouse, but look again. It is a brand-new (1979) two-family residence designed by Chicago architect Thomas Hall Beeby of Hammond Beeby and Babka. The clapboarding is actually metal siding, and the foundation walls, which look like brick, are actually poured concrete with a brick pattern scored on the surface. The french doors, columns, and wooden balustrades of the porch were salvaged from previously demolished houses and incorporated into the design. There are 3,500 square feet of interior space. Beeby's goal was to design a completely contemporary house that looks comfortable in its prosperous Wisconsin farm setting, and clearly he has succeeded.

PHOTO ELLIE BABKA

PHOTOS ELLIE BABKA

SECTION

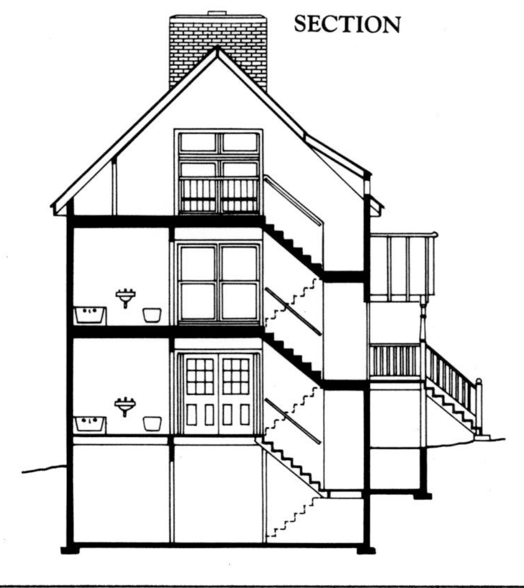

FIRST-FLOOR PLAN

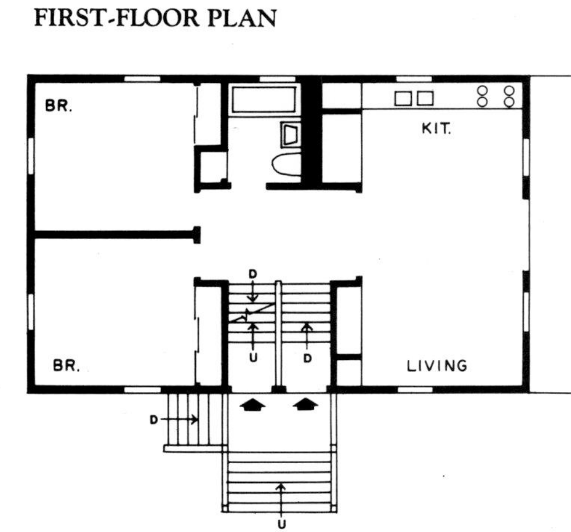

SECOND-FLOOR PLAN

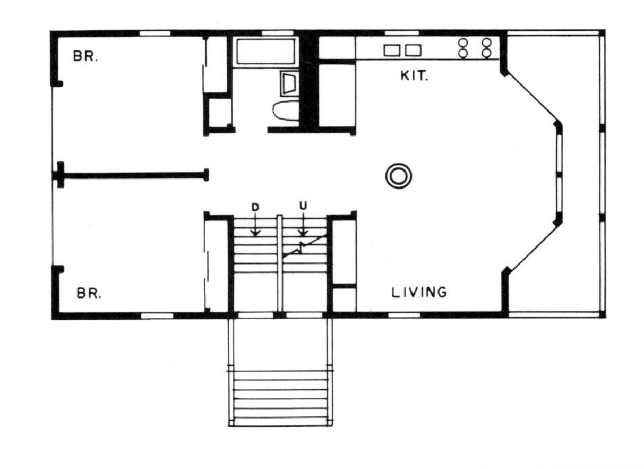

PHOTOS ROBERT JENSEN

ABOVE: The Tuscan house features an elaborate molding, BOTTOM LEFT, over its front door and painted metal acroteria, TOP LEFT, on the roof, which Smith salvaged from another building. The courtyard of the house, RIGHT, is enclosed by a two-story screen.

Tuscan and Laurentian Houses • Livermore, California

These two adjacent houses, built in 1979, are named after first-century A.D. villas described by the Roman historian Pliny in his letters about the life and architecture of that ancient empire. Architect Thomas Gordon Smith wanted to depict the spirit of Pliny's words in actual forms, made today. He has accomplished that goal using the standard wood-and-stucco construction of California builders, using salvaged Neoclassical ornament that he found and applied to the houses, then uniting these diverse forms into one idea with the bright, strong colors of the Mediterranean tradition. Color and ornament are the key: they bring this historical theme alive in the most contemporary way.

PHOTO ROBERT JENSEN

PHOTO DOUGLAS SYMES

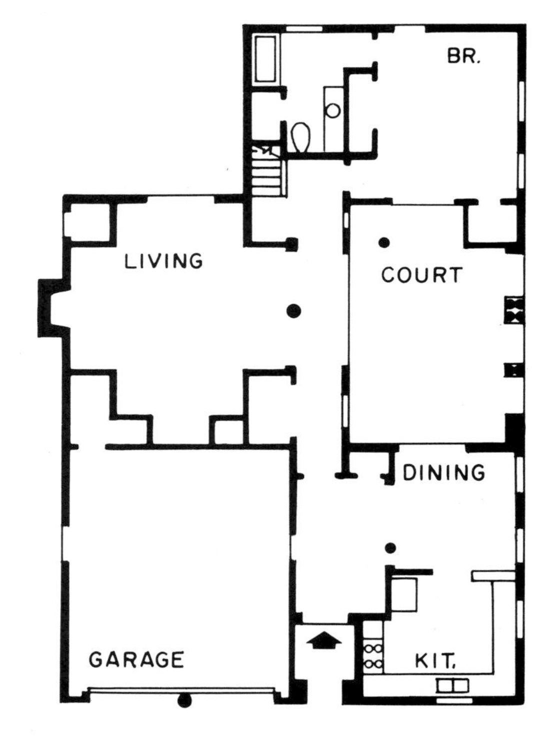

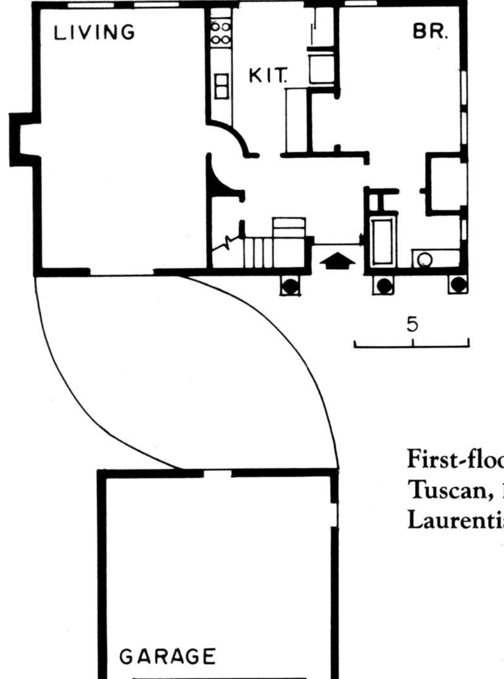

First-floor plan:
Tuscan, LEFT
Laurentian, RIGHT

ABOVE: The two houses are relatively small (about 1,900 square feet each) and fill most of their 100 × 50 ft. lots in this modest Livermore, California, neighborhood. The Tuscan house cost $105,000 to build; the Laurentian house, $90,000. OPPOSITE: Views of the front façade and garage of the Laurentian house. Three brightly painted wooden columns and an entablature mark the main entry. The central post of the garage is an unfinished tree trunk, with the bark left intact.

PHOTOS ROBERT JENSEN

PHOTO ROBERT JENSEN

PHOTO DOUGLAS SYMES

ABOVE: The Tuscan and Laurentian houses together form a courtyard that is a focus for the plan of both houses. Columns applied to the stucco wall stand out dramatically in both profile and elevation.

House of Virgil • Midwestern United States

Formally titled "The House of Virgil, Built in Anticipation of the Return of the Golden Age," this proposal depicts architect Thomas Hall Beeby's dream of what might be, or ought to be, in the world of the future. The house, to be built within the ruins of an abandoned midwestern farm, has a central half-domed pavilion rising from what remains of an old barn and a formal garden defined by the stone walls of what was once a livestock enclosure. The stalls of the former stable are converted to sleeping quarters. Part restoration, part pastoral fantasy, the project is presented in Magic Marker drawings on yellow tracing paper that show not only an architectural vision but a picture of mankind at peace with nature. Below is a plan of the farmstead, and on the following pages are a front view of the house by day (left) and a garden view at night.

PHOTO HEDRICH-BLESSING

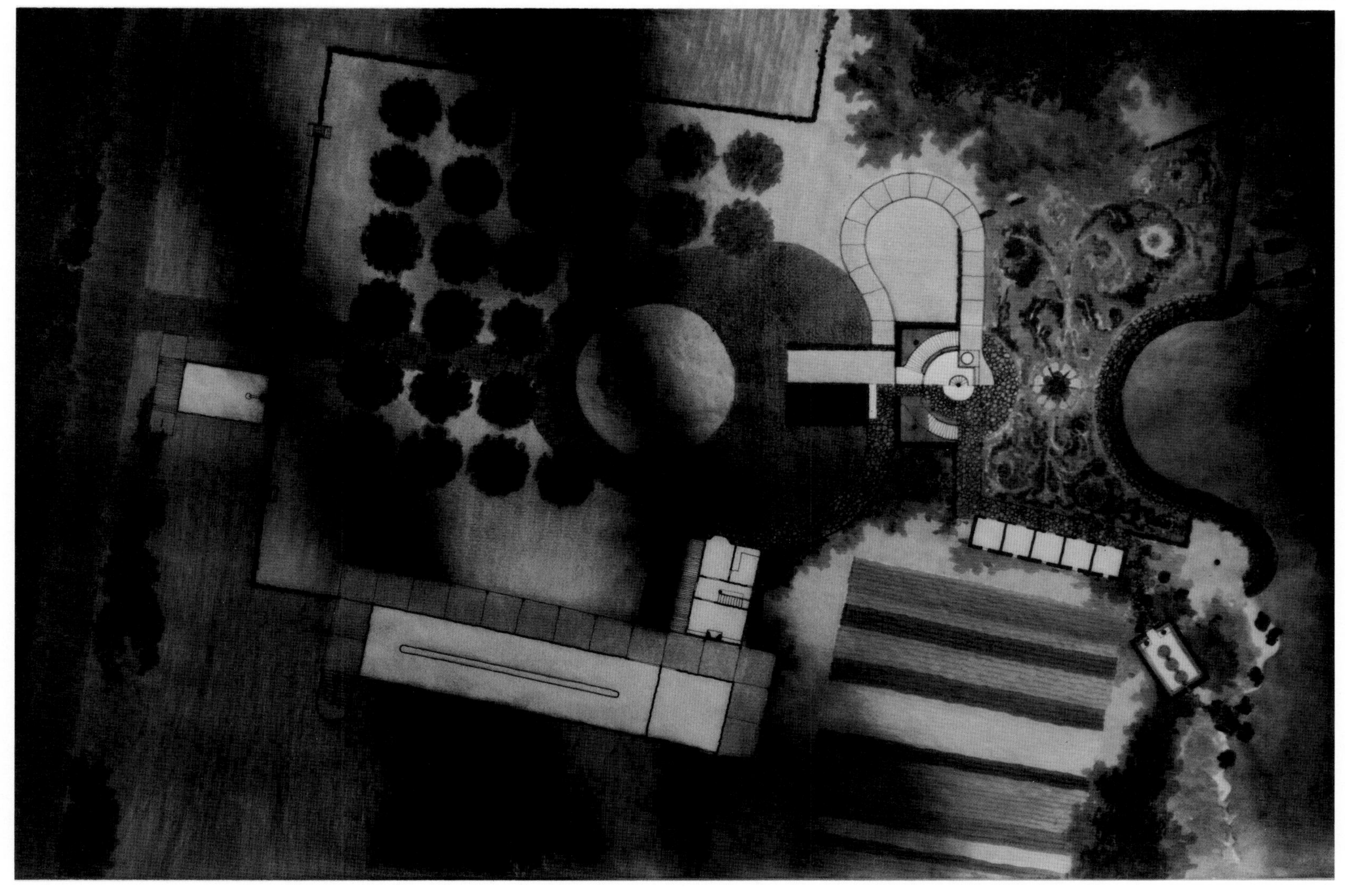

PHOTOS HEDRICH-BLESSING

Country House • Massachusetts

Symmetry, which until recently has been out of fashion in architecture, brings clarity and order to this brick residence designed in 1981 for a New England college professor. An entry porch with skylight and colonnades is the focus of the front elevation. Because it is nearly symmetrical around this entry, the house looks much larger than its 3,000 square feet. Stuccoed pavilions at each of the four corners provide a dining room, a utility entry, and two studies. As the plan shows, the house is filled with intricate spaces. It was designed by Robert Harper with Charles Moore and James Childress of Moore Grover Harper.

PHOTO ROBERT HARPER

OPPOSITE: Ornamental entry with painted wood columns and lattice. ABOVE: Front elevation, facing south, and plan.

PHOTO WAYNE BERG

Chancia Apartment • New York City

Architect Wayne Berg created this 600-square-foot apartment in 1981 on a budget so small he won't reveal it. Created for a woman and her child, the design springs from the need to make this efficiency apartment truly efficient. It is accomplished with an ornamental flourish that makes the space glow. Screened with bright fabric supported by a freestanding column-and-beam system, a bed has been added at one end of the living room, with a dining table next to it (below). In the "real" bedroom, which now belongs to the child (opposite), Berg has inserted a loft structure which frees most of the floor for sitting and working.

PHOTO WAYNE BERG

Shapleigh House • Massachusetts Coast

The adventure of this house is in its freestanding screens, its doorways that frame vistas but don't enclose space, its applied latticework, and its ladders to the sky. Through these devices, the internal courtyard becomes almost urban, a compressed cityscape. Boston architect Graham Gund releases fantasy and emotion with these ornamental forms, but in other respects the house remains close to the long, sweeping angles of traditional New England "salt-box" construction. The main house is winterized for year-round living, but the two guesthouse pavilions are unheated, built for members of the family who return every summer.

PHOTO STEVE ROSENTHAL

ABOVE: The main house is connected by a second-level walkway to the upper bedrooms of the guesthouse, the vantage point from which this photograph was taken. OPPOSITE: Wood clapboarding is the principal material of the courtyard. Note the fantasy tower with ladders standing above the garage.

PHOTO STEVE ROSENTHAL

PHOTOS NORMAN McGRATH

Maberry Loft • New York City

Phillip Maberry, an artist who makes ceramics, fabrics, and furniture, has designed his own loft with associate Scott Walker. Or rather, he and Walker redesign it continually, using ceramics, paint, fabrics, found objects, and even found wallpaper. The Maberry loft is applied decoration with a vengeance and clearly within the Modernist tradition of shocking the bourgeoisie. The photograph below shows the loft as it was early in 1981, with some of Maberry's ceramic pieces and fabric on the walls. The photographs opposite show it several months later with different wallpapers and painted patterns in a new arrangement.

PHOTO NORMAN McGRATH

OPPOSITE, TOP LEFT: Wall pattern is roll-on stencil over paint; the frieze above it is painted with a brush. TOP RIGHT: A Maberry silkscreened fabric is backlit in its alcove. BOTTOM: Ceramic bowls displayed on painted plywood shelf and illuminated by thrift-shop lamps, LEFT, are by Maberry, as is the slip-cast cone vase supported by wall-mounted brackets, RIGHT.

Nelson Entrance Hall • New York City

When architect Peter Nelson redesigned his loft in 1976, he commissioned artist Richard Haas to paint this entrance foyer. It is a masterpiece of architectural trompe l'oeil, a Neoclassical fantasy in which nearly every detail is painted. The walls below the skylight beam are oil-on-canvas so that the architectural details and painted scenes, particularly the arcade vista and garden vistas, can be removed by the owners if the loft is sold. The floor is made of standard Masonite sheets over wood and painted to look like inlaid stone. Even the exposed sprinkler pipe is occasionally painted "into" the wall. Haas first studied the loft space in model form; then the actual painting was completed by seven people in about five weeks.

PHOTOS CERVIN ROBINSON

ABOVE AND OPPOSITE: The entrance foyer is illuminated by a skylight, which adds to the magic of the space.

PHOTO OPPOSITE PAGE CERVIN ROBINSON

PHOTO NORMAN McGRATH

Park Avenue Apartment • New York City

The looming columns in this apartment are pure sculpture, freestanding and graduated in size from one room to the next. The pair in the library (below) is bigger than the pair in the foyer, and the single column of the living room (opposite) is the biggest of all. All are similar in form and linked by aluminum grid lines set into the terrazzo floor. The grid pattern is repeated by lines scored into the plaster ceiling, and the lines of both grids graduate in width as the columns graduate in size. The decorative effect of the columns and grids deliberately contradicts the existing layout of the apartment, which the designers did not want to disturb. Rather, they have linked individual rooms together conceptually, bringing the whole apartment powerfully into the present. The apartment was designed in 1978 by Italian architect Piero Sartogo in collaboration with American architect Jon Michael Schwarting, both of Design Collaborative. Italian sculptor Giulio Pollini created the columns, which are hollow and made of wood.

PHOTO NORMAN McGRATH

Hitzig Apartment • New York City

Located in one of the oldest apartment buildings in Manhattan, this apartment had Neoclassical characteristics which Robert A. M. Stern Architects wished not only to retain, but to embellish. A chair rail molding has been introduced throughout, appearing on walls, new cabinetry, and over doors. Major portals carry new columns and flat, abstracted pediments that could only have been designed today. The kitchen has been relocated behind a large freestanding cabinet wall which emulates an Edwardian china closet and screens the kitchen from the dining room. These ornamental strategies preserve the history of the apartment, but at the same time exude a humor and irony that place it very much in the present.

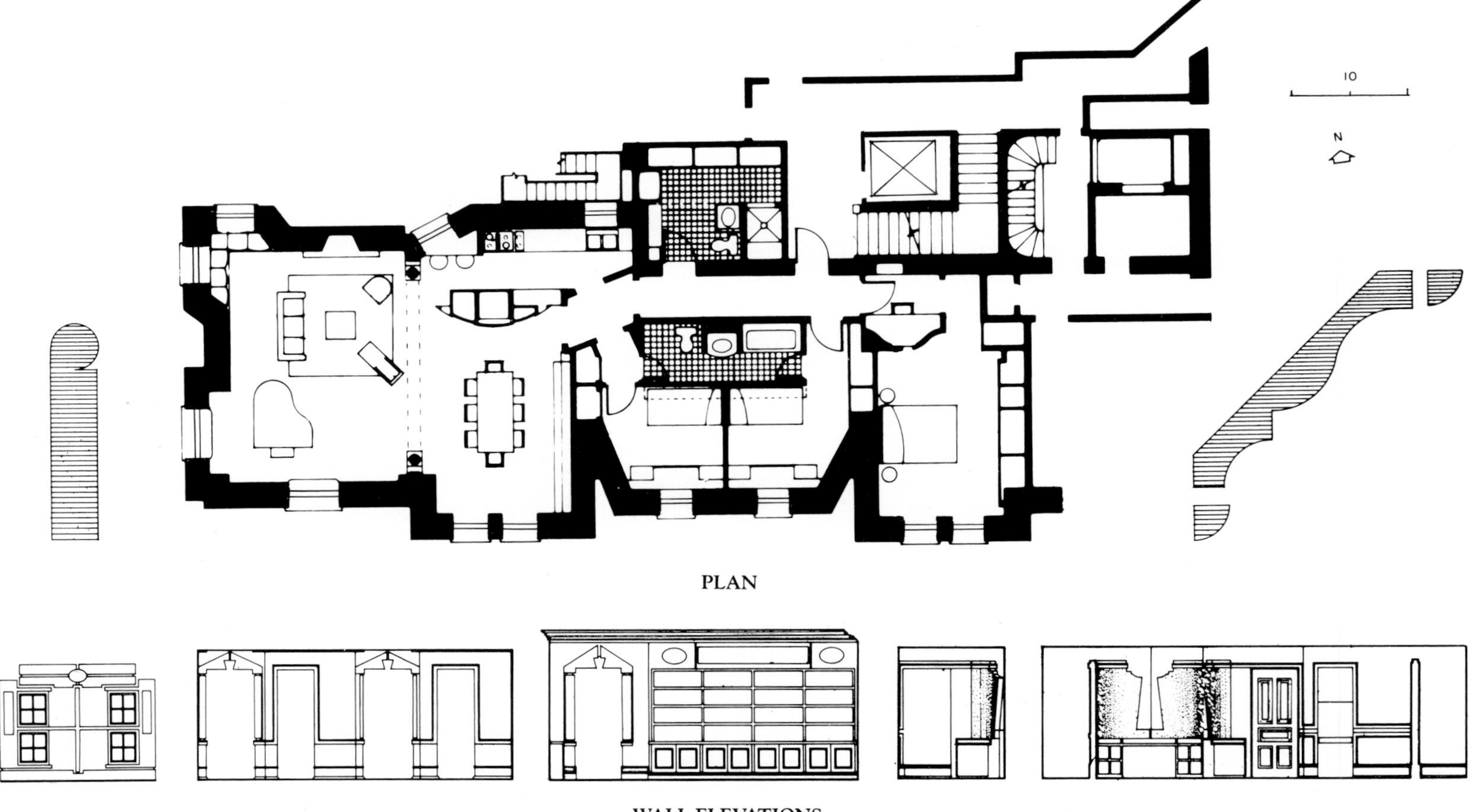

PLAN

WALL ELEVATIONS

ABOVE: Plan and wall elevations, with sections of the new chair rail and crown moldings. OPPOSITE, TOP: The dining room, LEFT, with curving, fantasy-Edwardian cabinetry screening the kitchen, and the bedroom, RIGHT, with new cabinets displaying Stern's decorative moldings. BOTTOM: An open screen between the master bedroom, LEFT, and the hall, RIGHT, creates a small study in which a Classical column appears as a negative silhouette.

PHOTOS EDMUND STOECKLEIN

PHOTO NORMAN McGRATH

Apartment Renovation • New York City

To bring a space alive, ornamental touches do not have to be lavish. Architect Peter Wilson designed tile bands and exposed neon lighting to accent his straightforward changes to this small New York apartment, and they are the whole show. Or rather, they complement the show. This owner displays no books and no paintings in the space; his favorite entertainment is inviting friends over for an evening in front of his huge Advent TV screen. The glitter of neon and glazed tile fit well with this contemporary lifestyle. Below is the living room and, opposite, the dining and kitchen area.

PHOTO NORMAN McGRATH

Eftekhari Apartment • New York City

Fantasy columns, freestanding screen walls, and a planter box eroded to look like a ruin are the devices used to embellish and enlarge this small apartment. Architect Wayne Berg is alluding to nature here, more than to past architectural styles. No Egyptian columns ever looked quite like these; they shape the space and bring humor and vitality to the room but support nothing at all. The columns are painted cardboard sonotubes, normally used as poured-concrete molds and inexpensively available. The capitals can be quickly made from stiff cardboard sheets, cut with a knife, glued, taped, and painted. Completed in 1979, all new work in this 800-square-foot apartment, including furniture, cost $16,000.

PHOTO WAYNE BERG

ABOVE: Eftekhari living room, looking back at the entry. OPPOSITE: Columns dominate the entry, TOP, and help to screen a small study, BOTTOM.

PHOTOS WAYNE BERG

Gillette Apartment • New York City

Richard Gillette is not an architect but an artist who has chosen to work on that most ubiquitous of all canvases, the twentieth-century apartment. He paints walls, ceilings, moldings, and floors, conceiving and executing surfaces as he goes, with no preliminary drawings. Like most painters, if he decides that what he did the day before isn't quite right, he changes it. Gillette's work has a haunting, ambiguous quality that asks: what time is this? what place is this? where exactly are we at this moment? The main space in this apartment, done in 1976 for his brother, is vaguely Art Deco, but the dripped paint and overlaid patterning of subsidiary spaces like the kitchen entrance (opposite) are pure 1980s.

PHOTO NORMAN McGRATH

ABOVE: The 1930s desk made by B. Altman & Co. was discovered at a sale after the living room was painted. OPPOSITE: All surfaces, including the metal fire door, have been given several coats of acrylic paint, rubbed with steel wool, then finished with clear acrylic.

PHOTO OPPOSITE PAGE DAVID GLOMB

PHOTOS NEAL SLAVIN

ABOVE: The main bedroom of the Von Wijnberge apartment, TOP LEFT, has plaster paneling painted to resemble yellow marble. The wood platform for the bed is painted similarly, with concealed headboard lights beneath frosted glass. The living room, RIGHT AND BOTTOM LEFT, displays a canvas by Gillette as well as his *faux marbre* and *faux bois* finishes.

Von Wijnberge Apartment • New York City

One of the Wijnberge bedrooms (below) has little natural light and no view. So, when artist Richard Gillette painted it in 1978, he filled the walls between existing moldings with a dreamy landscape that expands the space both visually and psychologically. A vaguely Classical pavilion is seen through pine trees while a sphinxlike creature admires herself in a mirror.

The desk is made from two metal filing cabinets painted *faux marbre* with a similarly painted wood top. On top of the desk is a wood column (probably salvaged from a house porch) found in a junk shop and painted to look like cement. The moldings on the walls are rubbed with bronzing powder and sealed with clear acrylic.

PHOTO NEAL SLAVIN

Tigerman Apartment • Los Angeles, California

Jim Tigerman, creative director of Tigerdale Studios in Los Angeles, brings to his own apartment the fabric-and-fantasy for which his furniture and lighting designs are known (see pages 233–35). The apartment, which he shares with his partner Norman List, is a bit like a tent in the desert, but other images are less familiar. Chunky ballerina legs support a table; a huge black horse stares out on the Los Angeles skyline; strange stuffed flowers and animals seem to inhabit the rooms.

The intrigue of Tigerman's space lies in little surprises and strange juxtaposition of scales, yet these surprising objects and spaces are constructed of the most straightforward materials and techniques. The ballerina legs are wooden, padded, and covered in canvas, while the black horse has a wood armature covered with stuffed muslin, Dacron, and a final layer of black suede. The two-floor apartment contains 1,750 square feet of interior space.

PHOTOS DAVID GLOMB

ABOVE: Miles of unbleached muslin drape the walls of the Tigerman bedroom. The bed, which faces a television set placed as if on a stage, has backs all around like a couch. OPPOSITE: The "Red Room" is just that, and in it a black carousel horse made by Tigerdale Studios pulls a red satin-trimmed cart.

PHOTO OPPOSITE PAGE DAVID GLOMB

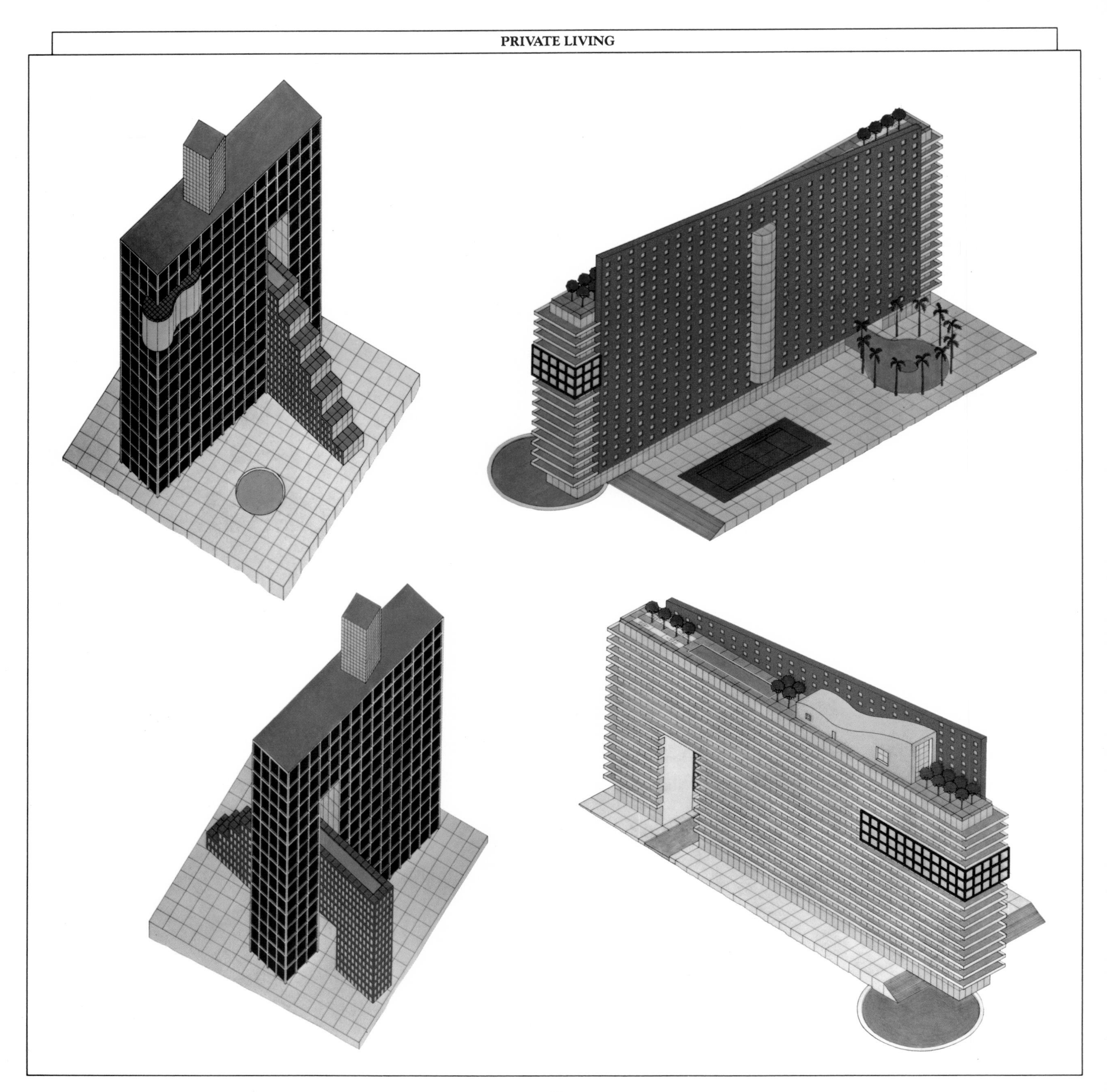

Atlantis, Palace, and Imperial Condominiums • Miami, Florida

These three luxury apartment buildings on Biscayne Bay in downtown Miami have been designed by a firm of young architects calling themselves Arquitectonica. Each building was commissioned by a different developer, but all three are scheduled for completion by late 1982. Their ornamental quality is their color and the way in which subsidiary forms seem to attach themselves to the basic slabs like gigantic decoration. The Atlantis appears to have a huge screen in front of its actual walls; the Palace has a six-story free-form curving cantilever of glass-encased space jutting out from its top; and the roof of the Imperial sprouts a wild yellow penthouse. Laurinda Spear, one of the principals of Arquitectonica, says of her firm's work, "We tend to use very large-scale 'decoration' which is usually functional, too."

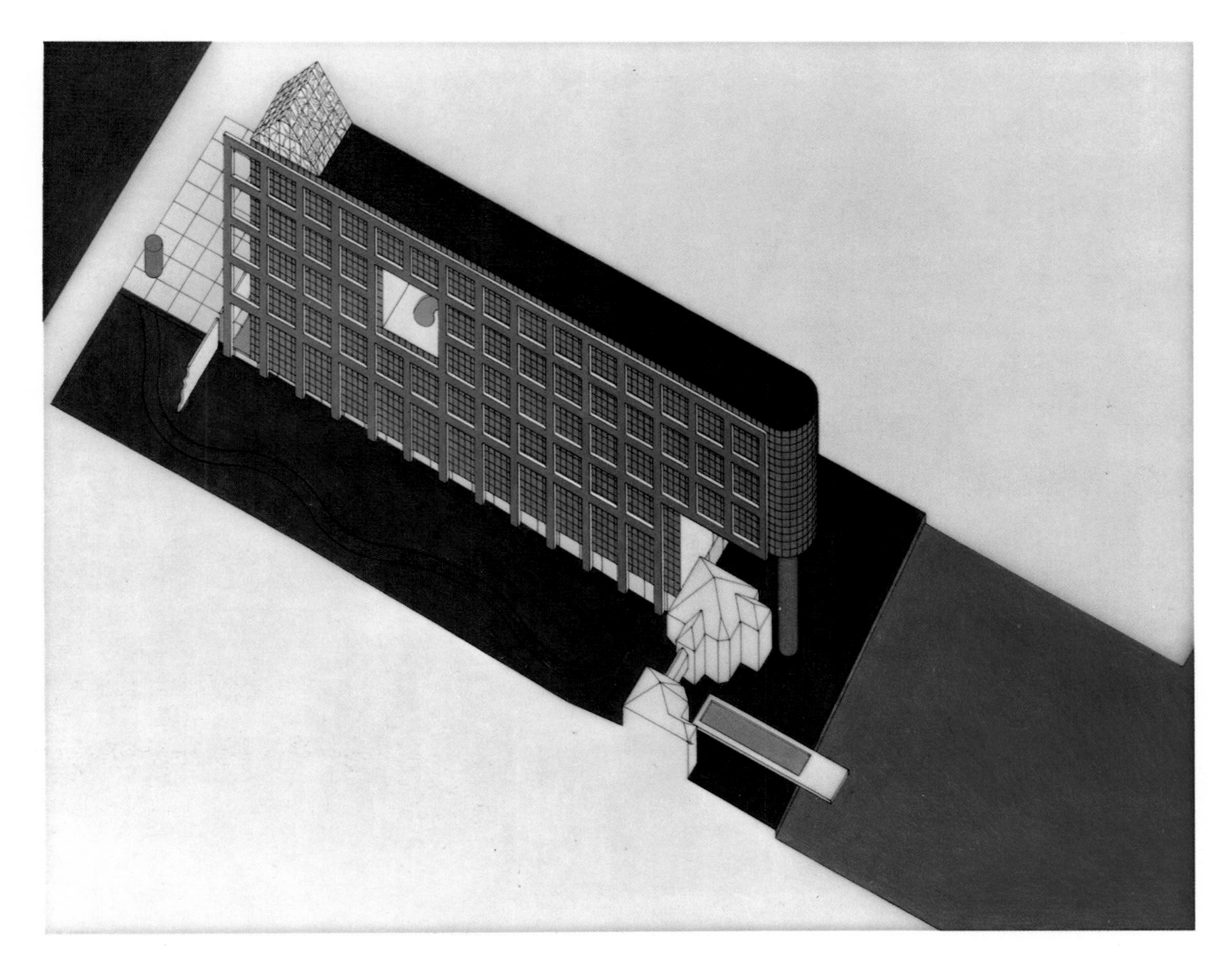

ABOVE: The Atlantis is a 21-story, 96-unit condominium on the site of an old mansion which will be restored as a clubhouse for apartment owners. OPPOSITE, LEFT: Two views of the Palace condominium, which contains 254 units in 41 stories. The giant "stairway," which houses a health club, seems to pierce the building. RIGHT: Two views of the Imperial, which offers 107 flats, 5 duplex townhouses, and a 2-story penthouse to be occupied by the developer of this Miami condominium.

Les Arcades du Lac • St. Quentin-en-Yvelines, France

Twenty-five kilometers from Paris, not far from Versailles, stands a project which substantiates, at a larger scale than any other recent example, the current revolution of style within architecture. It is a 322-unit social housing complex, including public spaces and some private commercial spaces within it. And it is industrialized housing: its exterior walls are of precast concrete, a system of construction in which concrete is formed into large panels on the ground, then lifted into place with a crane. Most industrialized housing projects look like endless rows of boxes, expressing only their technology. But Les Arcades du Lac is different: its arcades, Classical plan, and intricate embellishments express that order, human scale, and spatial balance that we associate with the best architecture of the past. The firm of Taller de Arquitectura designed Les Arcades du Lac and its adjoining wing, called Le Viaduc.

PHOTOS DEIDI VON SCHAEWEN

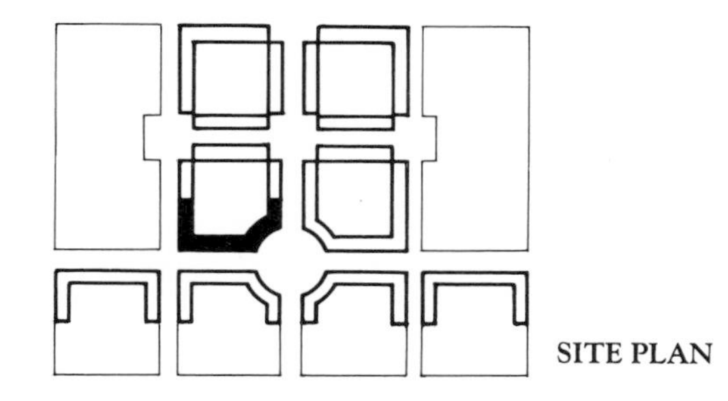

SITE PLAN

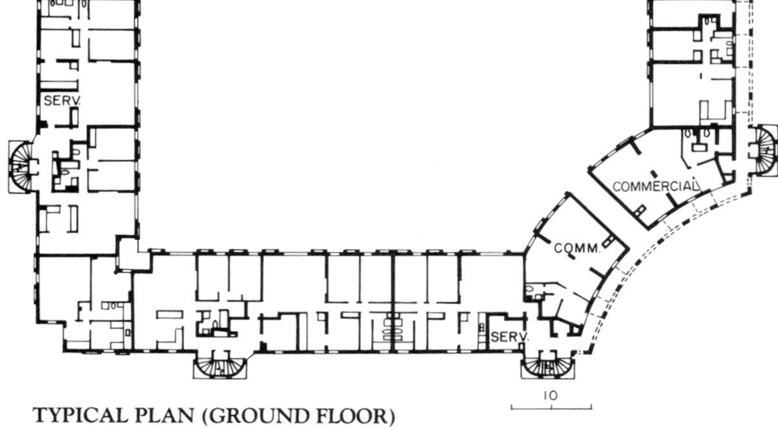

TYPICAL PLAN (GROUND FLOOR)

OPPOSITE: Aerial view of Les Arcades du Lac under construction. ABOVE: A portion of the ground-floor plan and the site plan, with photos of the arcades, courtyard, and arches taken just prior to completion.

PHOTOS DEIDI VON SCHAEWEN

Taller de Arquitectura is a group of architects based in Barcelona, Spain, and headed by Ricardo Bofill. Bofill has been responsible for housing complexes and apartment buildings around Barcelona over the last fifteen years, but none has been as large as Les Arcades du Lac. Construction began in 1978 and was completed late 1981.

ABOVE: End elevations, LEFT, of Le Viaduc, adjoining Les Arcades du Lac and similar in construction and materials. An arcade, RIGHT, shows precast concrete finished to expose the stones of its aggregate. OPPOSITE: A reflecting pool surrounding Le Viaduc lends it a monumental presence.

PHOTO OPPOSITE PAGE DEIDI VON SCHAEWEN

Le Viaduc

PHOTO JEREMY PRESTON

Byker Redevelopment • Newcastle-upon-Tyne, England

Rising like a walled medieval town, Byker is a new public housing estate for 7,000 people, designed by Swedish architect Ralph Erskine. The entire northern edge of its 200-acre site is bounded by a wall of housing up to eight stories high and decorated with brightly colored ventilators, occasional windows, and an intricate brick patterning that makes the complex look like a half-mile-long mural. The wall separates Byker from rail lines, a planned four-lane highway, and industrial squalor to the north. Residential units within the wall face south and overlook the walkways and gardens of the two- and three-story housing that forms the bulk of the estate. The smaller units, too, are colorful, witty, and decorative. The Byker Redevelopment, which began construction in 1970, is now about 85 percent complete.

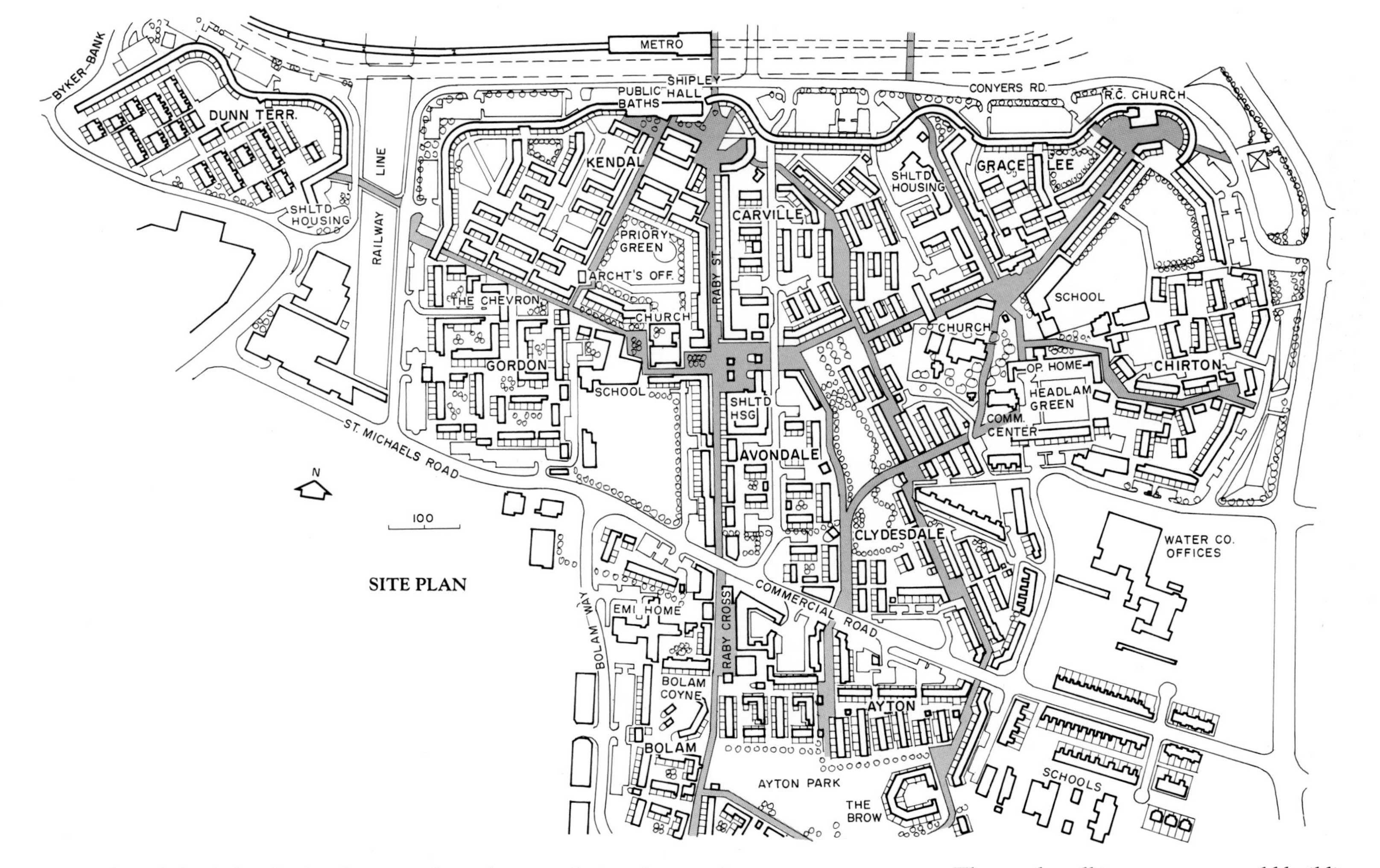

ABOVE: Plan of the Byker Redevelopment shows housing designed to take advantage of the contours of the land and grouped to enclose intimate spaces. OPPOSITE: The north wall incorporates an old building, now called Shipley Hall, which once contained public baths.

PHOTOS JEREMY PRESTON

PHOTO JEREMY PRESTON

OPPOSITE TOP: Northern wall of Byker Redevelopment surrounding Kendal and Dunn Terrace. BOTTOM: Three-story housing at Raby Street Crescent, LEFT, and units in the Bolam Coyne neighborhood, RIGHT. ABOVE: Raby Cross with garden in foreground. Erskine mixes brick, concrete, wood, metal, and bright color to enliven the surfaces of these buildings.

Offices, Shops & Restaurants

Lanvin Boutique • Zurich, Switzerland

Using a variety of illusionist techniques, Swiss architects Robert Haussmann and Trix Haussmann-Högl have achieved a sense of visual intrigue and almost limitless space in this small shop completed in 1977. Strips of mirror at 45-degree angles to the entrance of the double-height showroom create an illusory U-form that acts as counterpart to the U-shaped arrangement of niches in the walls of the remaining three sides. Similarly, narrow mirror-faced doors covering half of each niche create the illusion of slim apertures through which infinite expanses of floor and ceiling are revealed. Walls, balcony, niches, and coffered stucco ceiling are *faux marbre* patterned on the genuine Rosso norvegia marble inlay at the center of the floor. Leaded-glass curtains drape halfway down the windows to create a stagelike effect.

PHOTOS FRED WALDVOGEL

ABOVE: Views into, LEFT, and out of, RIGHT, the Lanvin boutique, looking through leaded-glass windows which imitate striped fabric drapery. OPPOSITE: Views of two-level shop interior with *faux marbre* painted finishes on niches and ceiling.

PHOTO OPPOSITE PAGE FRED WALDVOGEL

Franks for the Memory • San Francisco

Berkeley architects Richard Fernau, Scott Glendinning, and Laura Hartman have created architectural space through painting in this small (1,000-square-foot) lunchtime hot dog and hamburger restaurant completed in 1978. Located in a downtown highrise that imposes strict controls on signs and external appearance, the restaurant needed an identity strong enough to overcome its essentially subordinated situation and, in effect, to allow it to become its own sign. By setting the restaurant back from the window wall and containing the space within a playful screen wall punctured with oversized hot dog cutouts, the architects have created a distinct building within a building. Space is visually expanded with mirrors on one wall and a surrealistic mural designed by Richard Fernau and artist Patrick Kennedy on another.

PHOTO LEWIS WATTS

ABOVE AND OPPOSITE, TOP: Checkerboard floor pattern continues into the plane of the hot dog mural, extending the depth of the room. OPPOSITE, BOTTOM: Axonometric drawing of restaurant space with mural laid down flat shows change in size of floor tiles at threshold, another visual trick that expands the size of the space. Note hamburger pediment over hot dog cutout in center of front wall.

Jessica McClintock Boutique • San Francisco

Completed late 1980 by San Francisco architect Hanns Kainz & Associates, the McClintock Boutique occupies the ground floor and basement of a 15½-foot-wide building that dates to 1907. A decorative cornice with dentils is appliquéd to the length of the ground-floor walls, and nonstructural overscaled trusses of precast plaster are floated across the ceiling to visually expand the 80-foot-long space. Joined to these forms are half-arch panels painted with a misty trompe l'oeil sky, Classical columns, and ghosts of cyprus trees. These panels, which can be repainted seasonally and serve to divide merchandising areas, repeat the curve of the glass overdoor on the building façade. A view from the door through the layers of half-arches to the rear of the store is terminated by four freestanding truncated columns that screen the dressing rooms. A palette of soft pinks and blues, modulated by lighting dimmers or filters, completes the romantic fantasy.

PHOTOS COLIN McRAE

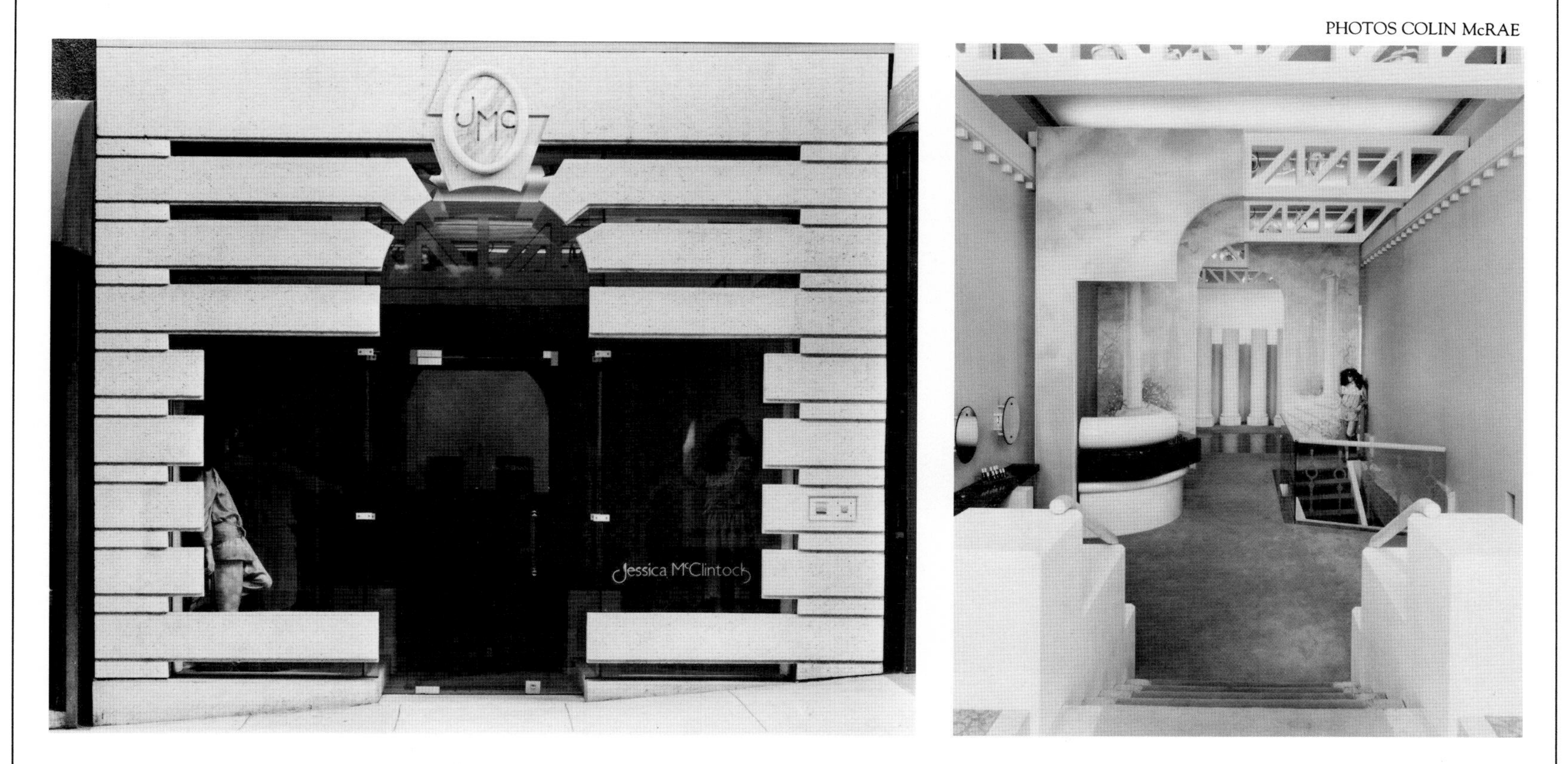

LEFT: Door and display windows are unified into a single element and cut into the precast concrete façade as a glass cruciform, above which a marble medallion carries the Jessica McClintock logo. RIGHT: Entry into the shop is dramatized by descent to the sales floor, which has been dropped 4 feet below street level. Sales desk is a massive slab of Carpathian elm burl sandwiched between two lacquer-finish pieces that suggest column fragments. Stairway to basement has an etched glass balustrade reminiscent of old San Francisco. OPPOSITE, TOP: On either side of truncated columns at rear of the store, mirrors set in undulating cove-lit niches opposite one another create multiple reflections that disappear off-axis. BOTTOM: In the basement an original pre-earthquake concrete wall is left exposed and highlighted by pearlescent paint. Floor is inset with marble stepping stones, individually lit by downlights placed above them.

Sunar Showrooms • Los Angeles & Houston

Princeton architect Michael Graves has relied on inexpensive wood framing, drywall, paint, and carefully manipulated lighting in the design of four historically evocative showrooms for Sunar, a manufacturer of modern office systems furniture. Shown here and on the following pages are the Los Angeles and Houston showrooms, completed in 1980. Both illustrate the complex color palettes through which Graves develops associations with nature and traditional building materials: terra cotta for earth/base/heaviness/warmth; white or gray for stone; green for landscape; azure for sky/top/lightness/coolness. "Rooms" are created with columns, which Graves sees as fragments of walls, and to which he attaches anthropomorphic meanings: bases are "feet," shafts are "bodies," and tops are "heads," a notion that goes back to Vitruvius.

PHOTO TIM STREET-PORTER

ABOVE: Columns, pilasters, and swags give architectural character to the exterior of the Los Angeles showroom fabric pavilion, which stands in sharp contrast to the building corridor off of which it is located. OPPOSITE: Entrance to fabric pavilion is through freestanding columns over which a beam is placed, signifying "portal." Rounded wall leading to doors is studded with ornamental brass dots.

PHOTO OPPOSITE PAGE TIM STREET-PORTER

PHOTO CHARLES McGRATH

ABOVE: In the systems furniture display area of Sunar's Houston showroom, a pale yellow ceiling with blue band, lit from below by cove lighting and sconces, recalls the sky and natural daylight. Floor-to-ceiling windows overlooking a parking lot are draped with translucent curtains, in front of which Graves has erected a latticework grid in the form of mullions symbolically echoing the real window behind. X-shaped Roman grilles at top suggest passage of light and air through a transom. OPPOSITE: Tapered passageway leads to conference-fabric room, TOP LEFT, off of an internal circulation corridor developed as a "loggia," TOP RIGHT. To reinforce sense of passage, Graves's palette is inverted, with light terra-cotta ceiling suggesting a clay tile roof, BOTTOM.

PHOTOS CHARLES McGRATH

Proposal for Marlborough Blenheim Hotel • Atlantic City, New Jersey

Before it fell to the wrecker's ball in 1978–79, the venerable Marlborough Blenheim enjoyed a brief moment of hope for continued operation as a greatly enlarged complex of shops, restaurants, parking, casino, hotel, and convention facilities. In the scheme proposed by Venturi, Rauch and Scott Brown, the interior of the old Byzantine-Moorish hotel would have been converted into meeting rooms and a new thirty-story hotel erected in a curved slab behind it. From the setbacks of the new slab to the upper portions of the old structure, the architects proposed to drape decorative cables strung with illuminated fiberglass shapes, creating the image of a three-strand necklace emblazoning the bosom of the Grand Old Lady of Atlantic City. Instead, the city now has on this site a new casino that looks not unlike an ordinary office building.

Best Products Showroom • Oxford Valley, Pennsylvania

The idea of the "decorated shed" set forth by Robert Venturi, Denise Scott Brown, and Steve Izenour in their book *Learning from Las Vegas* (1972) is realized in this catalogue-merchandising showroom completed in 1979 by Robert Venturi and David Vaughan of the Philadelphia firm Venturi, Rauch and Scott Brown. It is a simple windowless box ("shed") enveloped in gigantic flowers ("decorated") that wrap around corners and bleed up over the roof line in rough diagonals that contradict the basic structure. The floral pattern, borrowed from a French wallpaper, is hand-applied on porcelain enamel finish steel panels. It is the same pattern with which the husband-and-wife team of Venturi and Scott Brown allegedly have papered their home. Viewed from a distance (see over), the flowers seem to spring joyfully from the vegetation of an adjacent lot.

BEST

Schullin Jewellery Store • Vienna, Austria

This tiny shop was renovated in 1975 by Austrian architect Hans Hollein. By first establishing a grid over the marble façade, then cutting into the grid as though with a jeweler's tool, he achieves a scale transformation that makes the store front appear larger than it actually is (the door is just wide enough for one person to pass through). The fissure spills downward into sensual metal folds which form the door and, from within the fissure, metal tubes emerge end-lit so that one cannot see the air-conditioning unit located behind the opening. The tubes are brass and bronze, and gold-colored metals are used to clad the door and window frames. The result is shiny and luxurious, yet a bit mysterious and startlingly erotic.

PHOTO MARK MACK

Jewish Welcome Center • Vienna, Austria

An oasis of metal palm trees greets travelers arriving at the Jewish Welcome Center in Vienna. At the base of the trees a pool is cut in the mottled granite floor and fed by a small fountain. Another reminiscence of the Israeli homeland is the massive crumbled granite block wall which recalls the Wailing Wall in Jerusalem. The erosion of the wall is a device used frequently by Hollein, who completed the Welcome Center in 1979. The natural imagery of palms, pool (not visible in this photograph), and crumbled stone is dramatized by its opposition to the rigid, abstract grid of the ceiling, wall and floor, and the handsome modern seating.

PHOTO HANNS KAINZ

PHOTO HANNS KAINZ

Austrian Travel Bureau • Vienna, Austria

Opposite the Opera on Vienna's famed Ringstrasse is the Opernringhoff office building, the ground floor of which was redesigned by Hans Hollein in 1978 to house Austria's semigovernmental travel bureau. Visions of sun-filled vacations and faraway places are evoked by palm trees, a broken Classical column, and an Indian pavilion—all transformed in sleek, shiny metal and arranged on a patterned marble floor under a large vaulted skylight. A draped curtain, formed in metal, frames a woodcut comic scene by Serlio, transforming the theater-ticket sales desk into a stage set (see below). In front of the stage, four seating cubes are arranged on a portion of the floor patterned as a chessboard. These and numerous other symbolic elements in the space are designed to be movable or replaced with other objects so that changes in the function of the Bureau can be accommodated. The carefully crafted use of noble materials, like marble and bronze, distinguishes Hollein's Ornamentalism from that of many other architects who, for the moment at least, have to rely on inexpensive drywall, stucco, and paint to achieve their decorative effects.

PHOTO HANNS KAINZ

Americana Hotel Ballroom and Restaurant • Fort Worth, Texas

Images from nature have been used by New York City architect Roger Ferri, with Ben Baldwin and Jonathan Warwick, to give meaning to the lobby, ballroom, and restaurant of this hotel completed in 1981. Exploring what they term "harmonic resonance," the designers have introduced turbulence patterns, such as those found in waves, clouds, and stellar formations, as their principal ornamental motif. This motif is anticipated by naturalistic tapestries hung in the lobby adjacent to the ballroom, then exploded in the more stylized treatment of ceiling and wall panels in the ballroom itself. In the restaurant (see following page) the designers have created a "fictive outdoor room" to "domesticate" the Texas climate and bring it indoors.

PHOTOS CERVIN ROBINSON

ABOVE LEFT: One of three tapestries, each 20 × 30 ft., based on turbulence patterns in nature. This one flanks entrance to ballroom, OPPOSITE, in which ceiling is composed of free-floating acoustical baffles. The undersides of the baffles are cut to trochoid curves, the mathematical equivalent of ocean waves. The pattern is repeated in tones of gray that become progressively lighter as they descend to floor, set off by lighter piping and roundels. Doors, ABOVE RIGHT, are set in plaster frames leafed in silver.

PHOTO OPPOSITE PAGE CERVIN ROBINSON

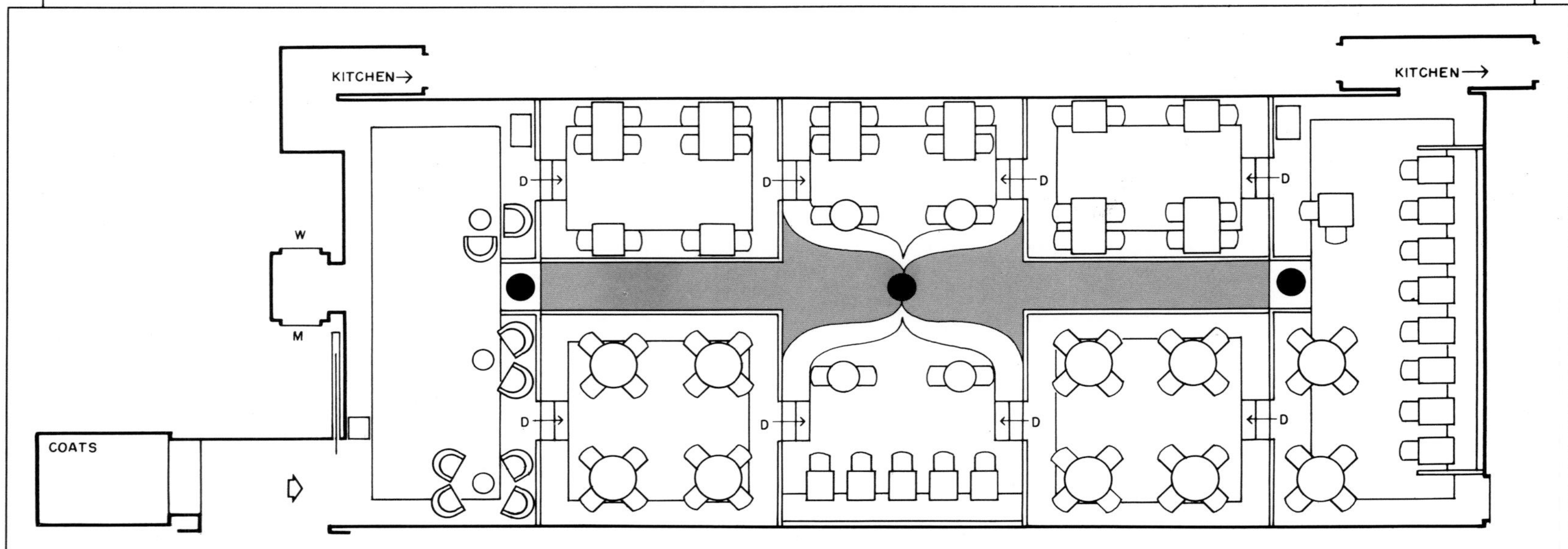

PHOTOS CERVIN ROBINSON

ABOVE: Reflections Restaurant in Americana Hotel—Tandy Center is organized around a reflecting pool (shaded area in plan, TOP), with floors terraced into parterres, BOTTOM LEFT, that create a garden amphitheater descending to water. Giant flower columns at each end, BOTTOM RIGHT, support a low ceiling open at center to an illusional night sky. A trellis springs from the central flower.

Proposal for Lutèce Restaurant • New York City

In 1976 Roger C. Ferri and Associates developed two schemes for transforming this well-known restaurant into an imaginary garden. The owners subsequently decided not to renovate: Ferri's drawings remain as early documents depicting nature as a metaphor in contemporary design. In Scheme II, shown here in plan, elevation, and axonometric drawings, columns introduced around the perimeter of the space take the shape of twisted stems, with buds concealing upspot lights. Stems and buds, finished in glazed terra cotta, appear to climb against a Corten steel trellis backed with panels of indigo velvet over sound-absorbing batting. A scrim canopy is hung beneath the existing glass shed roof to create a soft, diaphanous ceiling.

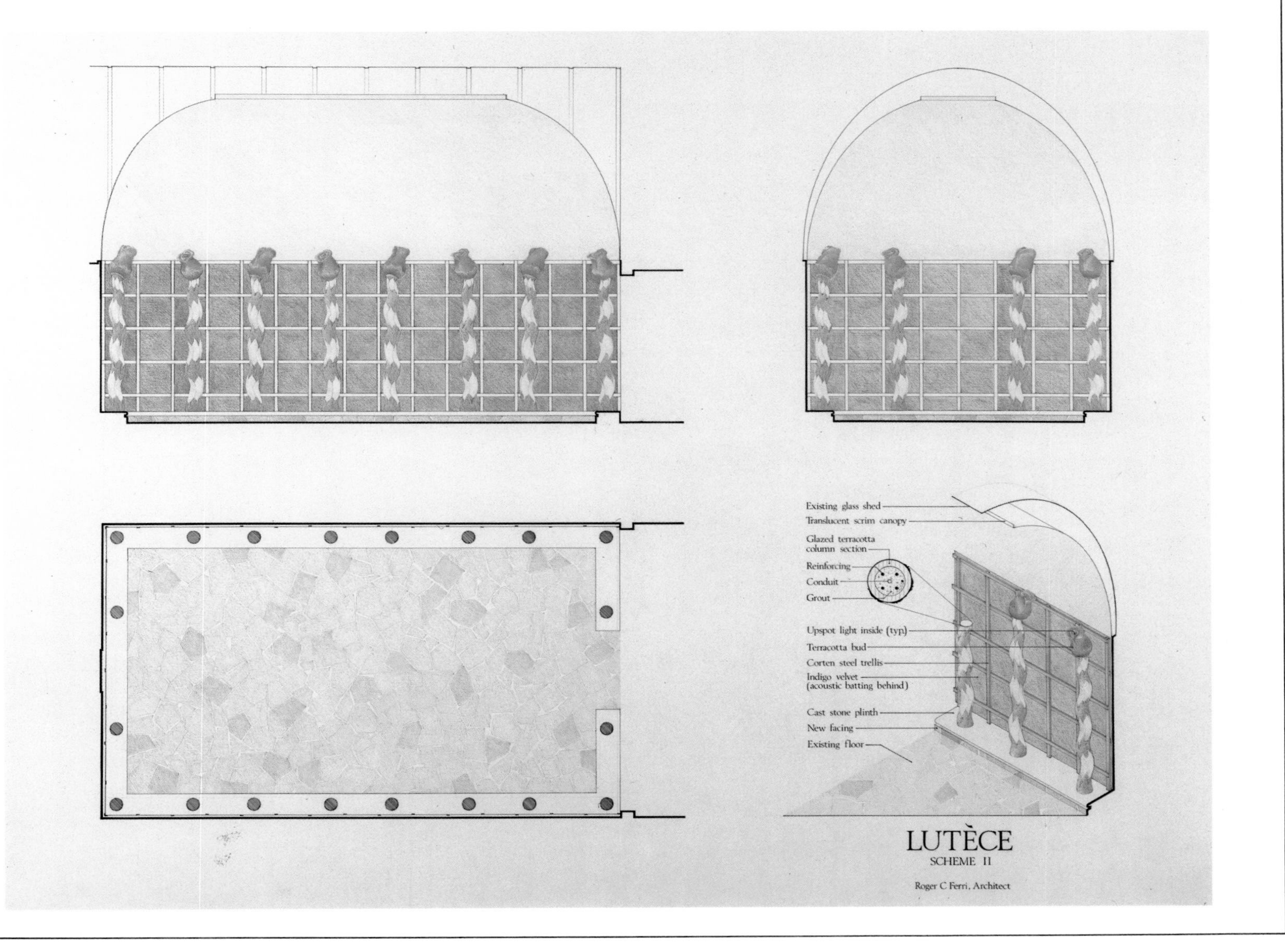

Backstreet Restaurant • New Haven, Connecticut

Architect Mark Simon of Moore Grover Harper, Essex, Connecticut, has manipulated bulbous curves, etched glass, mirror facets, and pressed-tin ceiling panels to evoke memories of Victorian saloons or steamships. The style, however, is unmistakably contemporary, with no attempt to make its historical references authentic. Located in New Haven's art center and completed in 1980, the restaurant is designed as a theatrical experience, with neon tubing used not only for lighting, but also as applied decoration and a source of architectural form. Around the bar, pink and orange neon is operated on dimmers to emit a seductive glow similar to candlelight; reflected in the shiny ceiling panels, it recalls the radiant coronas often hung above Baroque statues. A cool pastel palette tempers the excitement of the lighting.

PHOTOS NORMAN McGRATH

PHOTO NORMAN McGRATH

OPPOSITE: Flanked by fat beaded columns, the etched glass "swallow-tail" swinging doors, LEFT, lead into the bar, RIGHT, which is hand-crafted of solid walnut with cherry inlays and backed by a cityscape of mirrors, bottles, and neon. ABOVE: Another cityscape of neon sky-scrapers and streetlights ornaments the large plate-glass windows through which Backstreet is viewed from outside.

Le Cygne Restaurant • New York City

When the former site of this restaurant was acquired for construction of a new highrise office building and "vest pocket" park, Le Cygne moved one door east to a brownstone renovated for its use by architects Bartholomew Voorsanger, Richard Velsor, and Charles Crowley of the New York firm Voorsanger & Mills Associates. On the exterior, the designers worked up "layers of history and modernity." At the ground, they added a projecting façade for the first 20 feet in granite, with metal columns finished in baked enamel to match the new adjacent highrise. Above the new granite façade, the wall is stucco painted to relate to an old adjacent brownstone. At the roof line, an original ornamental cornice is retained. For zoning reasons, only two floors could be constructed within the five-story shell, creating the opportunity for a four-story entrance foyer leading to two levels of dining, each one-and-one-half story high. The new location will open in 1982.

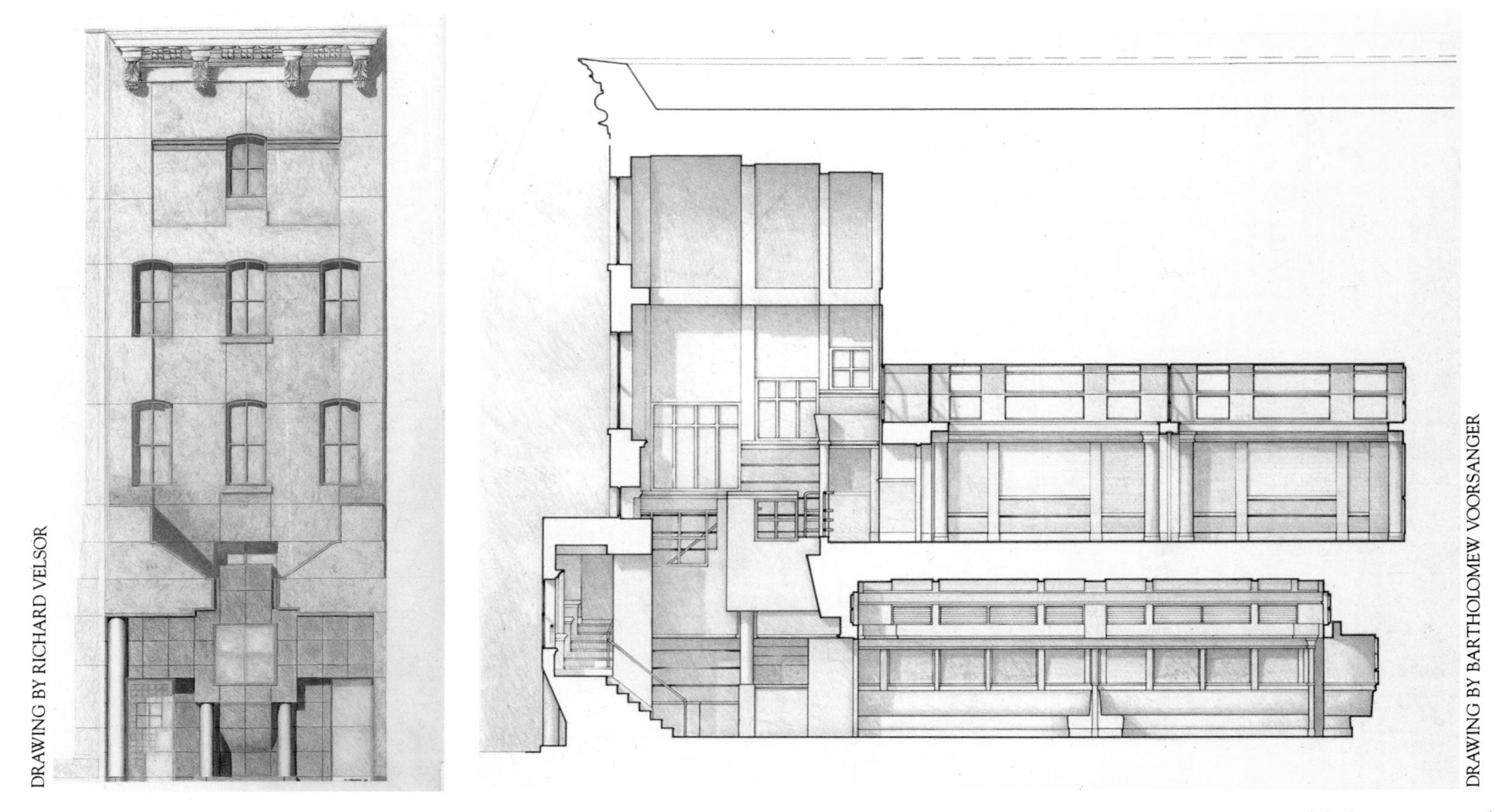

ABOVE: Heightening of corner column, LEFT, begins transition in scale from low brownstone to adjacent highrise. Painted stucco wall above signifies that entire building has one use and calls out the four-story entrance foyer, RIGHT, behind it. According to the architects, the interior evolved as a study of Impressionism, with pinks and lavenders in the lower level alluding to morning, and light orange and ocher in the upper level alluding to late afternoon. Spaces are intended to create the effect of a stacked arboretum, with light "squeezed" in from all sides. OPPOSITE: Interior elevations of front, LEFT, and rear, RIGHT, walls.

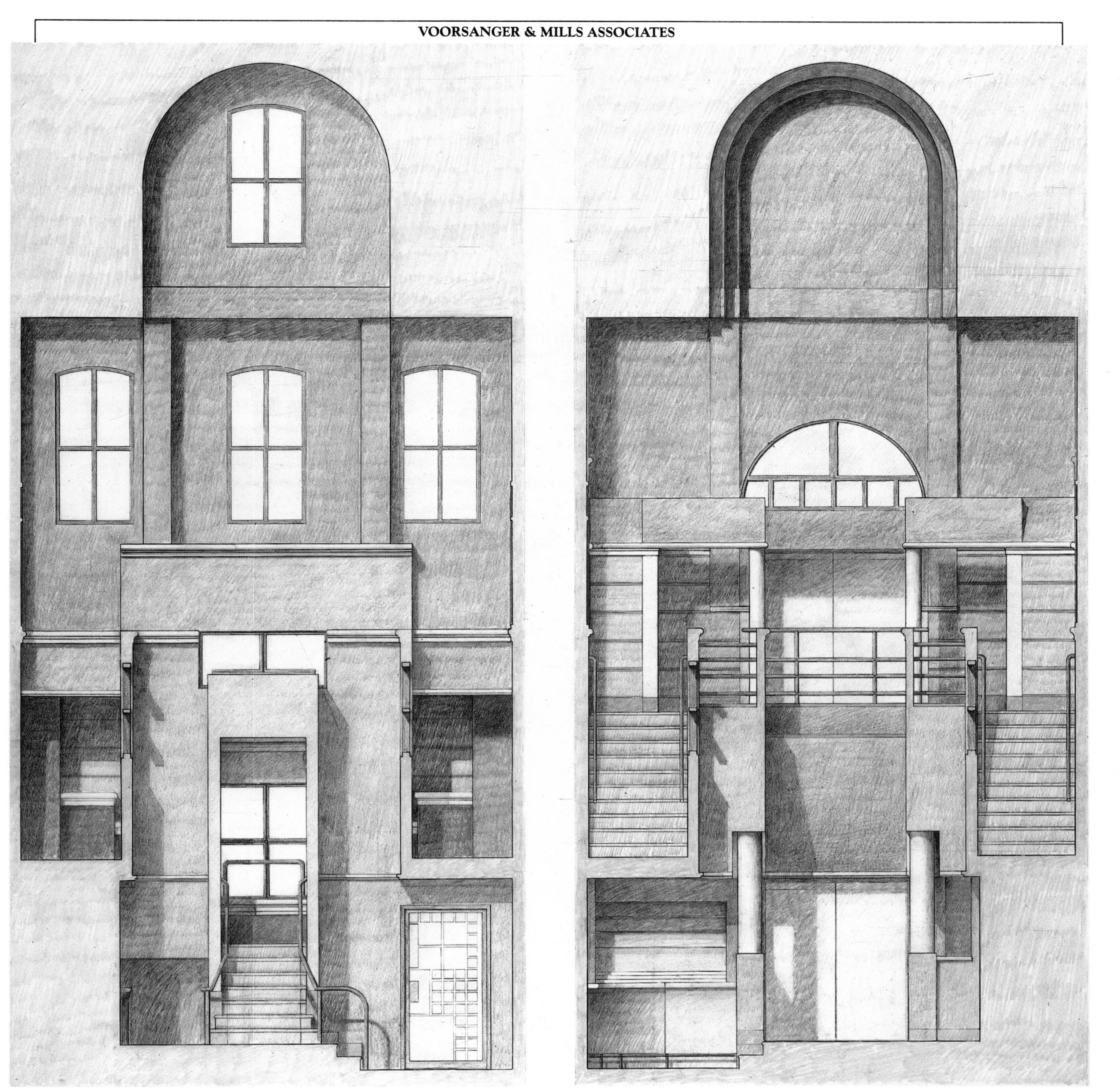

DRAWING BY CHARLES CROWLEY

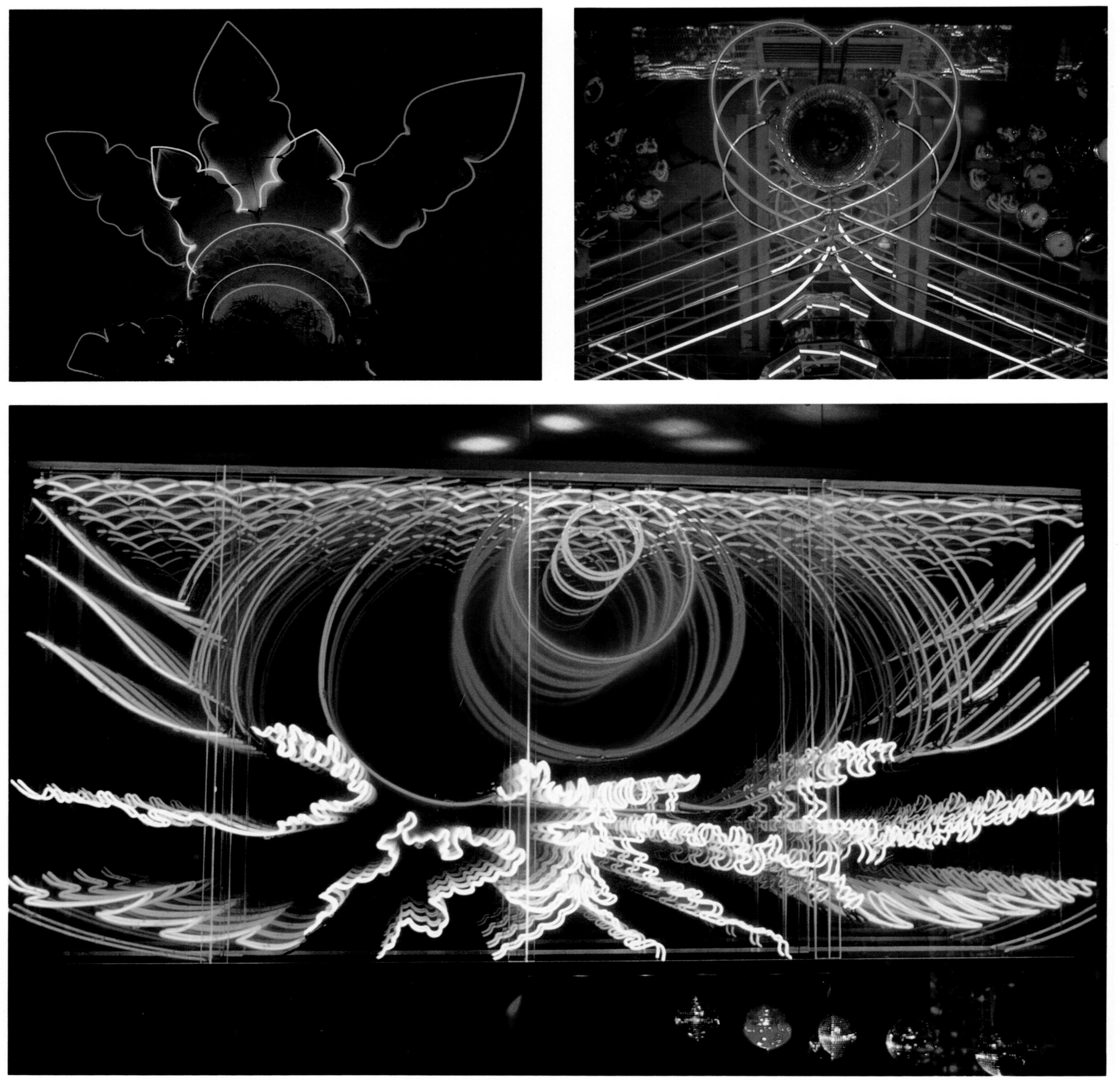

PHOTOS BELISSIMO/WRIGHT STUDIOS INC.

Electronic Ornament • Lighting as Kinetic Decoration

A new decorative medium available to designers today is electronically controlled lighting. Although its use in nonentertainment settings is just beginning to be explored, the ornamental possibilities of kinetic lighting are already apparent in discos, nightclubs, bars, and restaurants. Shown here are several installations created by Design Circuit Inc. of New York City, a pioneer in the field. With the exception of the "Scaramouche Wave," all are orchestrated on bioelectric keyboards to emit varying patterns of light synchronized to music. The visual effect of the "Wave," while not orchestrated, can be changed from time to time.

PHOTO BELISSIMO/WRIGHT STUDIOS INC.

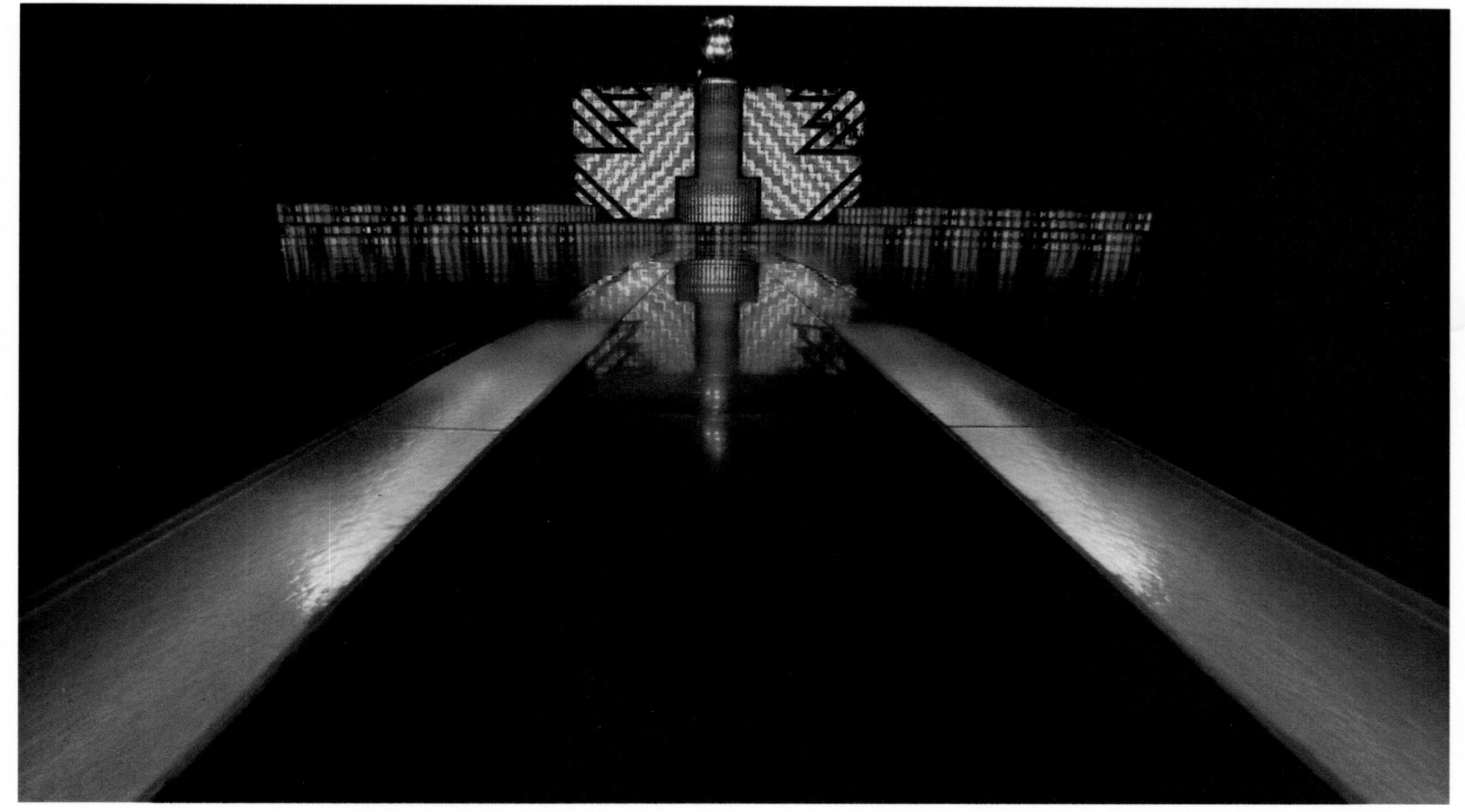

ABOVE: Back wall and focal point of Emerald City disco, Cherry Hill, New Jersey. Designed 1978 by George Heyward and Robert Lobi. Behind black parquet floor with inlaid glass panels rise two tiered dance platforms, wall, and 17-foot tower faced in original 1930s Art Deco glass block, and lit by 200 channels of sequential light and 24 channels of theatrical lighting. OPPOSITE, TOP LEFT: Original palm tree in the Copacabana, New York City, restored by Joe Spencer and Robert Lobi, 1976, and outlined in neon. TOP RIGHT: Three-dimensional neon heart in Régine's, New York City, designed by Michael Zaner and Robert Lobi, 1978. BOTTOM: "Scaramouche Wave," neon and Fresnell flood sculpture, Omni International Hotel, Miami, designed by George Heyward and Robert Lobi, 1978.

Best Products Headquarters • Richmond, Virginia

New York City architects Hardy Holzman Pfeiffer Associates have managed to "soften" technology with a cheerful sense of decorativeness in this 68,000-square-foot corporate office building completed late 1979. A curved glass block wall on the front of the building, topped by an ornamental glazed terra-cotta cornice, admits enough ambient light to reduce artificial lighting requirements, thus saving energy, while the arrangement of clear glass windows in a diamond pattern makes a strong decorative statement. Inside, the architects have taken advantage of the unusually high 13-foot ceilings by designing work-station dividers in the form of wardrobes or small-scale Colonial houses complete with cornices. The dividers contain storage space and all wiring and cables for telephones, task lighting, and computer terminals. While providing state-of-the-art functionalism, these work stations have a warmth and intimacy that go a long way toward humanizing the work environment, a problem not many open office furniture systems have really addressed.

PHOTO NORMAN McGRATH

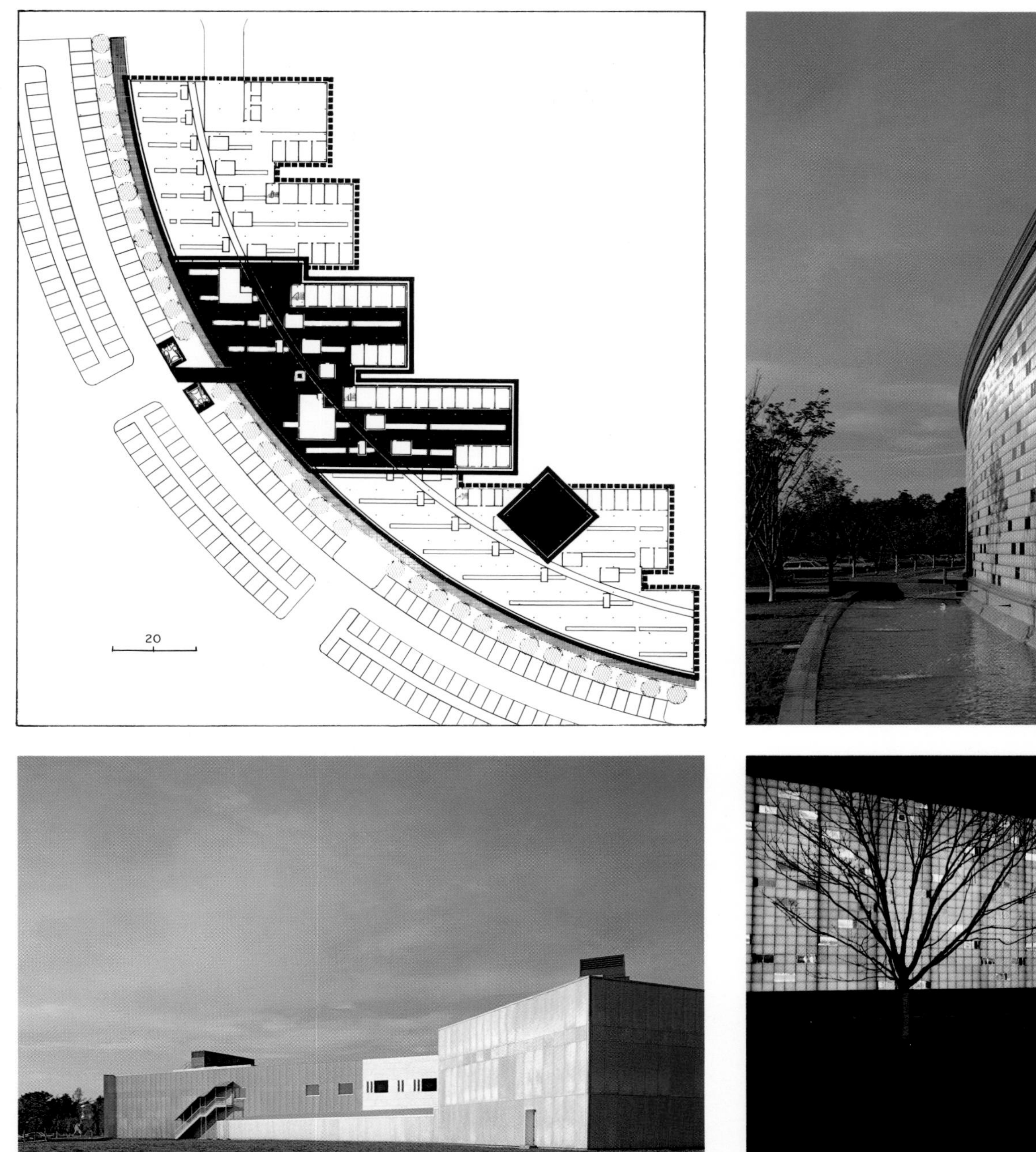

PHOTOS NORMAN McGRATH

OPPOSITE: Main entrance is given ceremonial presence by Moderne eagles salvaged from New York City's 1939 Airlines Building. TOP LEFT: Plan showing open office areas along translucent front wall, private offices to the rear, and potential for future expansion. TOP RIGHT: Curved glass block wall of front façade bordered by linear reflecting pool; same wall at night with diamond pattern of windows illuminated. BOTTOM: Straightforward treatment of rear façade, LEFT, underscores decorative intent of front wall which, when illuminated at night, RIGHT, reveals diamond pattern of windows even more clearly.

PHOTOS NORMAN McGRATH

PHOTO NORMAN McGRATH

OPPOSITE, TOP LEFT: Inside Best Products Headquarters, main circulation path follows curve of front façade, running counter to orthogonal grid of open office layout. TOP RIGHT: Part of company's major art collection displayed in double-height atrium. BOTTOM LEFT: Conference room with illuminated table by furniture maker Edward Zucca, whose work is also shown on page 220. BOTTOM RIGHT: Internal stair connecting two levels of open plan work area. ABOVE: A ceramic tile pattern reminiscent of nineteenth-century cafés marks the main circulation path, offset against water lily carpet designed by artist Jack Beal.

Tigerman Office • Chicago

Chicago architect Stanley Tigerman created this illusional setting for his own five-person office in 1978. Above the drawing boards, an oversized pencil is suspended as if drawing a line around the trompe l'oeil sky painted in a circular dome. The sky appears to illuminate the room with indirect light projected from the Corinthian capital that tops a freestanding acrylic column. Ceiling moldings, french doors, and other original architectural details are given decorative emphasis to heighten the play of modern, functional drafting equipment against the 1893 interior. Hats and apples on drawing boards are an homage to Magritte.

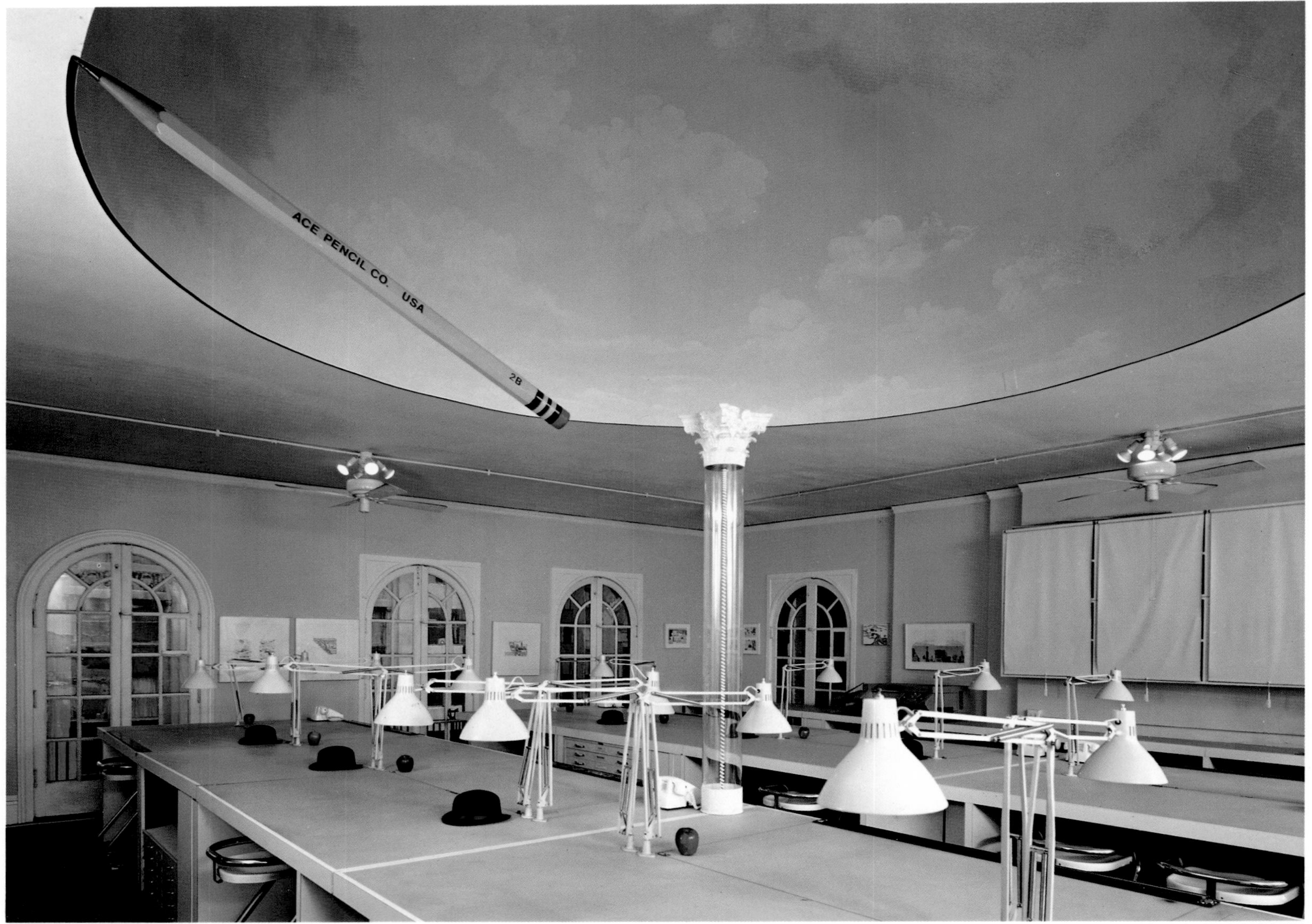

PHOTO SADIN/KARANT

Bank of San Paolo • New York City

Behind the slick glass skin of a new highrise on Park Avenue, architects Edward Mills, Wanatha Garner, and Zerline Joffe of Voorsanger & Mills Associates have designed headquarters for the Instituto Bancario San Paolo di Torino, evoking this bank's Italian origins. The arcades of Turin's Piazza San Carlo, where the bank's home office is located, are alluded to in drywall construction and inlaid carpet along the elevator lobby, through the reception area, and down the major circulation corridor (see plan, below). Important pieces of furniture, such as the reception desk, were designed by the architects and custom fabricated as part of the allusive cityscape. A complex layering of surfaces, articulated with seventeen different paint colors, nine lacquer colors, and six carpet colors, belies the tight budget for this project, completed late 1980.

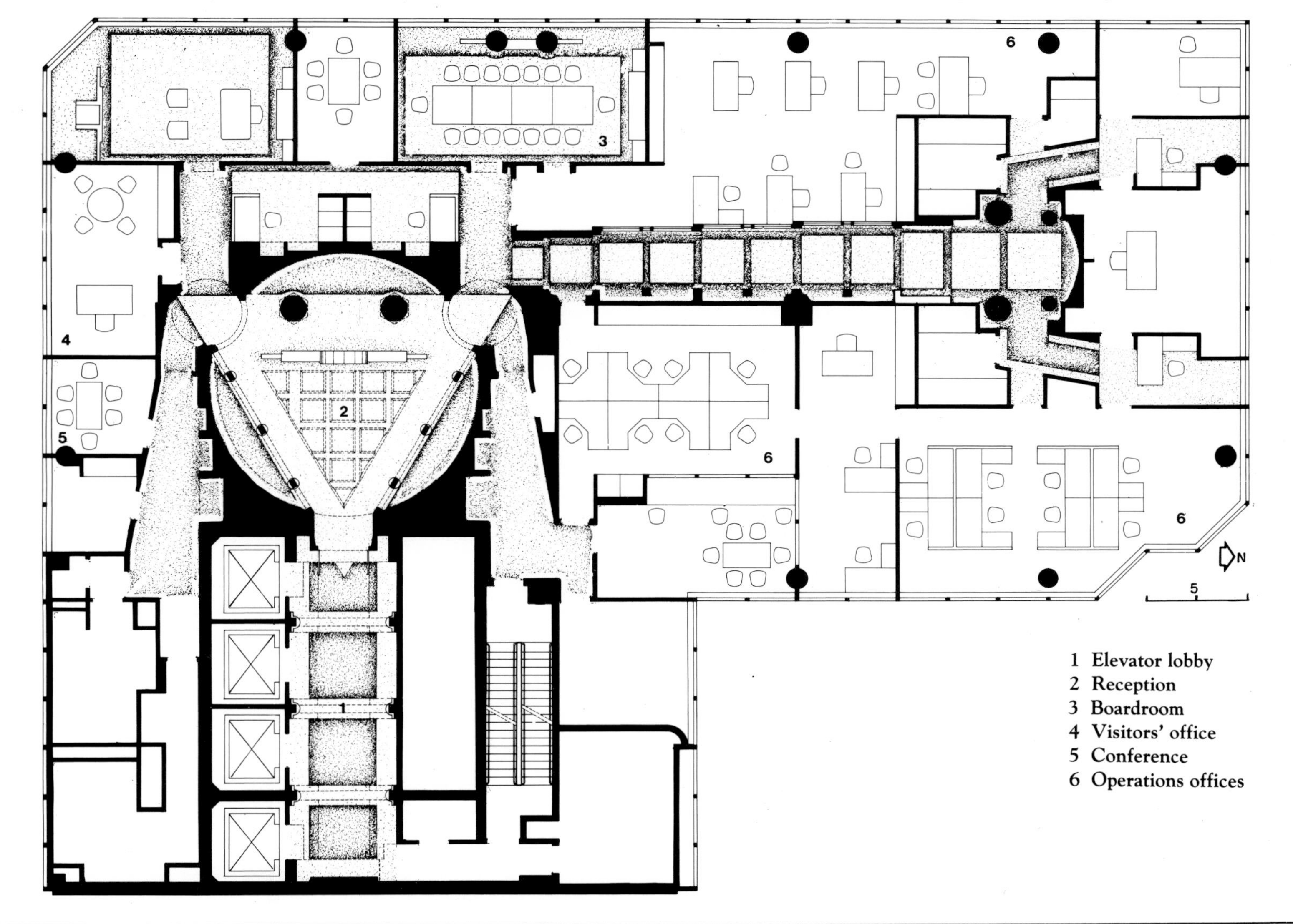

1 Elevator lobby
2 Reception
3 Boardroom
4 Visitors' office
5 Conference
6 Operations offices

PHOTO PETER AARON, ESTO

ABOVE: Custom-designed desk, with illuminated panel creating the illusion of columns supporting a slab, becomes an architectural element in the Bank of San Paolo reception area. Screen wall arcades on either side of reception area, multilayered partition behind the desk, and exposed structural concrete coffer above are all contained in a rotunda (note curved wall at rear illuminated by sconces) which inflects movement from elevator lobby off to circulation corridors at right and left. OPPOSITE, CLOCKWISE FROM BOTTOM LEFT: Looking into reception area from elevator lobby; view back to lobby endwall where statuary from bank's home office is to be installed; space between reception area screen wall and curved endwall punctuated by two oversized columns; and corner detail of reception desk set against multilayered screen wall.

PHOTOS PETER AARON, ESTO

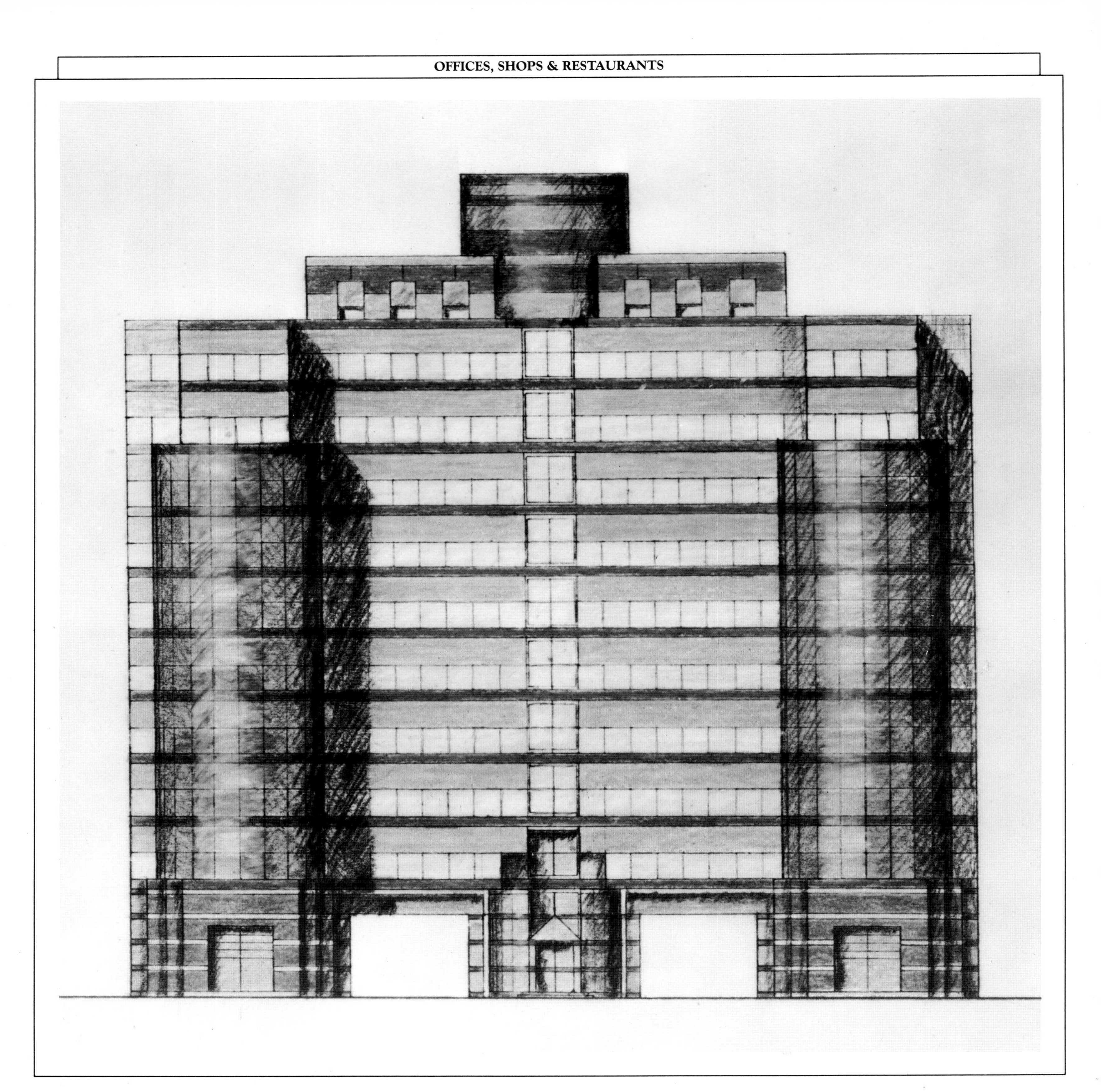

San Felipe Office Building • Houston, Texas

To achieve a strong visual image for this modestly budgeted speculative office building, architects Edward Mills, Conrad Wos, and Charles Crowley of Voorsanger & Mills Associates have developed the surface in bands of color that call attention to the building's most important features. Nine floors of typical office space are identified by bands of red-brown and dark gray painted fiberglass panels alternating with light gray glass. The glass color shifts to green on the rounded endwalls, which recall giant columns. These endwalls also help to direct traffic by marking the vehicular drives through the building into the garage at rear. Green vision glass distinguishes the tall lobby atrium at the center on the ground level as well as the office penthouse which is set in at the top of the building below the rounded mechanical penthouse. Scheduled for completion in 1983, the building contains 180,000 square feet of office space plus parking.

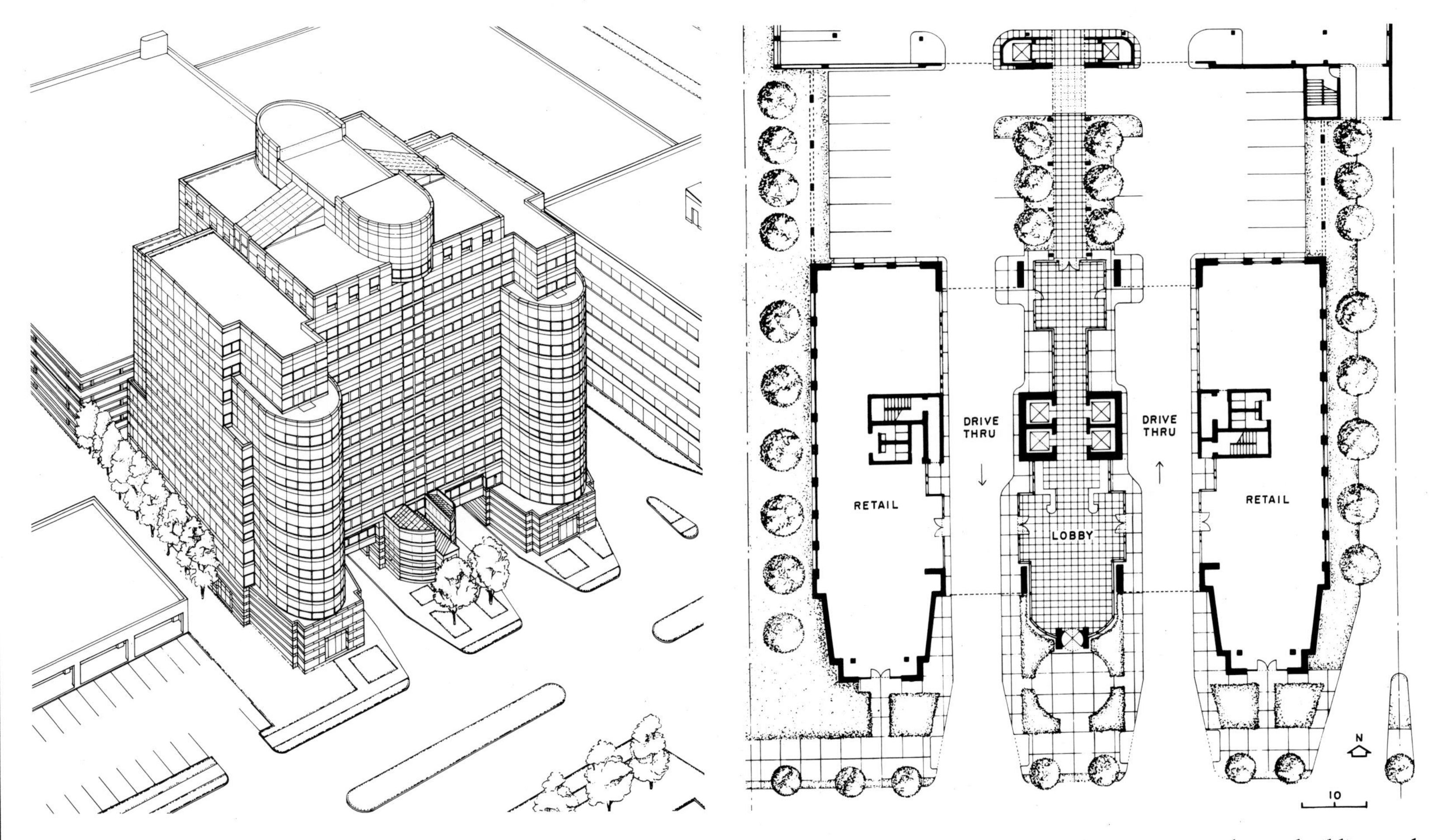

ABOVE: Perspective drawing, LEFT, and plan, RIGHT, show driveways through building to garage in rear. OPPOSITE: Round endwalls add visual interest to what could have been a very ordinary building and increase number of corners available for executive offices.

Institute for Scientific Information • Philadelphia

The new headquarters for ISI, an organization which provides secondary information services to the scientific-technical field, is a highly sophisticated version of the "decorated shed." Designed by Robert Venturi and David Vaughan of Venturi, Rauch and Scott Brown, and completed late 1979, this 132,000-square-foot building is located on a busy industrial-commercial street in Philadelphia's University City Science Center, a research park development. The street façade is decorated with a tightly ordered geometric pattern of brick inflected from predominant tan on the edges to white at the center, with horizontal accents of blue and black brick striping played against vertical metal panels of orange and rose. The symmetry of the façade is disrupted by a corner entrance cut in at an angle and flanked by flower panels that offer an inviting contrast to the abstract formality of the decorative brickwork. The flower panels are similar to those used by the architects to clad the Best Products Showroom (see pages 97–99).

ABOVE: Entrance to the ISI Building is called out by contrasting flower panels and raised blue brick line. OPPOSITE: Decorative brick patterning is inflected toward a strong central axis, creating an appropriately well-ordered "scientific" image.

INSTITUTE FOR SCIENTIFIC INFORMATION
isi 3501
INFORMATION

Proposal for Madison Square Skyscraper • New York City

In 1976 architect Roger Ferri developed this visionary scheme for a midtown highrise in which nature itself, not just images of nature, would become an ornament in the cityscape. Designed for the maximum floor area allowed by zoning, the building maintains the street wall for the first four floors, then steps back on the west side to allow for two-story-deep planting bins. These bins support a cascade of constantly changing landscape accessible from each office floor and composed of plants and animals native to the Hudson River Valley, including sheep shown grazing on the twenty-third floor. Conceived as an "active civic monument integrating the corporate aspiration for strong imagery, the public aspiration for shared amenity, and the individual aspiration for a sentient environment that fosters emotional life," the proposal was Ferri's protest against "real junk" then being built in the Madison Square area. Despite its romanticism, the building is feasible; it was designed with a team of mechanical and structural engineers and could be built using available building systems and construction technology.

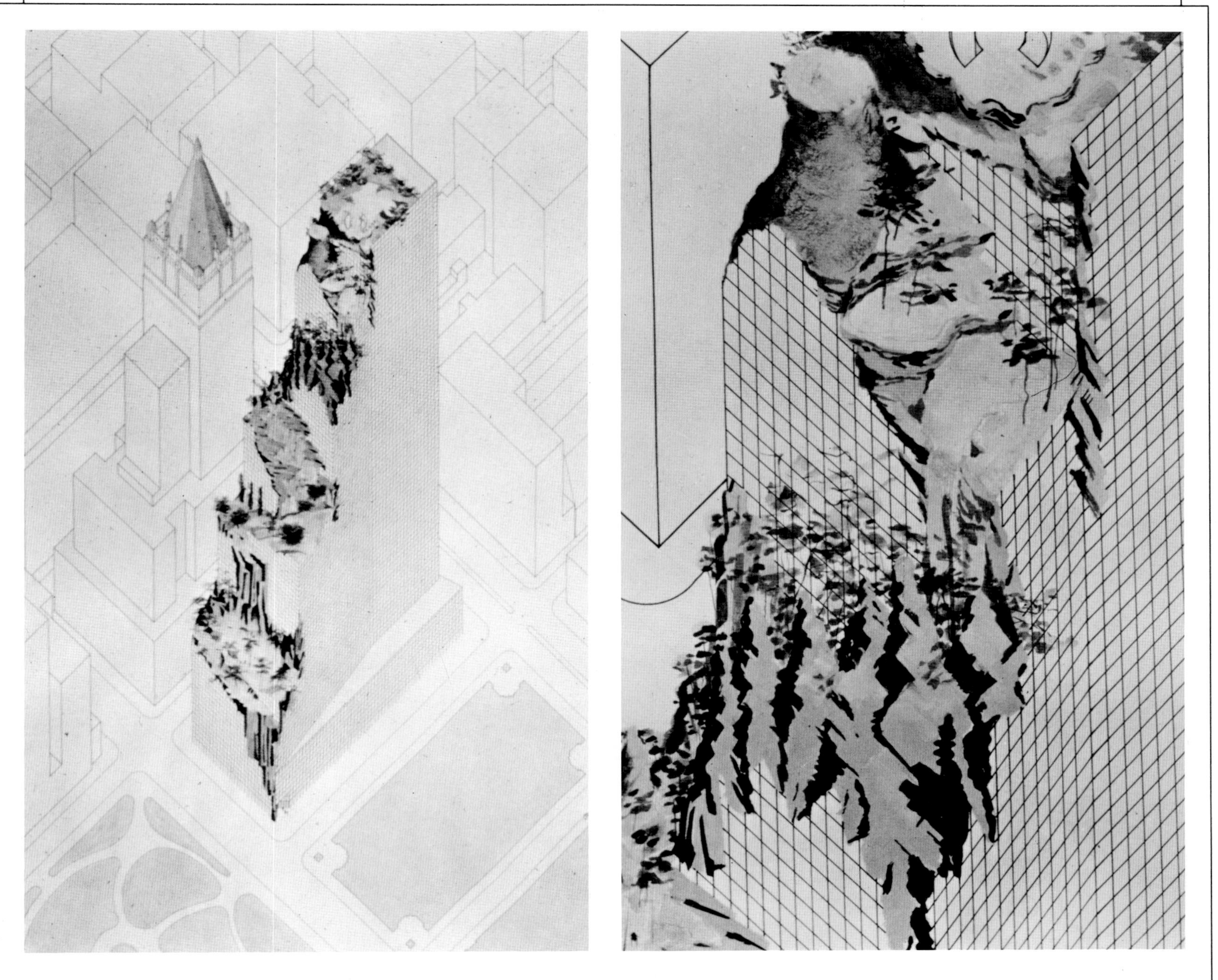

OPPOSITE: West elevation of proposed skyscraper viewed across Madison Square with the familiar New York Life Insurance Building on the left and the Metropolitan Life Insurance Building on the right. ABOVE: Isometric view of skyscraper from the southwest corner of Madison Square, LEFT, and detail of landscape on west side of building, RIGHT. Drawings collection of Augustus Paege.

333 Wacker Drive • Chicago

A powerful identity at ground level is achieved by the richly ornamented base of this thirty-five-story speculative office building located at a bend in the Chicago River. The first four stories, above which rises a curved and beveled glass tower, are surfaced in gray granite striped and patterned with green marble. This masonry base is stepped down over entrances on both the river and downtown sides of the building to call attention to points of arrival. A pedestrian arcade, which adds focus to the entrances, is designed as a monumental colonnade flanked by enormous exposed structural columns at the outside corners. On the downtown façade, circular air-intake grilles set in black granite panels become large-scale decorative elements. The rich patterning of the plaza extends the surface embellishment of this large building to the very edges of its site. Designed by William Pedersen with Alexander Ward and Gary Stluka of the New York firm Kohn Pedersen Fox, this 1,000,000-square-foot building is scheduled for 1983 occupancy.

DRAWING BY ALEXANDER WARD

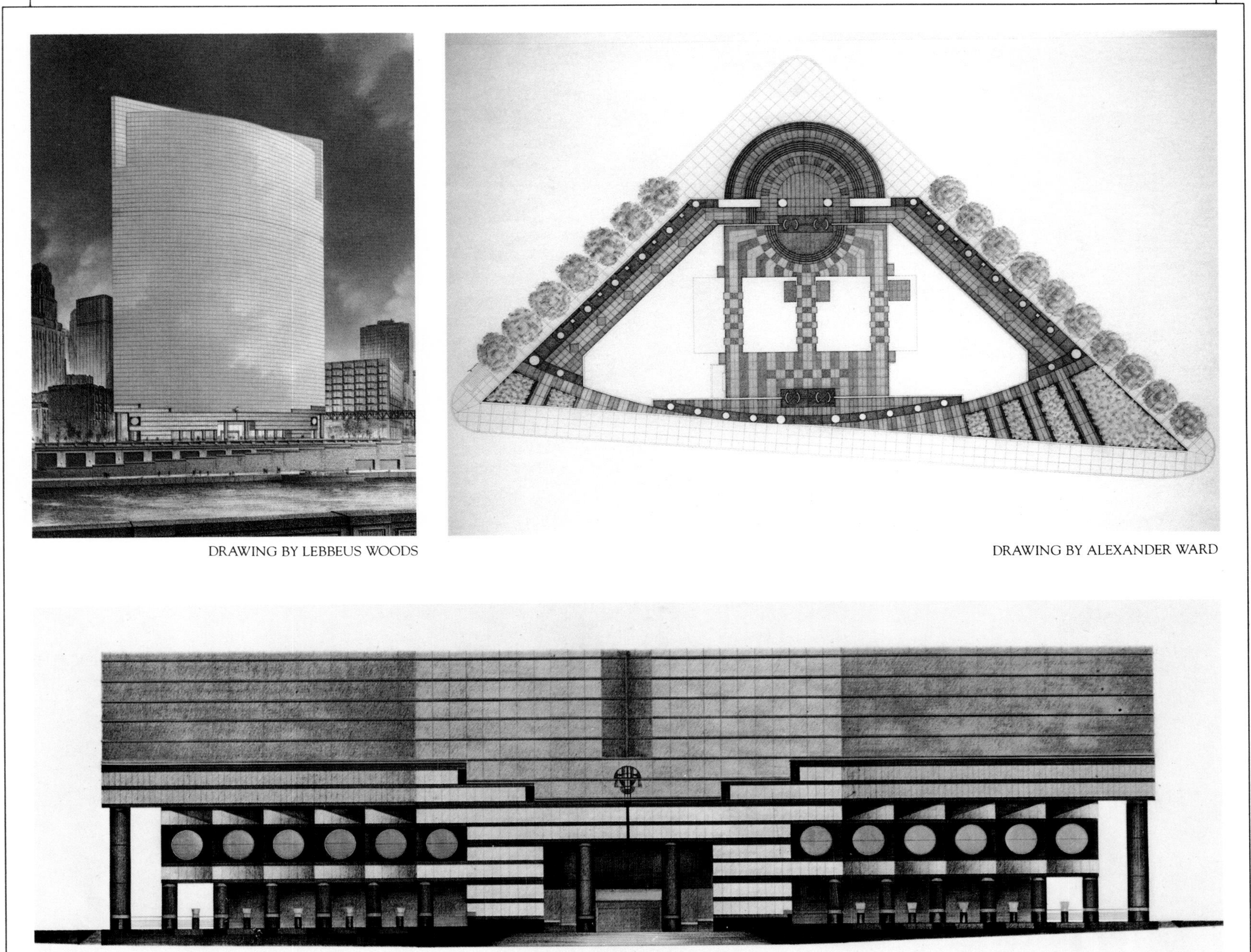

DRAWING BY LEBBEUS WOODS

DRAWING BY ALEXANDER WARD

DRAWING BY WILLIAM PEDERSEN

OPPOSITE: Arcade columns and lighting bollards are clad in dark green marble banded with polished black marble and matte stainless steel. ABOVE: Rendered elevations of 35-story tower, TOP LEFT, patterned terrazzo plaza, TOP RIGHT, and base of building on downtown side.

Public Buildings & Spaces

Public Service Building • Portland, Oregon

When the citizens of Portland elected to build a new municipal office building, they held a national design competition and selected this scheme by Princeton architect Michael Graves over more conventional entries. Their decision, reached amidst considerable controversy, scored a decisive victory for the notion that public buildings need not be drab and spiritless; that because they serve the public they should be expected to encourage visitors, delight viewers, and enliven the city. Graves's design does all these things, principally through the manipulation of surface elements in a manner only vaguely and symbolically related to the straightforward building plan and functions that take place inside. By working on the surface with color and inexpensive materials, Graves produced a building that not only relates to its urban context and is rich in historical allusion, but was the only competition entry that met the city's stringent budget.

PHOTO PRINCETON PHOTOGRAPHICS

DRAWING BY MICHAEL GRAVES

ABOVE: Model, LEFT, and rendering, RIGHT, of building scheduled for completion mid-1982. Base is developed as a continuous colonnade that recalls Portland's traditional arcades. Large paired columns and keystone are appliquéd in ceramic tile on aggregate concrete walls, forming a gigantic portal that reinforces the building's primary axis.

Original scheme for an elaborate roofscape with pavilions crowning the keystone images and housing storage areas, stair exits, and skylights, OPPOSITE, has been simplified in construction, but the ornamental garlands festooning the side columns may yet be spared the city's budget ax.

PHOTO OPPOSITE PAGE PRINCETON PHOTOGRAPHICS

Old Pine Community Center • Philadelphia

Brilliantly patterned quarry tile work, reminiscent of Victorian floors, is a cheerful alternative to the vinyl asbestos tile usually specified for buildings of this type. Completed by Friday Architects of Philadelphia in 1977, the Old Pine Community Center is another example of the "decorated shed": a rather ordinary-looking building transformed by surface decoration, in this case mostly on the interior. In the large community room (below), the tiles are laid in a pattern that looks like a giant Kilim rug spread out before the fireplace. Placing the patterned brick fireplace on axis with the "rug" symbolically reinforces the role of the community room as the social heart of Old Pine. In the ground-floor hallway (opposite) tile patterning lends warmth and elegance to a space that must withstand a lot of wear, yet still feel like "home" to people who use it.

PHOTO ROBERT HARRIS

PHOTO MARK SCHEYER

ABOVE: When viewed at a distance, TOP LEFT, the stucco overlay greatly increases the apparent size of the building, which has been scaled up by extension of the false front on either side and as a parapet above the roofline. OPPOSITE: Decorative glazed tile insignia, designed and executed by the architects, sometimes reads as stained glass.

Quail Valley Control Building • Missouri City, Texas

An addition to a sewage treatment plant might not seem to offer much opportunity for decorativeness, but the Quail Valley Utility District Municipal Control Building proves otherwise. Designed in 1979 by John Casbarian, Danny Samuels, and Robert Timme of the Houston firm Taft Architects, this tiny building (1,000 square feet of office and lunchroom space) recalls the "Classical" style of countless late nineteenth- and early twentieth-century public buildings in America, including the familiar WPA projects. The building is essentially a box with a false front composed of red-brown tile and beige stucco. The "falseness" of the façade is emphasized by its thinness, its projection beyond the corners of the box, and the fact that the tile grid does not "fit" the stucco overlay, thus giving the two materials the appearance of being in different planes. By contrast, the entrance has great depth, being composed of recessed arches which enlarge its scale and give it a ceremonial character. The huge globe lights flanking the entrance and the colorful tilework over the transom reinforce the building's associations with "Classical" public architecture.

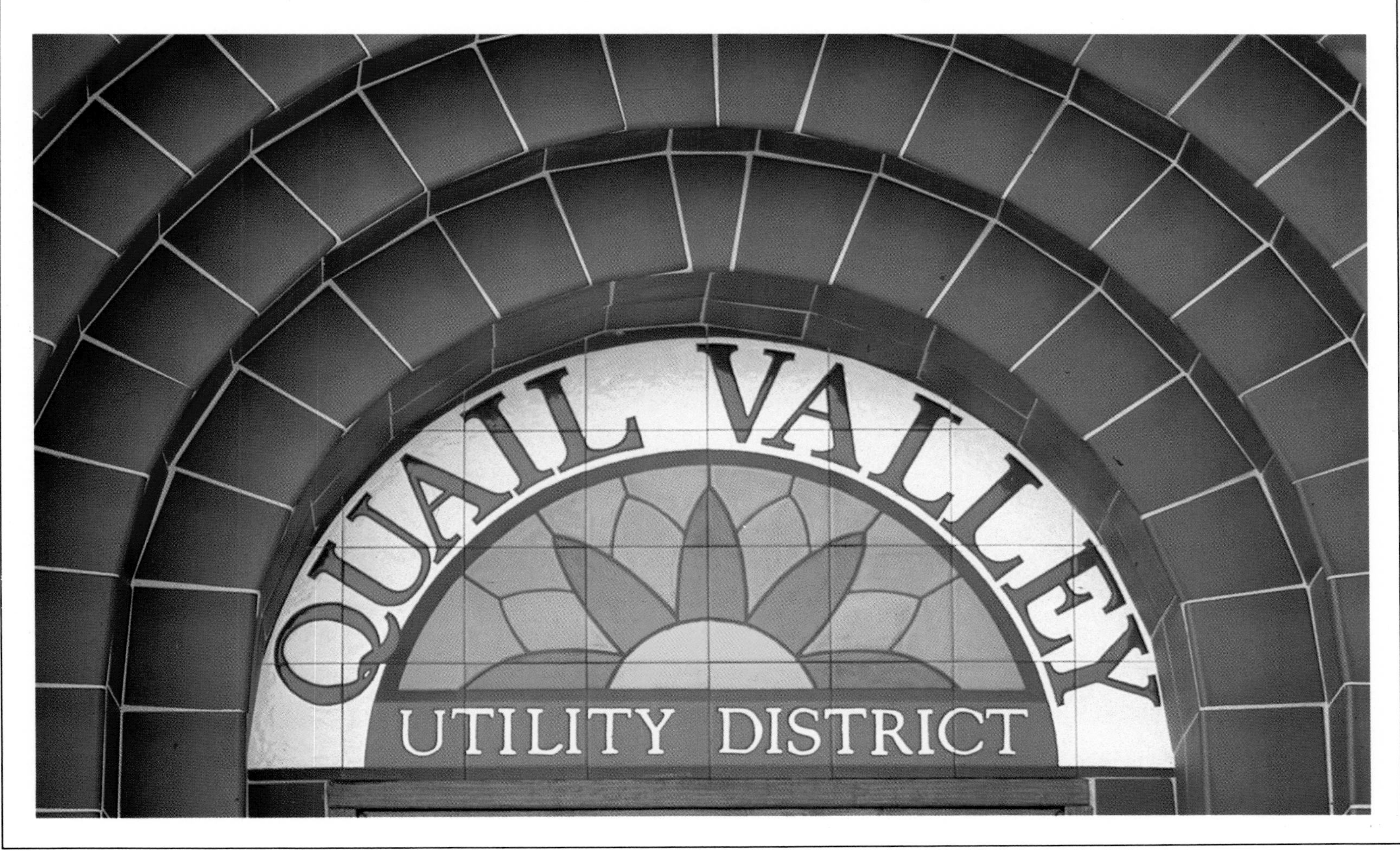

Temple University Student Center • Philadelphia

When students spurned the cafeteria in favor of street vendors, that part of their Student Center was renovated into a symbolic "campus" to provide a sense of identity and place lacking in many urban universities. Axial circulation spaces are defined by the walls of surrounding rooms and built-in seating alcoves which act as "buildings," and by false domes created with drywall and cove lighting to signify classical tradition. Existing columns are built up to monumental proportions, and around the perimeter a wainscot of ceramic tile depicts the university's history in four motifs: the Temple owl, the T, the university seal, and more than fifty plaques inscribed with information about the school. The decorative quality of the renovation, developed and completed in 1981 by Friday Architects of Philadelphia, greatly relieves the formerly stark, fortresslike character of the center, designed in 1969 by another architect.

PHOTO ROBERT HARRIS

ABOVE: The "Forum," or main circulation area, with false dome and oak-clad columns that stop short of ceiling to conceal uplighting and visually heighten space. OPPOSITE, TOP: Entrance to cinema with marquee outlined in incandescent bulbs. BOTTOM: Crossing of axis from cabaret, RIGHT, with main axis leading to "Forum," LEFT, is marked with mosaic tile version of the university seal.

PHOTOS ROBERT HARRIS

PHOTOS NORMAN McGRATH

Civic Center • Madison, Wisconsin

The conversion of an old Hispano-Moorish movie palace into a modern performing-arts theater as part of Madison's new Civic Center is an example of "interpretative restoration": not the painstakingly researched, historically accurate treatment given museum-quality buildings, but a looser kind of refurbishing through which less important but nevertheless valuable structures are adapted to new uses with the feeling of their period still intact. This process is becoming increasingly common as more and more older buildings are being recycled and calls upon the architect to invent decorative treatments that might not necessarily have been used in the original design, but look as though they could have been. In this case, New York architects Hardy Holzman Pfeiffer Associates, who completed the Civic Center in 1980, created a wholly new color palette using fourteen different values and finishes selected for the effects they produce in combination with a new three-color house lighting system. The walls were refinished and stenciled with new patterns designed by the architects in a style sympathetic to the original interior.

PHOTO NORMAN McGRATH

ABOVE AND OPPOSITE: "Restored" Capital Theater has original ceiling coves newly illuminated, walls newly stenciled, and two large new chandeliers fashioned from five smaller original ones.

Sammis Hall • Lloyd Harbor, New York

Sammis Hall is a two-story, sixteen-bedroom guesthouse for scientists attending week-long research seminars at the Banbury Conference Center, part of the Cold Spring Harbor Laboratory complex. Its massing and organization, inspired by Palladio, and its dignified exterior make it sit comfortably in the Georgian estate now occupied by the Center, giving the building a rather grand, formal image that offsets its relatively small size. Inside, the bedrooms are grouped around a double-height, skylighted "Great Hall" which serves as a meeting space and informal living room. This hall is enlivened by thin, abstract arches which appear to float beneath the skylights. The shapes of these arches continually "layer" into intricate, shifting patterns as the hall is experienced on different levels and from different vantage points. The building is constructed of stucco over wood frame and was completed in 1981 by architects Charles Moore, William Grover, and Glen Arbonies of Moore Grover Harper, located in Essex, Connecticut.

PHOTO PETER AARON, ESTO

ABOVE: Main entrance to Sammis Hall is given stature and importance by shape suspended over recessed doorway and surrounded by cutout openings. OPPOSITE: View into "Great Hall" at second level through narrow arch with negative keystone that frames the stair connecting the first and second levels.

PHOTO PETER AARON, ESTO

PHOTOS PETER AARON, ESTO

TOP LEFT: View into upper level of Sammis Hall through cut-out stucco screen wall behind which window is recessed. TOP RIGHT: View through floating arches of "Great Hall" from second level balcony. BOTTOM: View up into skylights from ground floor of "Great Hall."

Federal Design Assembly Delegates' Room • Washington, D.C.

The Fourth Federal Assembly, sponsored by the National Endowment for the Arts in an effort to improve all aspects of federal design, was held in September 1978 in the old Pension Building. For this occasion, several architects were invited to design temporary delegates' rooms using only products, furnishings, and materials stocked by the General Services Administration, the agency responsible for building and furnishing all federal facilities. Shown here are a graphic designers' conference room (bottom left) and an editors' lounge (top left and right) designed by New York architect Susana Torre. The use of color articulates the rooms' architectural elements and imparts symbolic meaning: vaulted ceilings in the graphic designers' room are painted light blue for day sky; editors' lounge ceilings are dark blue for night sky. The public character of the rooms is stated by introducing the ornamental lamppost found in the streets of Washington, D.C., and still being manufactured. The continuity and connection that once existed between the rooms is re-created through the use of mirrors which reflect the lampposts in endless rows.

PHOTOS NORMAN McGRATH

La Strada Novissima • Venice, Italy

In the fall of 1980 the First International Exhibition of Architecture took place as part of the Venice Biennale. The theme of that exhibition, directed by Italian architect Paolo Portoghesi, was "The Presence of the Past," and it brought together seventy-six architects from all over the world whose work is considered "postmodern," mostly in the sense that it pursues historical ideas. Twenty of these architects were chosen to design individual façades arranged as a "street" (La Strada Novissima) running through the Corderia, a rope factory dating to 1579. Amidst all the debate stirred, the exhibition made two things very clear: first, that the traditional street, which has been largely eradicated by the Modern Movement, is still a very exciting place to be; and second, that much of the excitement is generated by the decorative (nonfunctional) treatment of building façades that form the continuous "wall" of the street. Another point made by the exhibition is the extent to which the historicism in so-called postmodern architecture is dependent upon surface ornamentation and decoration. Even allowing for the fact that La Strada was a temporary indoor mockup, not real architecture, the ease with which these designers were able to express their ideas in the thinnest, most superficial construction—and the similarity of that construction to much of their "real" work—confirms the importance of the surface as a medium for conveying, in modern architectural terms, allusions to historical styles and the meanings associated with them.

ABOVE: Entrance to the First International Exhibition of Architecture, LEFT, and a portion of La Strada Novissima, RIGHT. Façade in foreground was designed by American architect Thomas Gordon Smith and the wall to the right by Studio GRAU, an Italian group.

PHOTOS COURTESY PAOLO PORTOGHESI

OPPOSITE: View along La Strada Novissima with façade by American architect Robert A. M. Stern in foreground, followed by façades of the Italian partnership of Franco Purini and Laura Thermes, American architect Stanley Tigerman, Studio GRAU, and Smith.

PHOTO OPPOSITE PAGE COURTESY PAOLO PORTOGHESI

PHOTO COURTESY DOMUS MAGAZINE

PHOTO COURTESY PAOLO PORTOGHESI

LEFT: Another view along La Strada Novissima with façade by Italian architect Paolo Portoghesi in foreground, followed by Ricardo Bofill of Spain and Charles Moore, U.S.A. RIGHT: Façade by West German architect Joseph Paul Kleihues. OPPOSITE: Façade by Austrian architect Hans Hollein.

PHOTO OPPOSITE PAGE COURTESY DOMUS MAGAZINE

LEIN

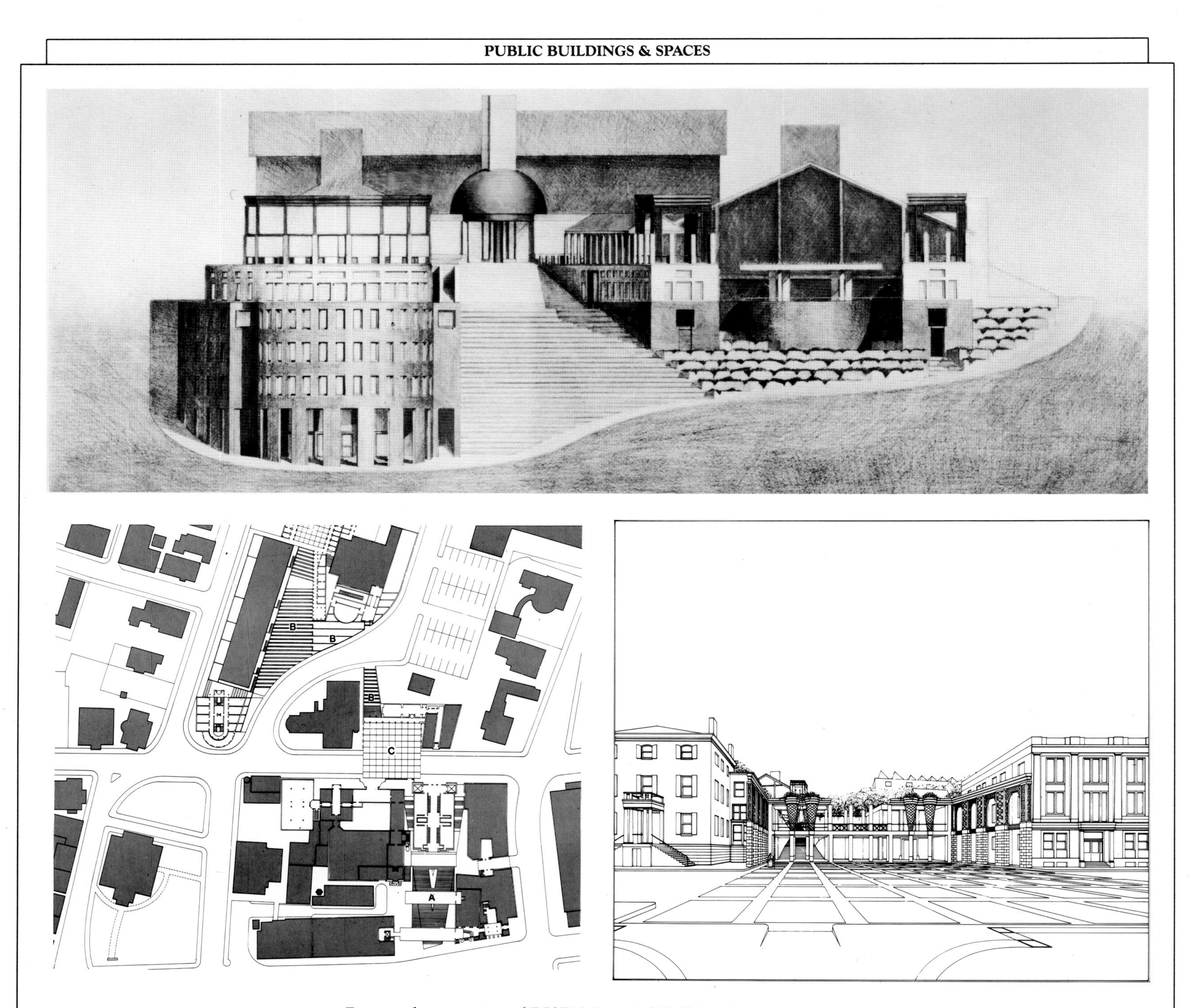

OPPOSITE: Proposed renovation of RISD Memorial Hall façade with proposed Memorial Steps, a ceremonial urban stair, leading up to it (A on keyed plan). ABOVE, TOP: More intimate, institutionally private stair leading to proposed RISD Studio Cloister with new dormitory facilities on the left and new Photography Club on the right (B on keyed plan). BOTTOM LEFT: Partial plan of area to be remodeled, with existing buildings shown in darker tones. BOTTOM RIGHT: Proposed Frazier Terrace (C on keyed plan) with stair in background connecting Department of Photography to Memorial Steps and the Studio Cloister.

The Steps of Providence • Rhode Island School of Design

In their proposal for the renovation and expansion of the RISD campus, Boston architects Rodolfo Machado and Jorge Silvetti have used "the stair" to tie together the school's facilities both functionally and symbolically. The school has no formal campus, having grown around and within original structures such as a bank, a church, factories, and private houses. This gradual physical infusion of the school into the urban fabric of Providence is here turned into an advantage. The intent is to create tangible, positive urban space by transforming what are now empty and leftover spaces into gardens and squares connected by steps. The visual unity created by these steps is enhanced by a careful imposition of new and renovated buildings which reinterpret classical principles of composition and design from among the three centuries of architectural styles accumulated in that part of Providence. While there is none of what the architects would regard as applied ornament, the combination of fragments produces an overall effect of ornateness.

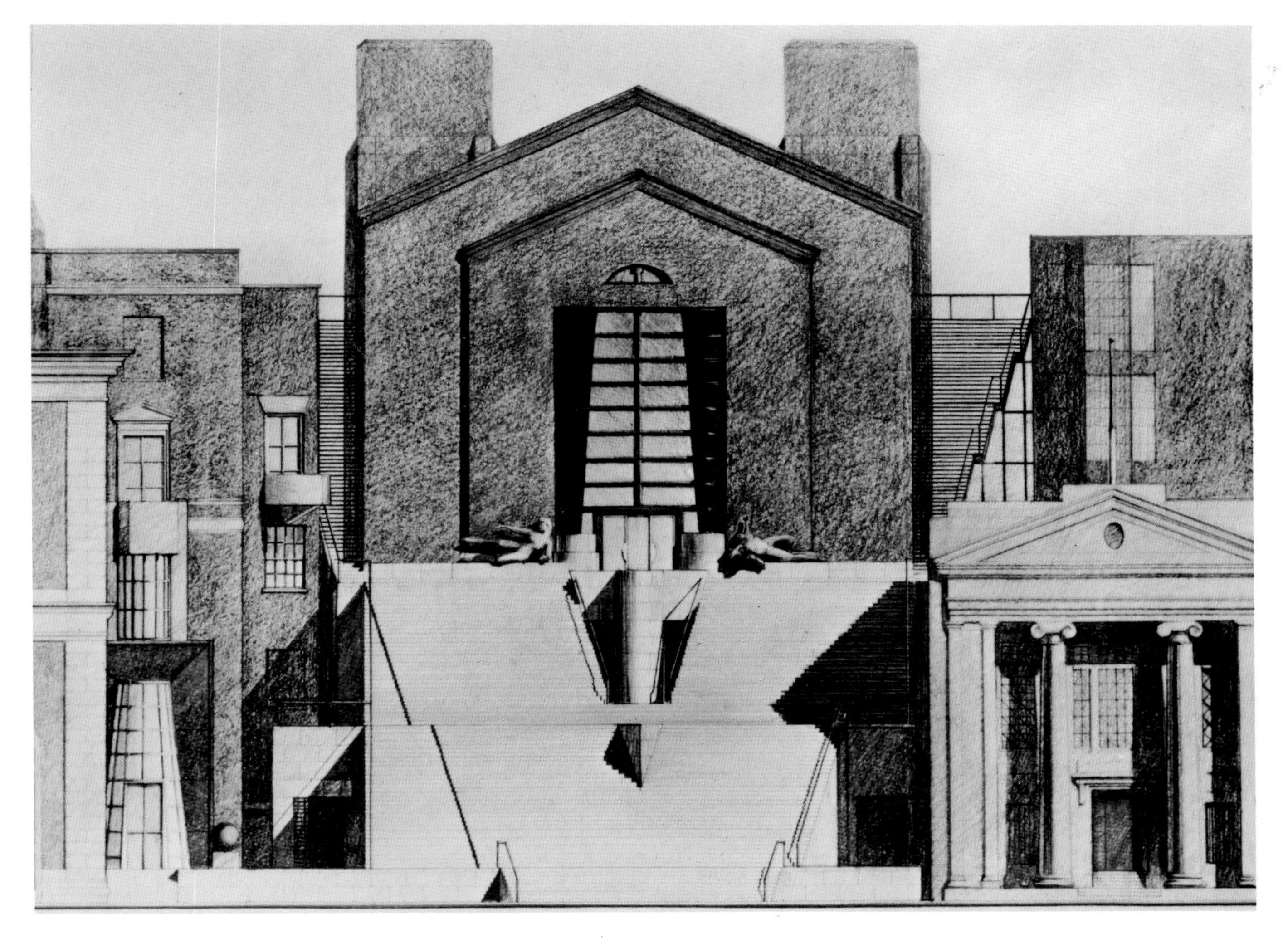

U.S. Ambassador's Residence and Consulate • Paris, France

Poetic License is an international team of young architects, artists, sculptors, poets, and construction workers asked in 1978 to refurbish the entry foyer of the U.S. Consulate and a blank wall flanking the entry to the U.S. ambassador's residence. Both problems were solved on a minimal budget by creating architecture with trompe l'oeil painting. In the consulate entry foyer, a narrow, awkward area made even less gracious by institutional décor and obligatory security procedures, the designers introduced a variety of *faux* textures and materials—linoleum, wood moldings, marble, stone, and sky—creating illusory doors, stairs, and arcades which expand the space and provide a psychological distraction from the necessary baggage searches and metal detectors. On the courtyard wall of the ambassador's residence, the designers continued the palace façade with trompe l'oeil windows, cornices, and architectural detail, visually expanding the residence and adding a touch of wit to the otherwise imposing structure.

PHOTOS V. CORBEILLE

ABOVE: Courtyard entrance to ambassador's residence, LEFT, "construction" in progress, CENTER, and completed trompe l'oeil window with painted reflections of clouds and sky, RIGHT. Where it was impossible or historically inappropriate to mimic the palace façade exactly, the architects improvised bas-relief garlands. OPPOSITE: Real-live tree and marine guard lend a touch of nonsimulation to the trompe l'oeil entry foyer of the U.S. Consulate in Paris.

PHOTO OPPOSITE PAGE ETIENNE REVAULT

NONIMMIGRANT
VISAS

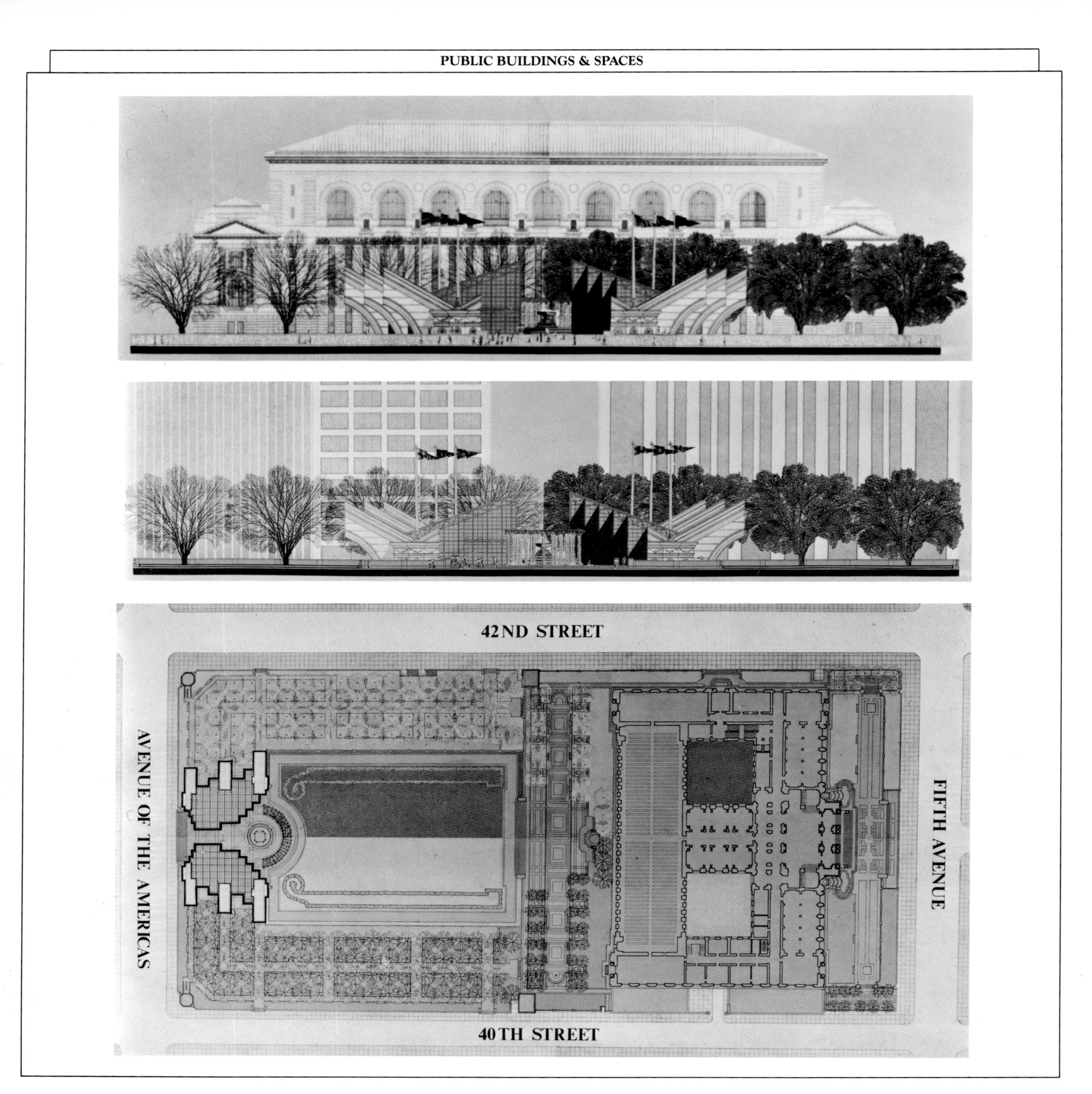
42ND STREET
AVENUE OF THE AMERICAS
FIFTH AVENUE
40TH STREET

Proposed Bryant Park Pavilions • New York City

In 1981 the Architectural League of New York celebrated its centennial by commissioning eleven architect-artist teams to design visionary projects for "Collaboration," an exhibition intended to foster association between architects and artists. For a period of more than fifty years the dominance of Modernism has largely frustrated such efforts. One project in this exhibition was a proposal by architect Hugh Hardy, with artists Jack Beal and Sondra Freckelton, to construct two new restaurant pavilions on the western edge of Bryant Park behind the New York Public Library. The pavilions are intended to reclaim socially degenerated park space by introducing the opportunity for "civilizing behavior," and to integrate into architecture certain aspects of nature. Artist Jack Beal created colored glass ceilings that recall the park's seasonal foliage, and carpet and paving designs that reflect the textures and materials of the park walkways; Sondra Freckelton contributed seasonal wall murals. To frame an existing fountain the architects proposed a semicircular pergola supported by Beal's fantasy Rococo ceramic columns, which are used inside as freestanding sculpture.

ABOVE: Four ceramic column types. OPPOSITE, TOP TO BOTTOM: Elevation of restaurant pavilions looking east from Avenue of the Americas; elevation looking west from inside park; and plan of library and Bryant Park with proposed pavilions and semicircular pergola at left.

Piazza D'Italia • New Orleans, Louisiana

Likely to become one of the most famous urban spaces in the United States, New Orleans' Piazza D'Italia was substantially completed in 1978–79, although peripheral development continues. Designed by architect Charles Moore with one of his several firms, the Urban Innovations Group of Los Angeles, in association with Perez Limited of New Orleans, the Piazza is a gift of that city's Italian community to "all the people." Set hard against a modern highrise on one side and an old warehouse district on another, the Piazza, like its Old World prototypes, is entered through tight spaces that reveal only tantalizing glimpses of the whole. Once inside the circular plaza, awareness of the adjacent skyscraper diminishes and attention is focused on St. Joseph's Fountain, a series of concentric, semicircular colonnades, each composed of one of the five Classical orders (Doric, Ionic, Corinthian, Tuscan, and Composite), plus a sixth, dubbed the "Delicatessen" order by Moore and intended to frame the entrance to a restaurant opening out onto the plaza. Each of the five orders is transformed by water: for example, the metopes of the Tuscan order are jets of water, and the fluting is created by tiny streams washing down a stainless-steel column. The "Delicatessen" order is appropriately ringed with neon. Pointing inward from the proposed restaurant entrance at the perimeter of the plaza is an 80-foot-long relief map of Italy, washed by three rivulets representing the Arno, the Po, and the Tiber rivers. At the very center of the plaza is Sicily, on which is focused a concentric paving pattern of alternating granite blocks and black slate salvaged from a local street demolition. The total effect is a statement of Moore's belief that in public architecture "you have to have things familiar so that people will feel comfortable and then a surprise to make things seem more vivid than ever."

PHOTO ALAN KARCHMER

PHOTO NORMAN McGRATH

ABOVE: Lafayette Arch, LEFT, and pergola, RIGHT, marking entrances to the Piazza from Lafayette and Poydras streets, respectively. Pergola takes the shape of a Classical temple but its columns are poured concrete and its entablature, pediments, and roof are formed from standard plumbing pipe. OPPOSITE: St. Joseph's Fountain at night, bathed in neon.

PHOTO OPPOSITE PAGE NORMAN McGRATH

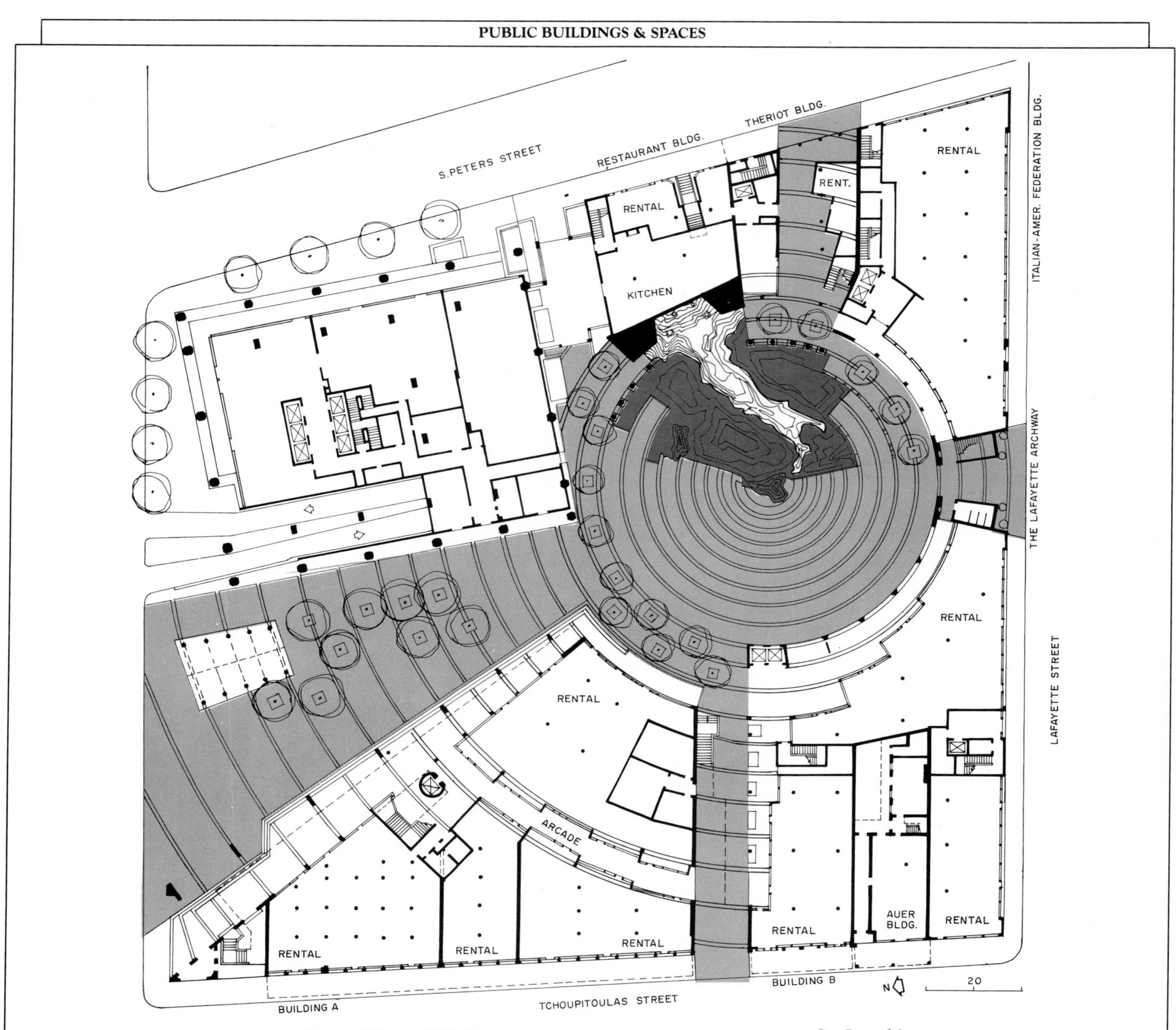

ABOVE: Plan of Piazza D'Italia. OPPOSITE, CLOCKWISE FROM TOP LEFT: St. Joseph's Fountain by day, with relief map of Italy descending in tiers of slate, marble, cobblestones, and mirrored tiles (raised area in foreground represents Sardinia); Ionic (foreground) and Corinthian colonnades; Doric column in stainless steel, slotted to reveal water pouring down inside; Composite column ringed in neon; and Corinthian capital in stainless steel.

PHOTO NORMAN McGRATH

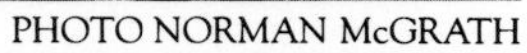

PHOTO NORMAN McGRATH

PHOTO ROBERT JENSEN

PHOTO ROBERT JENSEN

PHOTO ROBERT JENSEN

OPPOSITE: Albert Paley's New York State Senate chamber gates, one of a pair installed in 1981, Albany, New York. The largest work of their type commissioned in the last fifty years, the Albany gates bespeak an increasingly sympathetic attitude toward the use of new ornamental craftwork in architecture. Forged and fabricated mild steel, brass, and bronze, each gate 174 × 144 in.

THE DECORATIVE CRAFTS

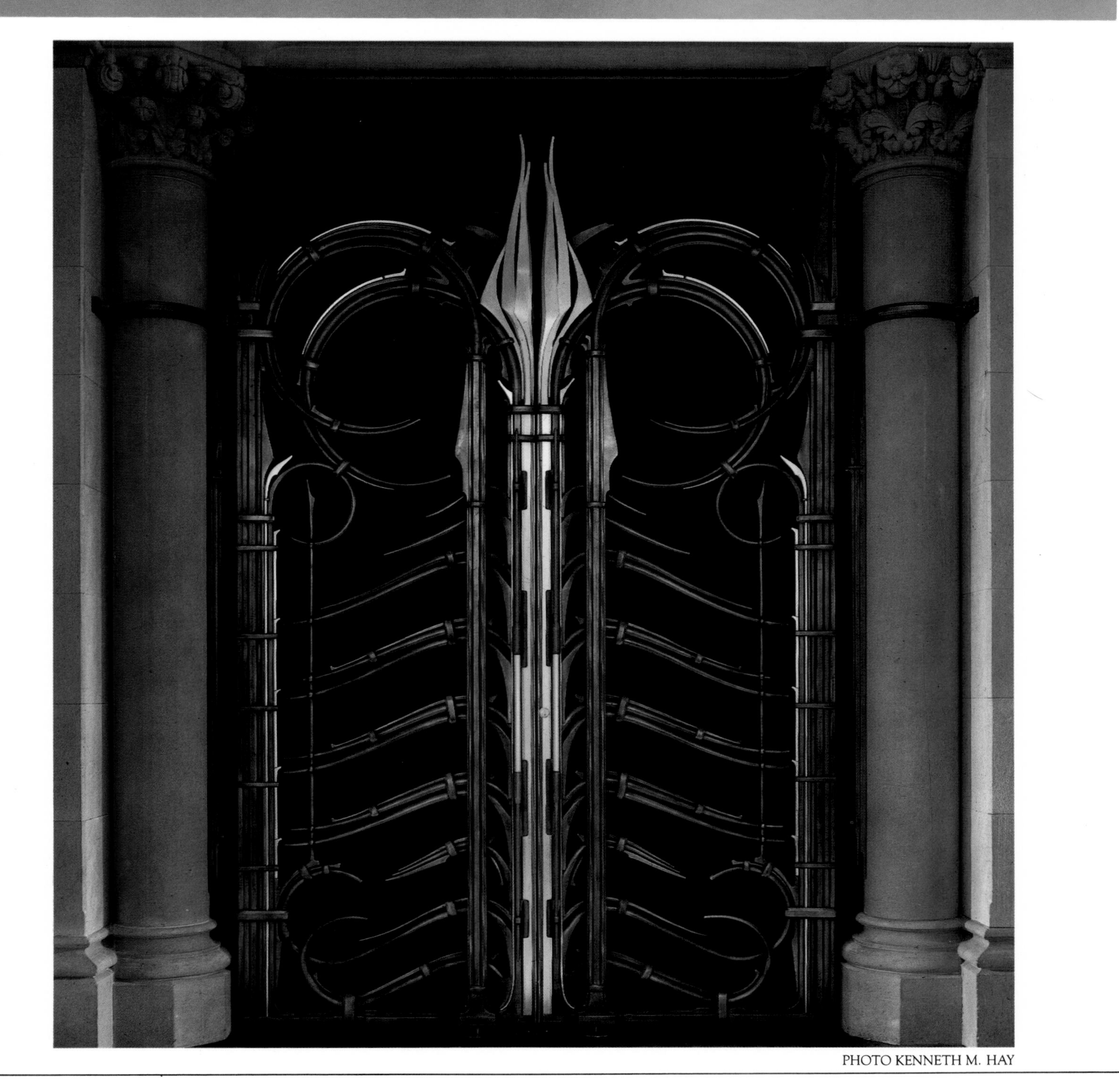

PHOTO KENNETH M. HAY

Most of what we recognize as ornament in architecture—the decorative stonework, cast plaster, stained and beveled glass, iron grilles, railings, woodwork, and painted surfaces—has been the work of craftspeople. What became of these craftspeople when the Modern Movement rejected ornament more than fifty years ago? Their participation since then in new construction has been negligible, and the limited demand for reproduction and repair work has afforded little opportunity for creative development. But, contrary to the claim of the Modernists, the crafts did not disappear; they simply retreated from the building process into the studio.

In some cases, this retreat to the studio has allowed the crafts to gather more original force than was ever before possible within the larger constraints of architecture. They have had the option, in essence, of becoming autonomous, and at the most creative end of this newly autonomous spectrum the lines between "high art" and "craft" have blurred. Like painting and sculpture, they now can be freed from utility. Stained glass, for example, is no longer limited to performing the function of "window"; it can hang in a room like a canvas, no more nor less than the expression of one artist's unique vision.

Yet another kind of retreat has taken place, not to the studio but to what, in the elite circles of Modern art and design, is regarded as the subculture of interior decorating. There the expensive taste for ornament was never rooted out, and it is there that many talented muralists, trompe l'oeil artists, and other decorative craftspeople have survived. These people are usually not decorators themselves, but rather the resources that decorators tap to provide the Old World ambiance that their clients demand. This persistent desire for decorative embellishment has preserved painting and finishing techniques which, but for the unregenerate tastes of a wealthy few, surely would have been lost to the Modern Movement.

This section of *Ornamentalism* looks at three areas of craftsmanship that traditionally have been integral to the architectural process and are potentially most important to the Ornamental Movement: glasswork, wrought-ironwork, and brushwork. Not only do these crafts perform the function of ornamenting or decorating architecture but, in the case of wrought-ironwork particularly, each in its own aesthetic development has recently become more explicitly ornamental, more decorative. Those familiar with the craft renaissance that has taken place since the mid-1960s will recognize the fundamental dichotomy that has developed, most noticeably in glass and wrought-ironwork. The rejection of technology has produced a group of organicists, historicists, and folklorists whose work stresses the individual hand of the artist, the use of natural materials and preindustrial techniques, sometimes to the point of coyness. The modernists, on the other hand, continue to invent new forms, using industrial materials and machine techniques. The glass and ironwork shown here represents more the latter attitude toward invention, though its aesthetic is clearly nonindustrial.

Glasswork

Perhaps the most ancient of the decorative crafts is glassmaking, the earliest examples of which are tiny colored inlay pieces found in Egypt and Babylonia and dated to the third millennium B.C. The oldest stained glass as we know it today dates to the twelfth century at St. Denis in France. Throughout the Middle Ages, the principal function of stained glass in church windows was to teach the gospel to an illiterate population. Later, as its function became less didactic and more freely decorative, architectural stained glass evolved stylistically in tandem with contemporary movements such as Art Nouveau and Art Deco. The Victorians made lavish use of stained, etched, and beveled glass in buildings of all types and, from the turn of the century up through the 1930s, decorative glass windows, doors, transoms, and sidelights were mass-produced by the thousands for installation in urban tract housing throughout America.

With the advent of Modernism, decorative architectural glass all but disappeared, except for the continued use of stained glass in churches and synagogues. Then, about fifteen years ago, there occurred a renaissance in stained glass, during which this age-old architectural craft emerged as an autonomous medium of artistic expression. A tremendous number of people started buying new or antique stained glass, but not just to install in doors and windows.

For the first time, stained-glass panels were made or salvaged as independent art objects to be displayed like paintings and sculpture. A similar renaissance has occurred in etched and beveled glass, and the decorative glass crafts are now pretty well divided between those people who believe that the full artistic potential of these media can be realized only through autonomous development, and those who maintain that the proper role of decorative glass is still as an architectural element—that, indeed, the continued survival of the glass crafts depends on closer collaboration with architects. Today there are an estimated five thousand stained-glass artisans alone working in the United States, and many studios produce both architectural and autonomous work. Examples of both are shown on the following pages, and the use of decorative glasswork in Ornamentalist architecture is illustrated also by the leaded-glass windows in Robert Haussmann and Trix Haussmann-Högl's Lanvin Boutique (pages 86, 87) and the etched glass in Moore Grover Harper's Backstreet Restaurant (pages 108, 109).

Wrought-Ironwork

Wrought iron, worked by hand at an anvil or by machine at a forge, is generally light in appearance, with subtle variations in shape and tool marks that give each piece a unique artistic expression. One of the earliest known pieces of wrought-ironwork is a grille excavated from beneath the ashes of Pompeii, the Roman resort town destroyed by the eruption of Mt. Vesuvius in A.D. 79. During the first centuries A.D., decorative wrought-ironwork appeared in Europe in the form of hinges and pull rings on church doors and, from the eleventh century on, wrought-iron grilles were commonly used to partition chapels and chancels from the naves or main interior portions of churches. In the twelfth and thirteenth centuries, wrought-iron pieces were fitted horizontally across vertical wooden door planks for additional strength. By the thirteenth century in France, the emphasis in this type of construction shifted from functionalism to decorativeness, as attested by the wrought-iron fittings on the west doors of Notre Dame, one of the most magnificent pieces of architectural ornament ever produced. Like stained glass, wrought-ironwork achieved what many consider to be the height of its expression in the Gothic style. Also like stained glass, it participated grandly in the decorative excess of the Victorians, was transformed by the organicism of Art Nouveau, then was all but banished by Modernism.

Wrought iron, in the form of grilles, galleries, stair railings, and fences, was certainly one of the most popular forms of premodern architectural ornament in the United States, but it was not the only metalcraft once integral to the building industry. Throughout the 1800s, cast-iron columns and fronts were widely used for ornamental as well as structural purposes. Cast-iron street furniture, elaborate bronze tellers' cages, brass elevator doors, and stainless-steel grilles are a large part of what remains of this country's decorative heritage. And some of the best examples of Art Deco and Moderne ornament are the metal grilles and doors installed in buildings of the 1920s and 1930s. Nevertheless, the only metalcraft that seems to be making a strong comeback in the wake of Modernism is wrought-ironwork, or more precisely, mild steelwork.

With few horses to shoe, the local blacksmith was until recently an endangered species. Then, about ten years ago, the founding of the Artists-Blacksmiths Association of North America signaled the beginning of a renaissance in wrought-ironwork. From 1971 to 1980, the membership of this organization grew from thirty-five to thirteen hundred. In 1981, the installation of two monumental gates in the Senate chamber of the New York State Capitol Building in Albany (page 159) marked completion of the largest such work commissioned in the United States in the last fifty years. The resurgence of wrought-ironwork owes much to the Restoration Movement, as exemplified by the Albany project, but the real challenges to this ancient craft lie in the potential for collaboration on new architecture as well.

Brushwork

In many ways the most intimate and personal of the decorative crafts is brushwork: stenciling, painted finishes, trompe l'oeil, and mural painting. These, with the exception of occasional monumental mural commissions, are also the crafts most alienated from the Modern Movement. Stencilwork particularly is a favorite of hobbyists and, given its origins in folk art, as likely to be executed by amateurs as by professionals. All this is changing, however, and over the last ten years there has been a revival of interest in decorative brushwork similar to the renaissance in glass and wrought-ironwork. Fortunately, this revival has been accompanied by the publication of several excellent "how-to" books and many programs of instruction so that the personal touch need not be lost to the growing number of professionals practicing these arts.

Stenciling is defined by Adele Bishop and Cile Lord, whose work is shown on pages 206–8, as "any method of decorating that involves using a brush or other implement to apply color through shapes cut out of a sheet of impervious material" (*The Art of Decorative Stenciling,* 1976). It may have been used by the Egyptians as early as 2500 B.C. to decorate their mummy cases, and some scholars believe that the process was invented by the Chinese before 3000 B.C. In Japan, India, Siam, and Persia, stenciling appeared as early as A.D. 600, then was carried by trade routes to the West where it enjoyed great popularity in France during the Middle Ages. By the seventeenth century, stencils were being used in Rouen to produce wallpaper that was "flocked" by brushing shredded wool remnants onto the still-wet pattern.

The Golden Age of stenciling seems to have occurred in Europe between the late seventeenth and early nineteenth centuries, a period that coincided with the settlement of North America. There, in that vast wilderness across the Atlantic, early settlers tried to emulate Old World elegance by stenciling carpetlike patterns on wooden floors and canvas floor cloths. Plaster walls, a gradual refinement of early rough-hewn construction, were decorated with stenciled borders. Most of this work was done by house painters or itinerant artists who, for room, board, and a small fee, would stencil crude but cheerful designs around ceilings, doorways, and fireplaces.

By the late nineteenth century, stenciling had become a much more precise, intricate craft in the hands of people like Louis Comfort Tiffany, who filled in all the spaces between his opulent stained-glass windows with elaborate stencilwork patterns; and architect Louis Sullivan who used rows of stencilwork to outline covings, walls, eaves, and domes of his early Modern buildings. Right up through the 1920s and 1930s, mass-produced stencil patterns were repeated, with varying artistic results, in homes and other buildings throughout America. Then, with the clean sweep of Modernism, stencilwork all but disappeared. Today, the restoration and recycling of older buildings is calling upon architects to resurrect this technique, and in new architecture, such as the house recently completed by Venturi, Rauch and Scott Brown (pages 34, 35), stencilwork is once more being seen in original patterns.

A very different kind of brushwork is the painted finish, the development of which is rooted, not in folk art, but in the fine artist's studio. Technically, the term *painted* describes a variety of finishes applied by hand or machine and used mostly on furniture. The current revival of interest in decorative finishes, however, focuses principally on three types: the lacquer finishes first introduced to the Western world by Marco Polo on his return from China in 1295; gilding, which dates back to the pharaohs and flourished during the Baroque, Regency, Rococo, and Empire periods; and the *faux* ("false") or "fantasy" finishes that simulate, with paint on ordinary wood or plaster, semiprecious stones and exotic woods. The *faux* finishes, which also can be traced to the Egyptians and Chinese, are particularly interesting because the French and Italians, who developed this craft to its zenith during the seventeenth and eighteenth centuries, used these "fantasies" primarily to conceal inferior materials or because they could not afford the exorbitant cost of real marble, lapis, malachite, and tortoise shell. Today commercial designers are reviving this ancient deception in part because the cost of "real" or "good" materials has once more escalated beyond the budgets of most clients. Fortunately, the technique has been lovingly preserved by devotees like Isabel O'Neil, whose book on the subject (*The Art of the Painted Finish,* 1971) is definitive and whose New York City school turns hobbyists into skilled artisans like Kakia Livanos (pages 200, 201). Whether for aesthetic or economic reasons, fine painted finishes are now being revived commercially, not only in furniture such as the Baker line recently designed by Alessandro (page 230), but as an architectural craft (see the Haussmanns' Lanvin Boutique interior, pages 86, 87, and Richard Gillette's apartments, pages 70–73).

The *faux* or "fantasy" finish is just part of a whole tradition of illusionist painting known as *trompe l'oeil,* a French term that translates literally to "deceive the eye." Pliny the Elder (d. A.D. 79) tells a story in his *Natural History* that describes what must be one of the earliest examples of trompe l'oeil. Around 400 B.C., the most celebrated artist of his time, the Greek Xeuxis, was challenged by a rival painter, Parrhasius, to see who could paint the most realistic image. Xeuxis drew aside a curtain from a painting of grapes so realistic that some birds attempted to peck at it. Triumphantly Xeuxis turned to his rival and asked him to draw aside the curtain on his painting, only to be defeated when it was realized that Parrhasius' curtain was, itself, painted. Architectural trompe l'oeil flourished in Europe during the seventeenth and eighteenth centuries when many galleries, ballrooms, and churches were built as shells on the interior, then transformed into Baroque, Rococo, or Neoclassical fantasies by anonymous artisans who painted columns, bas reliefs, and statues in niches on what, structurally, were just bare walls—a transformation not unlike that applied by Poetic License to the courtyard of the U.S. Ambassador's residence in Paris (page 150), or by artist Richard Haas to the Nelson loft entrance hall (pages 60, 61).

After the Industrial Revolution, trompe l'oeil declined from an architectural craft to a somewhat esoteric studio art, then was revived briefly by the Surrealist Movement. Today it is being picked up by serious modern architects for reasons best expressed by one of its leading practitioners, Richard Lowell Neas (page 204): "People are frustrated being stuck in apartments with no warmth, no charm, no real architecture. With 'trompe l'oeil' they can do something that they could never afford in reality—create the materials and the architecture that new buildings just don't have."

Restoring and Salvaging Craftwork

Both the studio crafts and the decorator arts are valuable resources upon which Ornamentalist architecture draws. An equally valuable resource is the Restoration Movement itself which has not only inspired a new appreciation for traditional ornament, but has renewed demand for craft skills that lay almost dormant for two generations. To meet this demand, workers in the building industry are being trained in techniques like stone casting, dressing, and carving, skills that can be applied to new Ornamentalist buildings as well as to the restoration and preservation of older buildings. Even more important, much of the recycling of older buildings involves "interpretative" restoration: a looser, more creative process than historically accurate reproduction. In interpretive restoration projects, such as the Madison Civic Center shown on pages 138 and 139, the architect is often required to invent decorative treatments that, although applied with traditional craft skills and stylistically compatible with the original décor of a building, are completely new. This process of inventing "new/old" decoration is greatly influencing the development of modern Ornamentalist design.

An alternative to inventing new ornamental craftwork or faithfully reproducing the old is to snatch original craftwork from the wrecker's ball. Beginning in the early 1960s, disenchantment with modern residential building drove many homeowners to rummage in junkyards for old mantelpieces, stained-glass windows, terra-cotta trim, and wrought-iron gates. Since then, salvage has become big business and what was once junk is now architectural antiques. Although most salvaged building craftwork is used to decorate homes or create instant nostalgia in period restaurants, some appears in modern Ornamentalist buildings like the Best Products Headquarters (page 114). Ironically, the Restoration Movement that touched off the salvage boom now threatens to defeat it. As more old buildings are recycled, fewer are torn down and the supply of salvage dries up. But the demand for old building craftwork continues and manufacturers are now making more and more reproductions of pre-Modern architectural components: fiberglass imitations of cast-iron imitations of Classical columns originally hand carved in stone.

To what extent all of this prefigures a reintegration of the ornamental crafts with architecture is uncertain. However, there is evidence in the previous section of this book that such a movement already is underway, and the work on the following pages begins to suggest the possibilities for a more active collaboration between architects, interior designers, and craftspeople.

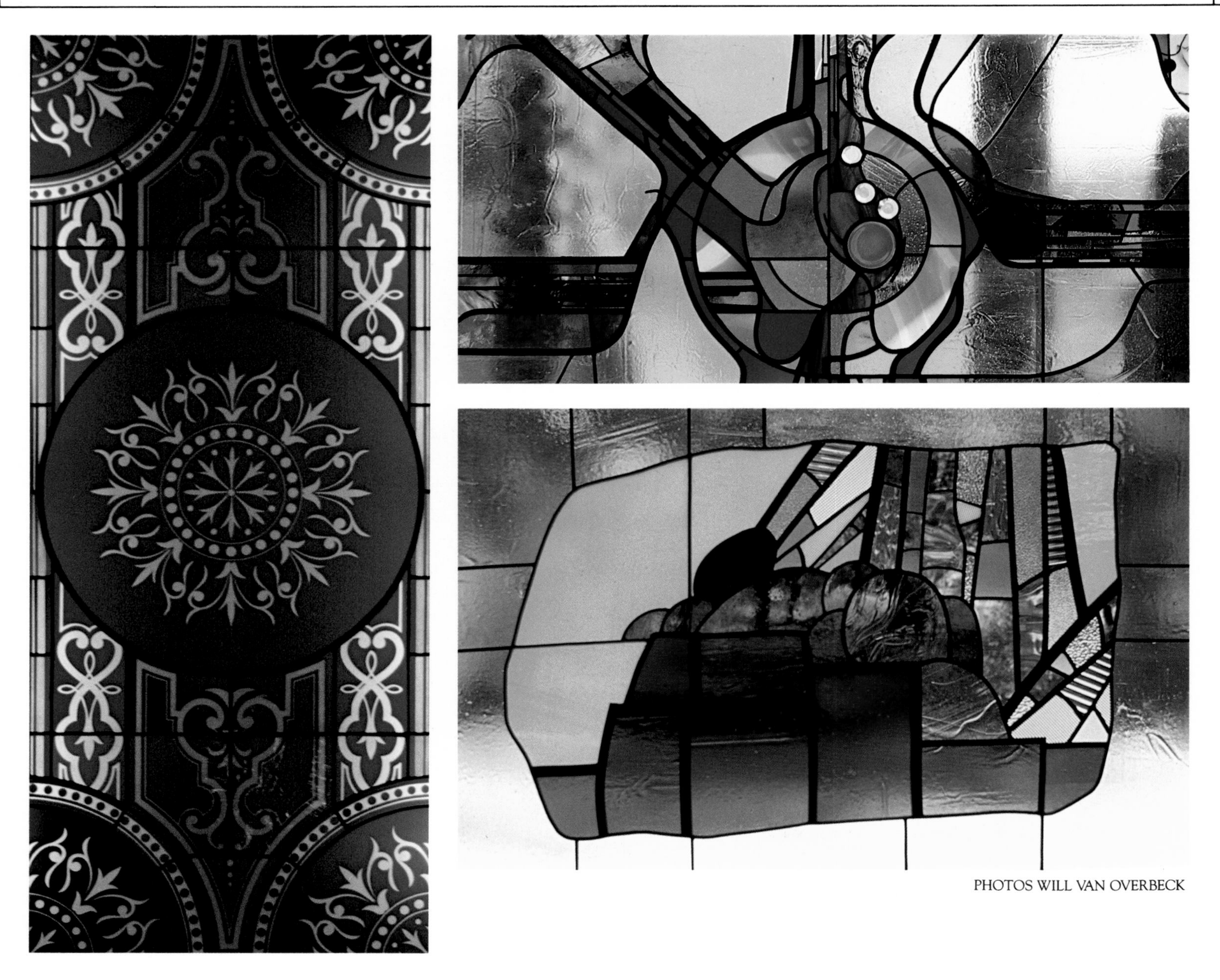

PHOTOS WILL VAN OVERBECK

Susan Stinsmuehlen started the Renaissance Glass Company in Austin, Texas, in 1973 with her partner Rodney Smith. As designer for the company, her glasswork has been installed in the Texas Governor's Mansion, as well as in restaurants and private residences throughout that state. These commissioned installations exhibit intricate patterning or strong complementary color in abstract shapes. LEFT: Decorative panel, 1979, illuminated etched glass, 90 × 42 in. Governor's Mansion, Austin, Texas. TOP RIGHT: Leaded-glass panel, 1979, 36 × 72 in. Pelican's Wharf Restaurant, San Antonio, Texas. BOTTOM RIGHT: "Radiation and Form," 1977, leaded-glass panel, 28 × 48 in. Private commission. OPPOSITE: "Morning Glory I," 1979, copper foiled technique with antique glass, 24 in. diameter. Private commission.

Glasswork

PHOTO WILL VAN OVERBECK

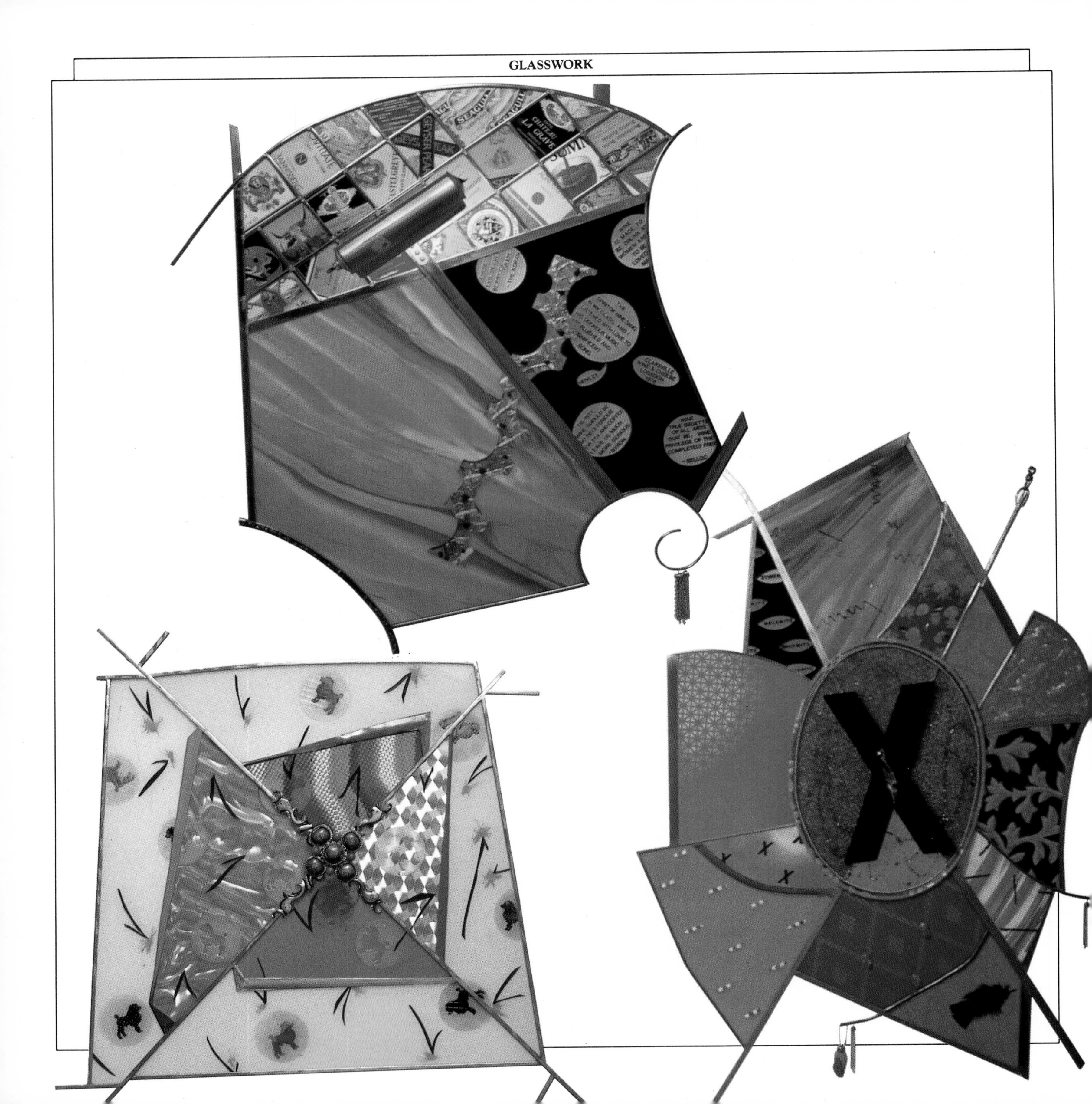
GEYSER PEAK
SEAGULL
CHATEAU
LA GRAVE
— SELLOC

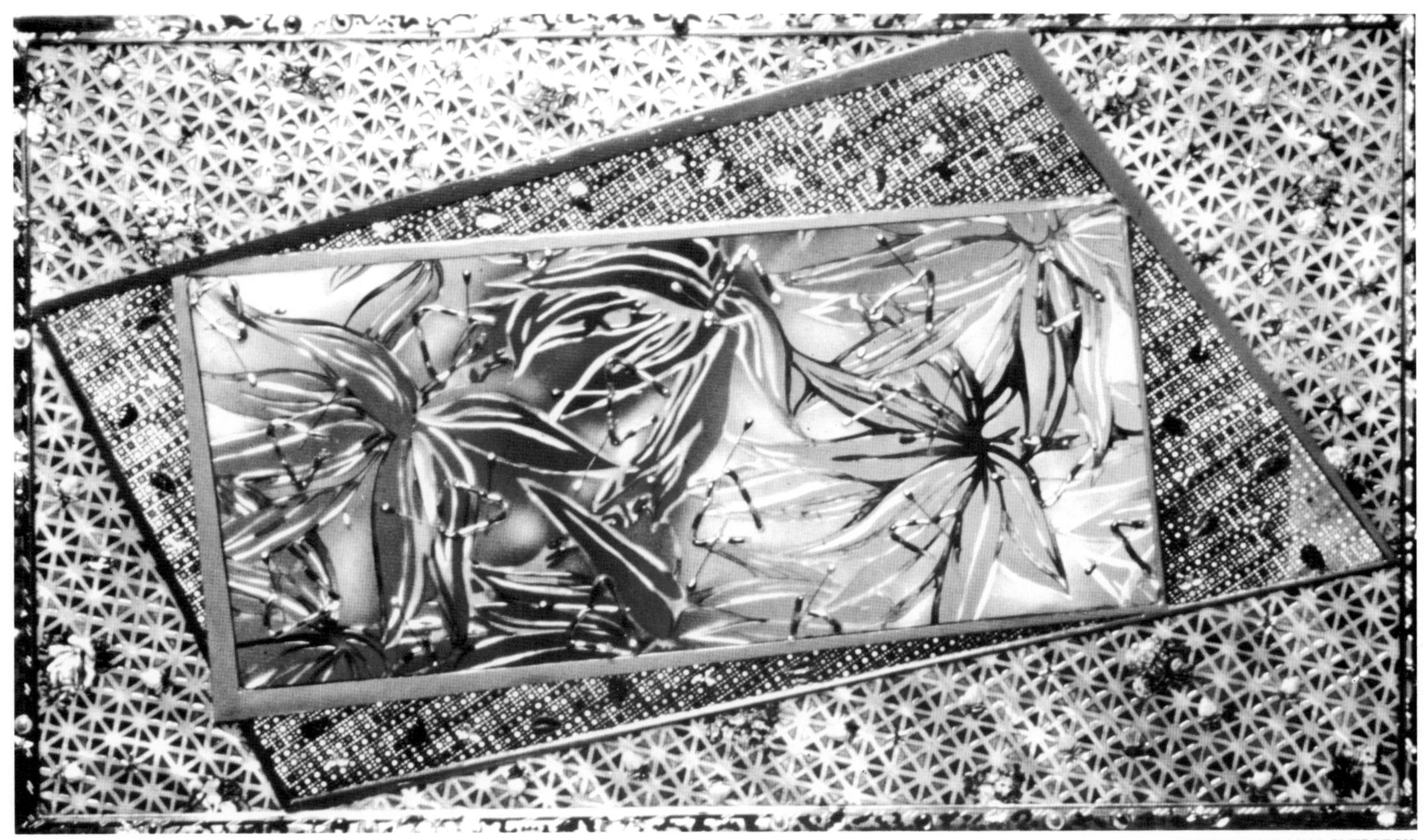

PHOTO WILL VAN OVERBECK

Stinsmuehlen also uses glass as an artist, making pieces for gallery exhibition and sale. The X form, which has become a symbol in her work, is associated in most cultures with caution, error, the act of crossing-out. For Stinsmuehlen, the emotional basis of her imagery is a desire to "X-out" people's habitual notion of what glass ought to look like: organic, fluid, romantic, and sweet. Stinsmuehlen's work denies such preconceptions. OPPOSITE TOP: "Clarxville X," 1980, glass lamination, etching, wood, paint, and light fixture, 36 × 30 in. Clarksville Wine and Cheese Shop, Austin, Texas. OPPOSITE LEFT: "X Poodle Bubble Memorial," 1980, laminated defraction grading, etched glass, brass, paint, costume jewels, 24 × 24 in. Collection of the artist. OPPOSITE RIGHT: "Xtinxion," 1980, laminated glass, fabrics, etching, jewels, paint, brass, 50 × 30 in. Traver/Sutton Gallery, Seattle, Washington. ABOVE: "Xtravaganza," 1980, etched glass, mirror, deca paint, foils, jewels, pins, 22 × 38 in. Collection, Leigh Yawkey Woodson Museum, Wausau, Wisconsin.

PHOTOS OPPOSITE PAGE WILL VAN OVERBECK

Paul Dufour heads the glass arts program at Louisiana State University, where Samuel Corso and Charles Devillier were at one time his students. Together they now comprise Dufour Glass Studios, Ltd., which has an enviable record of completed architectural commissions in stained glass throughout the Southwest. The three men share design and fabrication responsibilities for these architectural commissions, but independent of one another they also create autonomous panels for exhibition and sale. Their individual approaches to glass as an artistic medium come through in these panels, some of which are shown here. LEFT: Charles Devillier, "Wounded Shield: New Heart Stillborn," 1978, leaded antique glass with German opak, 36 × 24 in. Collection of the artist. RIGHT: Samuel Corso, "Yellow Rose of Texas," 1979, leaded antique reamies, 30 × 24 in. Collection of the artist. OPPOSITE, LEFT: Paul Dufour, "D.N.A. Galaxy," 1980, leaded glass with etched and fused rondels, 50 × 32 in. Collection of the artist. TOP RIGHT: Samuel Corso, "Sundance," 1980, antique reamy, opaks, opals, and lead, 43 × 25½ in. Collection of the artist. BOTTOM RIGHT: Charles Devillier, "The Law," 1978, leaded European antique glass, 60 × 36 in. Jackson Street Presbyterian Church, Alexandria, Louisiana.

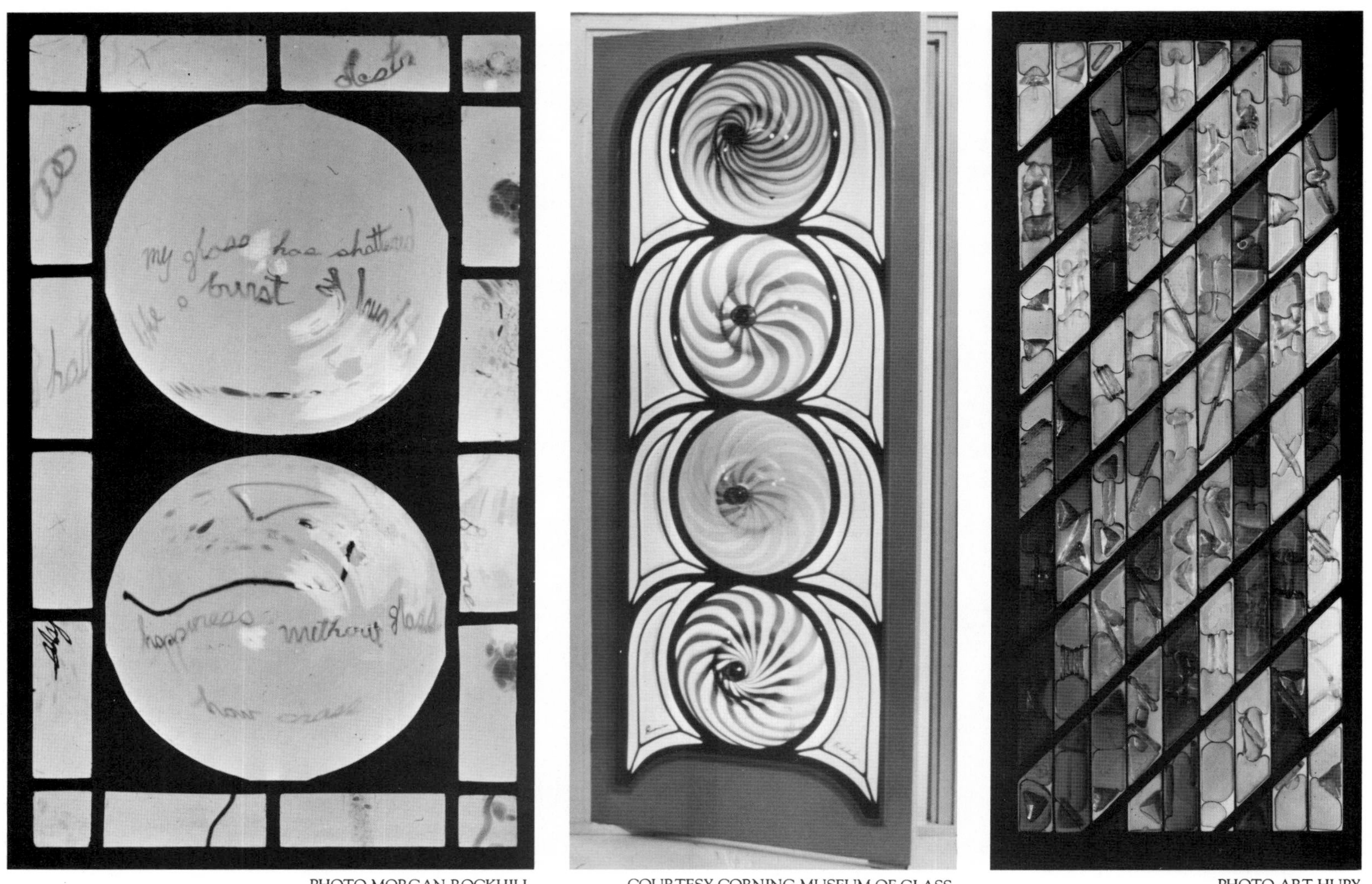

PHOTO MORGAN ROCKHILL

COURTESY CORNING MUSEUM OF GLASS

PHOTO ART HUPY

Since James Carpenter and Dale Chihuly began their collaboration in the early 1970s, they have emphasized glasswork as an architectural medium—doors, screens, and whole walls. They are frankly interested in the decorative arts and in the magical power of glass in light. Carpenter, who has formed his own design firm in New York City, believes that society has now reached the limit of its satisfaction with low-budget construction and mass-produced objects. Chihuly, artist-in-residence at the Rhode Island School of Design, says simply: "People are getting bored with technology and plastics." All of the glasswork shown here is the joint effort of Chihuly and Carpenter, except the panel above left, which is by Carpenter alone. LEFT: "My Glass Has Shattered," 1973, hand-blown panel with writing in glass thread, 54 × 30 in. Collection, Museum fur Kunsthandwerk, Frankfurt, West Germany. CENTER: Glass door with blown rondels, 1973, 84 x 30 in. Collection, Corning Museum of Glass. RIGHT: Cast glass door, 1973, 84 × 36 in. Collection, Pacific Northwest Arts Commission, Seattle Art Museum.

PHOTOS SEAVER LESLIE

The glass door above has an iridized surface stained with stannous chloride which gives it a deep, bronzelike sheen. Each rondel has been blown separately, then set into metal. Details show the power and interest of this piece at any distance. Collection of the artists.

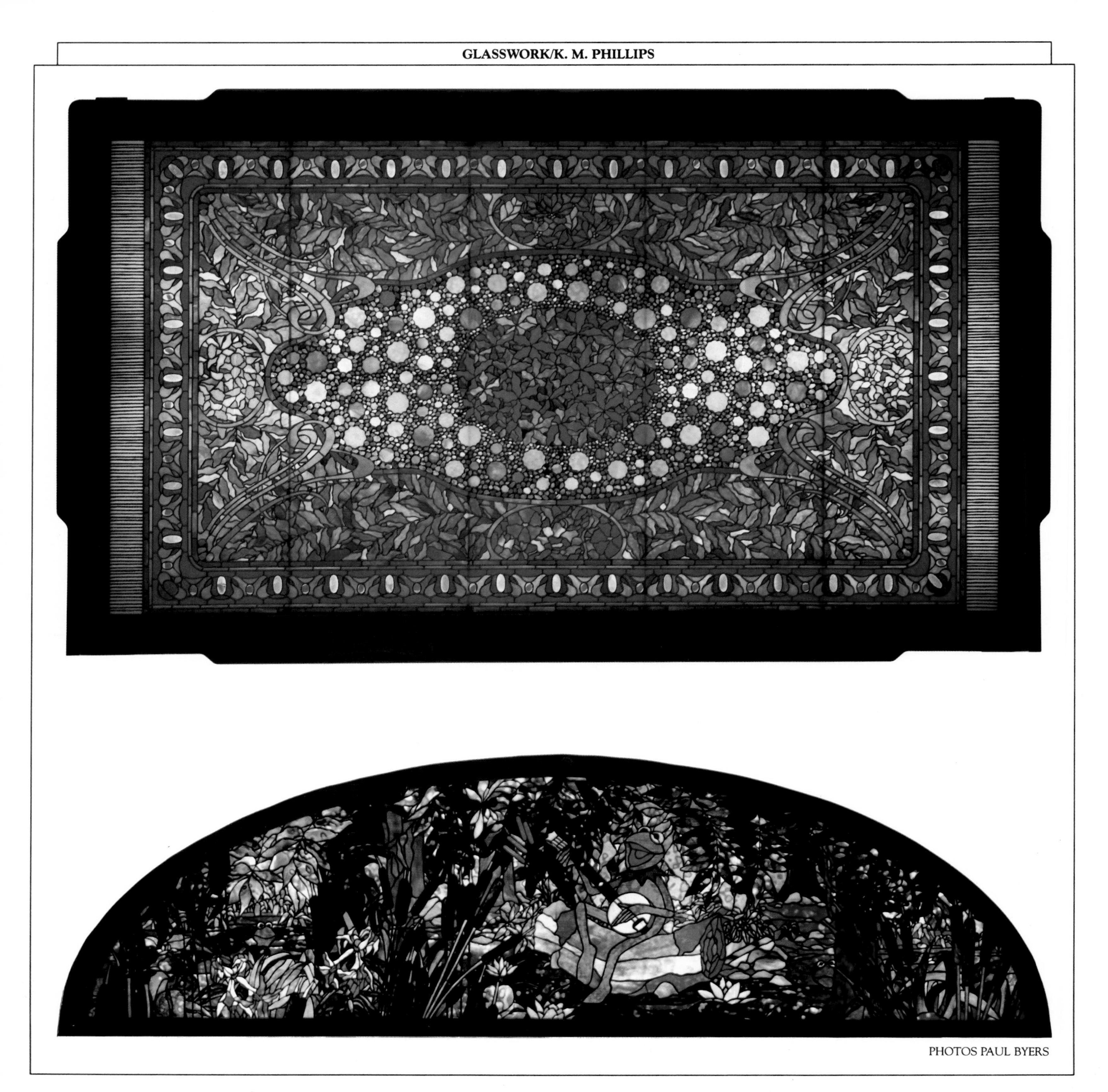

PHOTOS PAUL BYERS

PHOTO PAUL BYERS

Ken Phillips's decorative screens and windows often depict floral motifs, vibrating with color and intricate detail. They are made in his three-person Pittsburgh studio, almost exclusively on commissions from private clients. Phillips, who is noted for his craftsmanship, won the Athena Award in 1980 from McCall's Needlework & Crafts, as the magazine's artist of the year. OPPOSITE, TOP: "Oriental Carpet," 1979, freestanding screen of glass, pebbles, walnut, and ebony, 48 × 88 in. Collection, Mr. and Mrs. Vernon Pfile. BOTTOM: "Kermit the Frog," 1980, glass and wood window, 26 × 90 in. Henson Associates offices, New York City. ABOVE: Oval floral fire screen, 1978, glass, pebbles, and teak, 40 × 48 in. Private collection.

PHOTO STAN RIES

OPPOSITE: The beveled glass coffee table, 48 × 42 × 15 in. high, is but one example of the work of Ingo Williams, who founded Bedford-Downing Glass in New York City in 1971. His handmade glass objects, from furniture to candelabra, are exquisitely crafted, and the larger pieces of furniture glass are now made almost exclusively on commission. The window, BELOW, is by Robert Sowers of Brooklyn, New York, and is fabricated of black and opal-flashed white glass, 72 × 36 in. Sowers works in black and white in order to open rooms to light rather than close them. Crafted black-and-white glass has, for him, a strong decorative power without the "sweetness" of color. His book is *The Language of Stained Glass* (Timber Press, 1981).

ABOVE: In an extraordinary example of design collaboration, twenty-eight artisans and artists were commissioned in 1980 by Clyde's Restaurant, Vienna, Virginia, to create original glasswork, ironwork, woodwork, and fixtures for its interiors. The windows are by Kenneth vonRoenn, Branford, Connecticut, who designed 45 feet of interior glass partitions for the restaurant, as well as the principal windows for its three dining rooms. The breakfast-room window shown here is 8 × 9 ft. long on its curve, and is made of clear antique reamy glass and opal glass. The architect for Clyde's was J. Richard Andrews, and vonRoenn's glasswork was fabricated by Penco Studios, Louisville, Kentucky.

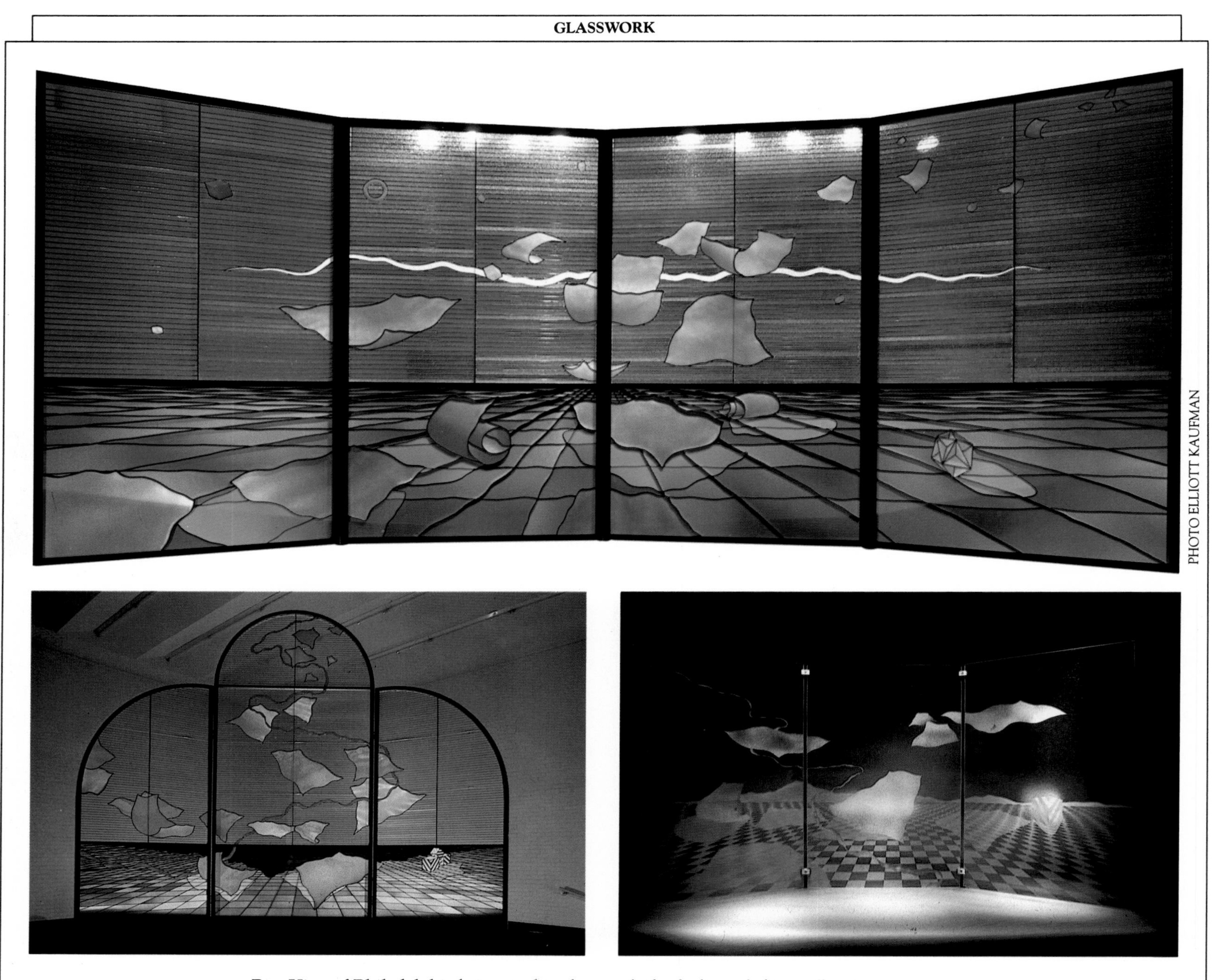

PHOTO ELLIOTT KAUFMAN

Ray King of Philadelphia brings to his glasswork the feeling of objects floating in space, of vast distances to be traveled. His recent large autonomous screens seem to envelop the viewer, creating a world of their own. He has exhibited at the Renwick Gallery, Washington, D.C., and at the Museum of Contemporary Crafts in New York, among other places. TOP: "Formlings II," 1980, colored and clear glass screen with lead, brass, and aluminum, 90 × 216 in. Collection of the artist. LEFT: "Mistral," 1980, colored and clear glass screen with lead, glass, and aluminum, 144 × 183 in. Collection of the artist. RIGHT: "Etched Triptych," 1979, etched glass, tinted with plastic dye, 36 × 72 in. Collection of the artist. OPPOSITE: "Disc VI," 1977, colored and clear glass, lead and brass, 34 inches diameter. Collection, Mr. and Mrs. Martin Ezra.

PHOTO OPPOSITE PAGE ELLIOTT KAUFMAN

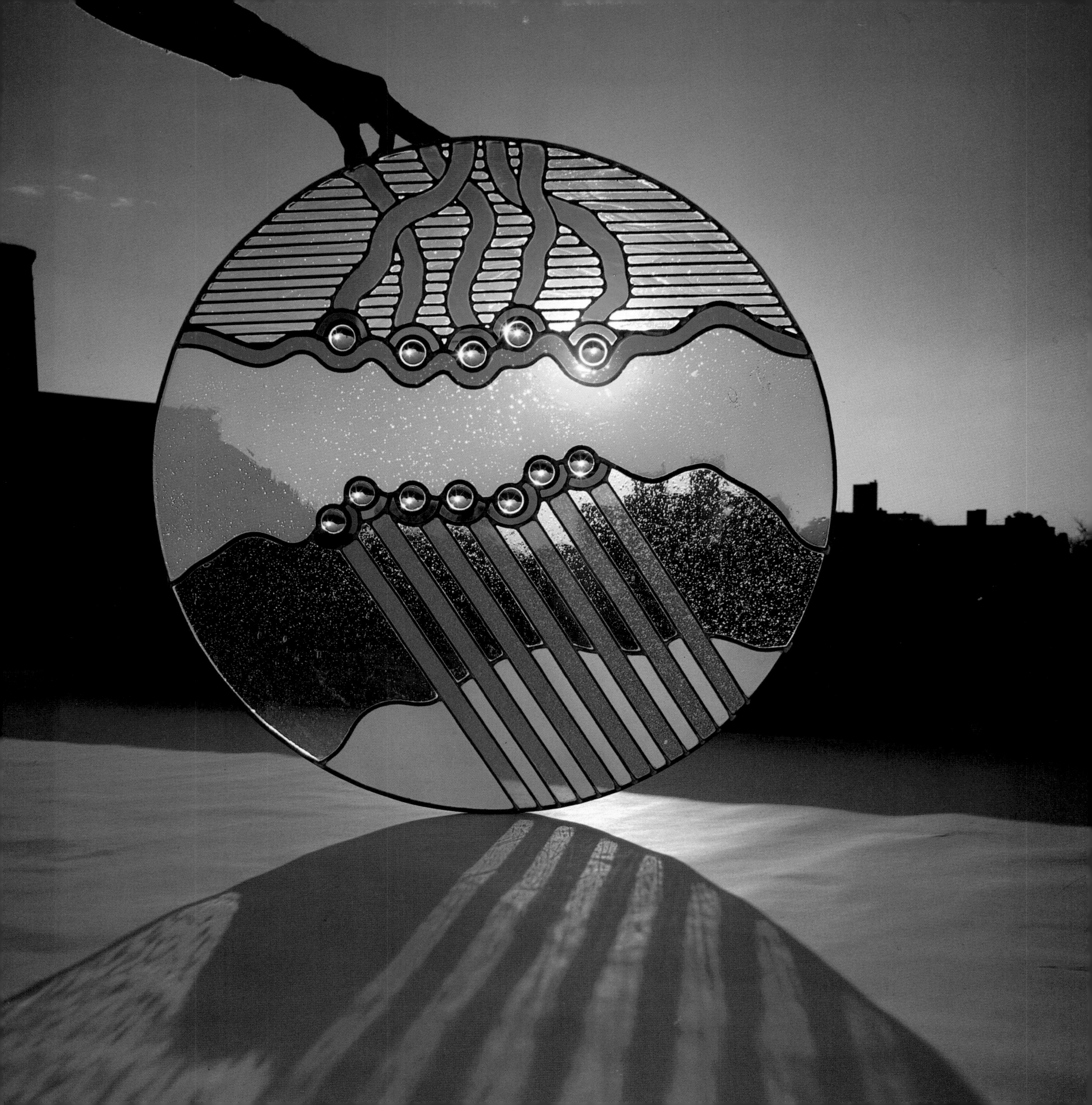

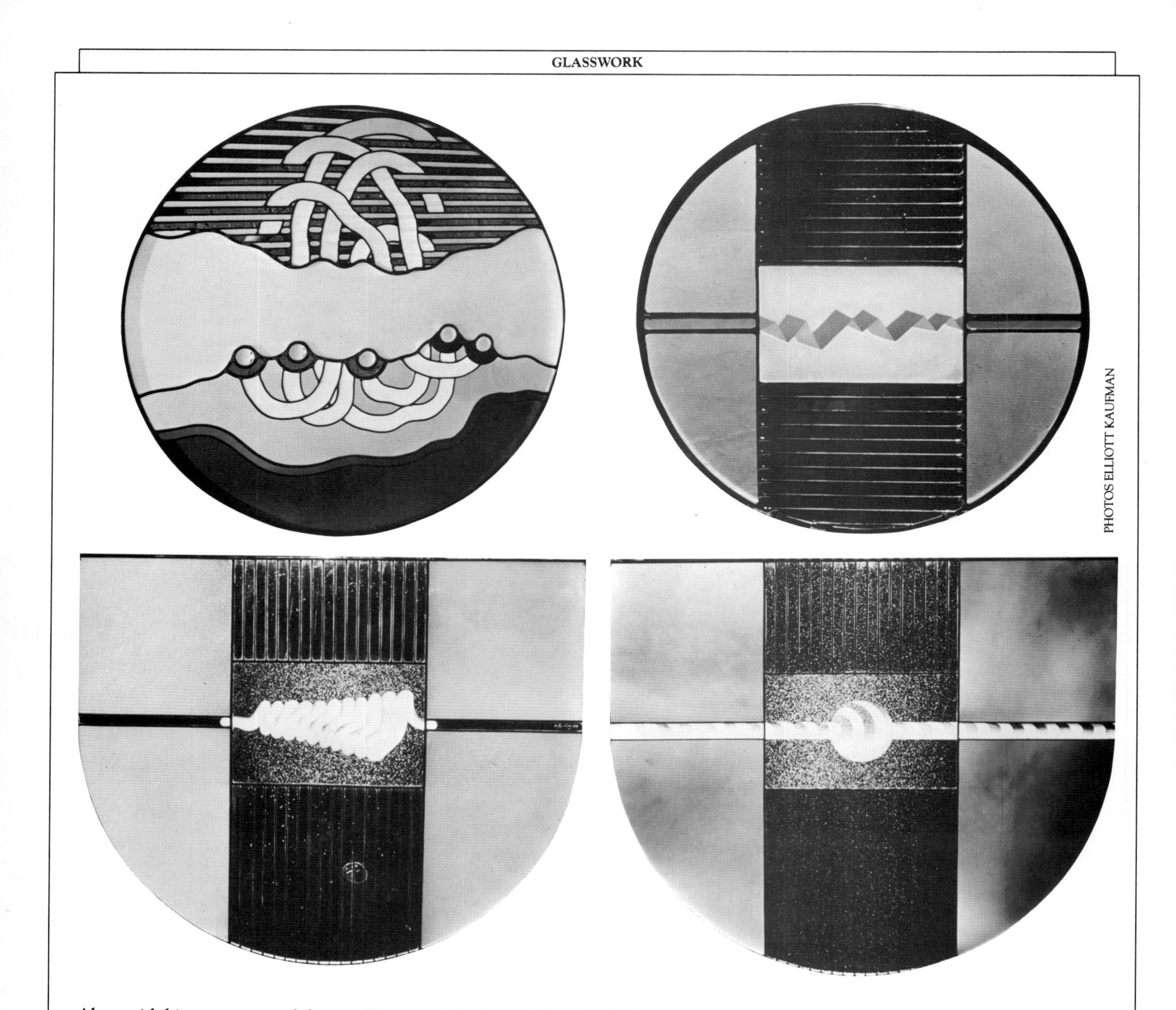

Along with his screens, an exhibition of Ray King's "Ghost Shields" series opened as a one-person show in 1980 at the Center for the Arts, Muhlenberg College in Allentown, Pennsylvania. One of his "Disc" series works is in the collection of the Victoria and Albert Museum, London. TOP LEFT: "Disc X," 1978, colored and clear glass, lead and brass, 34 inches diameter. Private collection. TOP RIGHT: "Small Disc," 1980, colored and clear glass, lead and brass, 18 inches diameter. Private collection. BOTTOM: "Ghost Shield I," 1978, LEFT, and "Ghost Shield VIII," 1980, RIGHT, colored and etched glass, lead and brass, 38 × 45 in. Private collection.

Wrought-Ironwork

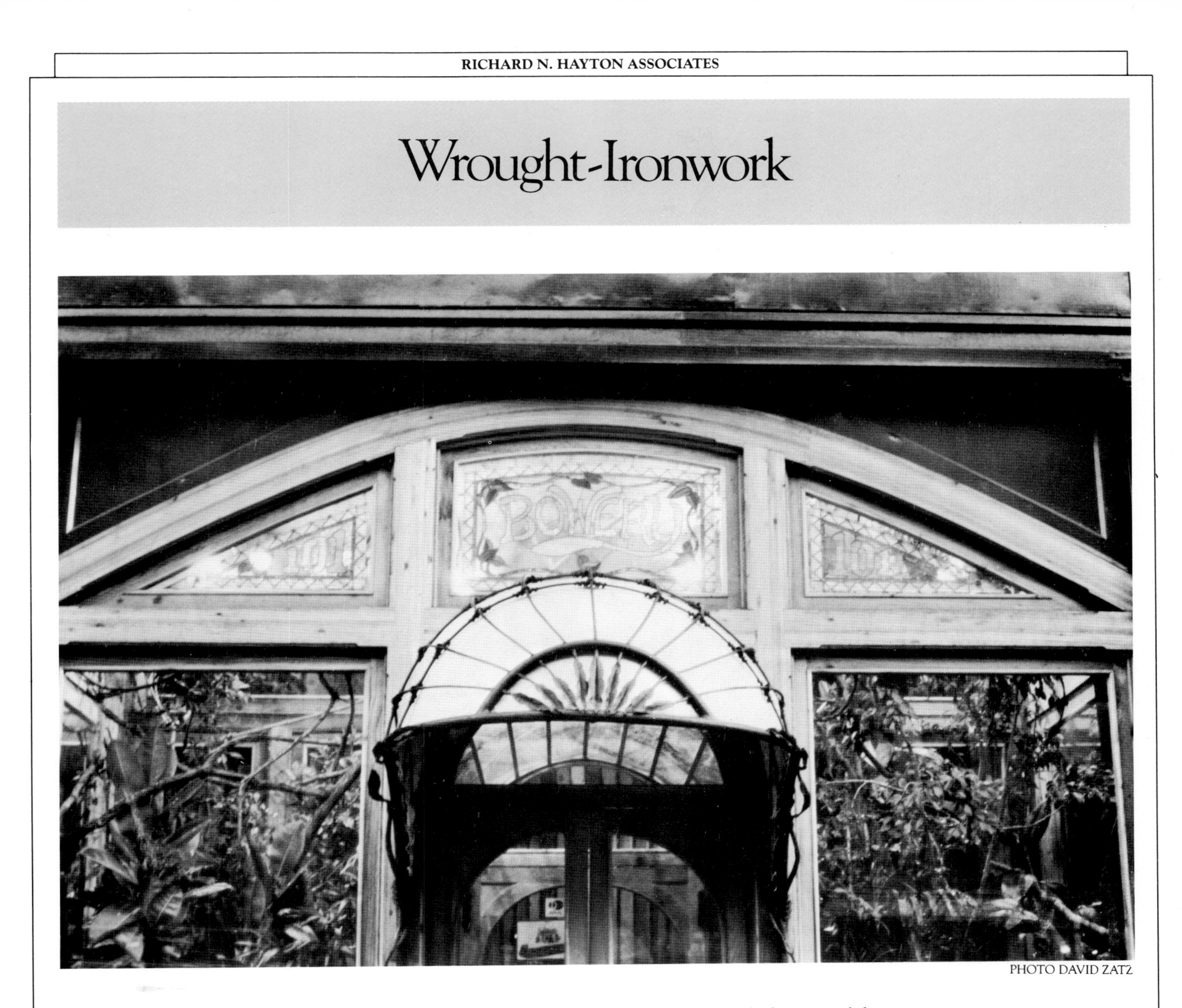

PHOTO DAVID ZATZ

The exterior and interior of 101 Bowery, ABOVE, a New York City jazz club, were created in 1978 by a group of designers and craftsmen who work together at Richard N. Hayton Associates, a Brooklyn firm that builds what it designs. For the façade and entrance canopy of the jazz club shown here, Richard Hayton himself developed the preliminary concept and designed the glass. Ernest Porcelli executed the glasswork and David Zatz, whose work is shown on the following pages, designed the structural and ornamental iron and constructed the canopy.

PHOTOS DAVID ZATZ

PHOTOS DAVID ZATZ

The integration of iron, glass, and wood in the 101 Bowery jazz club is brilliantly conceived and executed, as these general views and details of the exterior façade, OPPOSITE AND ABOVE, attest. David Zatz's ironwork, at once structural and ornamental as in the wrought-iron clamps and leaves directly above, is particularly illustrative of what craftsmanship can be today. The philosophy of Hayton Associates is based on design, craftsmanship, and construction as one unified endeavor. This, Hayton says, ". . . provides a level of satisfaction for the participants which, we feel, can contribute dramatically to the quality of the finished product." Their facilities in Brooklyn include a complete woodworking shop, a forge and metalworks, a greenhouse, and a design studio.

PHOTO BRUCE MILLER, COURTESY FENDRICK GALLERY, WASHINGTON, D.C.

Albert Paley's reputation as a metalworker has grown each year since his graduation as a sculptor from the Tyler School of Art in Philadelphia in 1966. Beginning with jewelry, Paley has been working at an architectural scale since 1974. At both the large and smaller scales, his designs have challenged the anonymity and simplicity that have been the rule in modern metalwork. Paley's work expresses an almost Rococo complexity combined with a clarity of conception that delights the mind. His pieces are forged and fabricated in a five-person studio and foundry in Rochester, New York. Most of the large commissions are constructed at the foundry to preset dimensions, then shipped to the site for installation. Paley was commissioned in 1980 by the Pennsylvania Avenue Development Corporation in Washington, D.C., to design cast-iron lampposts, park benches, and tree grates that are now being installed in the nation's capital. ABOVE: Security screen, 1978, wrought iron, 72 × 54 in. OPPOSITE: Portal gates, 1974, forged, fabricated, and inlaid mild steel, brass, bronze, and copper, 90½ × 72½ in. Installed in the Smithsonian Institution's Renwick Gallery, Washington, D.C.

PHOTO JOE WATSON

PHOTOS BRUCE MILLER

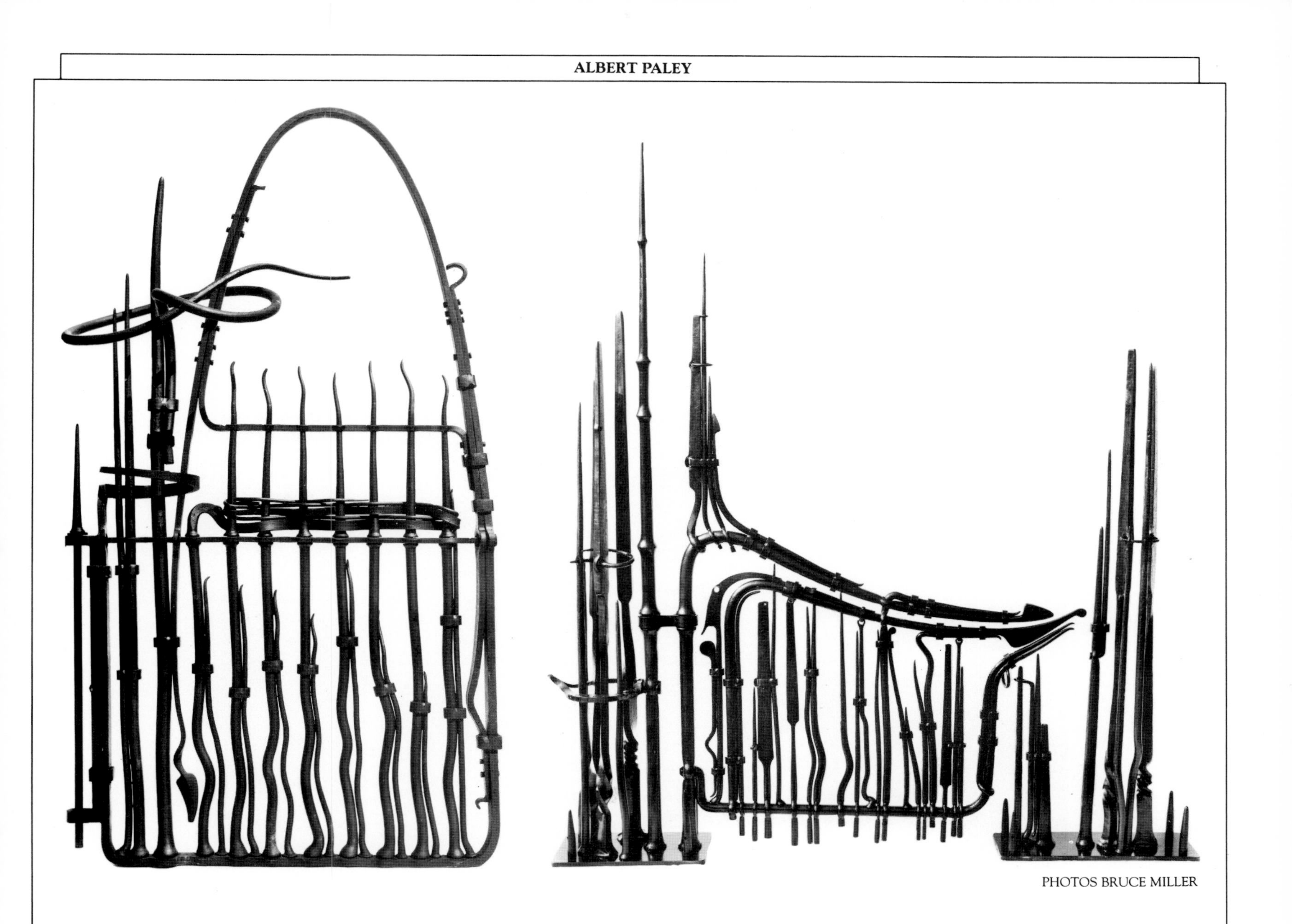

PHOTOS BRUCE MILLER

OPPOSITE, TOP LEFT: Albert Paley, balcony railing, 1979, forged and fabricated mild steel, 108 × 114 in. Collection, Karen Burns and Stephen Moscowitz. BOTTOM LEFT: Dining table with glass top, 1979, wrought iron, 29 × 40 in. diameter. Courtesy Fendrick Gallery, Washington, D.C. BOTTOM RIGHT: Clock stand, 1981, forged and fabricated mild steel, 14 feet high. Commissioned for Prospect Place Mall, Georgetown, Washington, D.C. ABOVE LEFT: Parabolic gate, 1976, mild steel, 96 × 48 in. RIGHT: Garden gate, 1976, forged and fabricated mild steel, 126 × 120 in.

PHOTO ROBERT PERRON

PHOTOS ROBERT PERRON

Sculptor Christopher Ray studied at the Pennsylvania Academy of Fine Arts and since 1964 has been working almost exclusively in metal. In addition to numerous private commissions, he has completed more than forty public and corporate installations since 1967. Ray works out of a forge and metalworks in Philadelphia. OPPOSITE: "Spiderweb" gate, 1969, forged iron, 80 inches high. Private residence, Society Hill, Philadelphia. LEFT: Handle detail, "Tree Door," 1968, forged iron and tempered glass. H. Cline Co., Philadelphia. RIGHT: Bolt lock with handle, TOP, and kitchen door handle, 1975, forged iron. Ray house, Mt. Airy, Pennsylvania.

PHOTOS MARY GERAKARIS

Joel Schwartz, whose work is shown on the opposite page, maintains a forge and metalworks in Deansboro, New York. Most of his commissions are architectural, and his work is distinguished by its sinuous, floral quality. Schwartz's pieces have been shown at the Museum of Contemporary Crafts in New York City and at the Renwick Gallery in Washington, D.C. OPPOSITE, TOP: Security grille, 1978, forged iron, 84 × 84 in. Commissioned for private residence, Brooklyn, New York. BOTTOM: Garden gate, 1980, forged iron, 48 × 36 in.

Dimitri Gerakaris of North Canaan, New Hampshire, whose work is shown above, speaks of the "spaces between" as a primary design element of his metalwork. The 20-foot-wide wrought-iron entry gates, TOP, AND DETAIL, RIGHT, to Windswept, an 800-acre unfenced New Hampshire estate, are intended as portal announcements as much as gates; they prohibit vehicular traffic only. A smaller courtyard gate at Windswept, LEFT, continues the theme of airy weightlessness that Gerakaris brings to his designs. Both gates were completed in 1979.

PHOTOS ROBERT PERRON

Greg Leavitt, founder of Upper Bank Forge in Wawa, a suburb of Philadelphia, is a sculptor who works in metal, primarily with architects and interior designers. His grilles and gates, as well as his sculpture, are more figurative than abstract, depicting flowers, birds, and fantasy beasts. Most of Leavitt's commissions have been in eastern Pennsylvania, and the Philadelphia Redevelopment Authority is currently incorporating his work in one of its housing projects.

PHOTOS ROBERT PERRON

OPPOSITE AND ABOVE LEFT: General view and details (demounted), "Flamen Gorey" grilles, 1978, forged iron, each 72 × 32 in. Private residence, Society Hill, Philadelphia. RIGHT: "Tomato Vine" gate, 1977, forged iron and copper, 48 × 48 in. Private residence, Princeton, New Jersey.

PHOTO GIL AMIAGA

Eloi Bordelon's murals are a frank continuation of eighteenth- and nineteenth-century Neoclassicism. His marble-bordered gardens spring from ceilings and walls, filled with trelliswork, plant life, and exotic birds. Bordelon, who learned trompe l'oeil mural technique in Europe, has lived and worked in New York City since 1965. ABOVE: Entrance foyer done in 1970 for the Simon apartment, New York City. Wall and ceiling panels are oil on canvas with painting over mirror set in the endwall. OPPOSITE: Entrance lobby ceiling, 1981, St. Regis Hotel, New York City. The 22 × 22 ft. ceiling panel is oil on canvas.

Brushwork

PHOTOS LESLEY BRILL

Megan Parry, whose studio is in Boulder, Colorado, describes herself as an architectural painter. Her stencil- and muralwork has a flat, contemporary power that avoids historical precedent. The Van Zante residence in Boulder, ABOVE, was designed in the 1950s for clients who required a large number of doors (one bedroom has four ways in and out). When new owners bought the house in 1978, something had to be done with all those doors. Parry was commissioned and, with a combination of stenciling and painting, transformed a liability into a decorative fantasy. Eleven doors in the house were each given a slightly different color and pattern.

PHOTOS LESLEY BRILL

ABOVE: Bedroom, LEFT, and front hall, RIGHT, of the Brill residence, Boulder, Colorado. Walls and chest are decorated with stencilwork, while painted detail adds visual emphasis to stair risers and banister.

PHOTO LESLEY BRILL

PHOTO LESLEY BRILL

PHOTO LESLEY BRILL

Using a combination of freehand painting and stenciling, Megan Parry created what she calls the "birdbath" corner, TOP LEFT AND RIGHT, for a residence in Yorkville, Illinois. A simple border pattern and tree stencil, BOTTOM LEFT, add interest to a small Denver bathroom. The executive bathroom for a corporate headquarters in Denver, BOTTOM RIGHT, was hand-painted in a pattern that borrows from traditional southwestern Indian designs. OPPOSITE: Megan Parry's murals are the main event for the Rendez-Vous Restaurant and Ice Cream Parlor in Denver, Colorado, which was completed in 1978 on Larimer Street in the historic section of the city.

PHOTO LESLEY BRILL

PHOTO WILLIAM BELL

PHOTOS WILLIAM BELL

William Bell, whose studio is in Norwalk, Connecticut, is a decorative-finish artist who uses photographic silkscreening as his medium, a technique allowing great intricacy of color and pattern. Bell, who was once a professional photographer, designs and executes finishes for furnishings, cloth, and even for wood flowers in a snowy backyard. OPPOSITE: A silkscreen-painted pattern has been applied to this 24-inch-high plywood chest, then sealed with a polyurethane finish.

TOP LEFT: Bell created all the patterns and finishes for this *House and Garden* room in 1971. CENTER: Bell printed the porch awning, table, planters, and woman's robe. TOP RIGHT: The table and T sculpture are for a private residence in Purchase, New York. BOTTOM: The painted wooden flowers are about 8 inches in diameter and were done by Bell in 1978. Bell hand-painted and then printed about a hundred of these flowers for a friend.

PHOTOS TOM SANCH

All of the objects on these pages are made of wood. They have been transformed into things of intricate delicacy by Kakia Livanos of New York City, using paint and hand-rubbed finishes. A complete finish might require eighty coats of varnish, with sanding between each coat. Livanos learned her craft from Isabel O'Neil who, through her New York school, has kept the techniques of fine painted finishes alive in this country. TOP LEFT: Miniature chest of drawers, 1978, painted eggshell inlay, 8 inches high. TOP RIGHT: Chest of drawers, 1976, stylized Arabic design with lacquer finish, 27 inches high. BOTTOM LEFT: Geese with fantasy surface, gold leaf and paint, 6 inches high. CENTER: Hexagonal box with lid, 1979, enameled paisley pattern over gold leaf, 6¼ inches diameter. RIGHT: Ginger jar, 1980, white eggshell over black lacquer, 18 inches high. OPPOSITE, TOP: Miniature for a two-sided screen, 1980, English black lacquer with gold inlay on one side, coromandel with ivory inlay on the other, 18 inches high. BOTTOM: Lacquered inlay box, 1977, 5 inches high.

PHOTOS TOM SANCH

Muralist Philip Standish Read has studios in Long Island, New York, and Palm Beac
Florida, where his work is a feature of many large residences. Read's murals are reali
tic, but with an eerie, subtle sense of humor that urges the viewer to look again, ar
then again. ABOVE: Read painted the foyer of this Palm Beach house in 1978. It
acrylic on canvas, painted in his studio and then applied to the wall. OPPOSITE, TC
RIGHT: Palm mural, 1980, painted for the lobby of a large private house in Palm Beach
TOP LEFT AND BELOW: This elaborate undersea scene, with facsimile coral, was painte
in 1979 for a house in Manaplan, Florida.

PHOTOS MICHAEL MERLE

Richard Lowell Neas is a trompe l'oeil artist who has done numerous residential and commercial spaces in New York City. He is a master at painting large surfaces and turning plain wood floors into marble inlay or intricate parquet. This elevator entrance foyer, OPPOSITE, complete with monkey in the oculus, was done in 1970 for the Copeland apartment, New York City.

The engaged column arcade, ABOVE LEFT, in a New York City apartment building lobby was originally unadorned plaster and stucco. Artist Nicholas Crowell transformed it with this painted *faux marbre* finish in 1980, using an airbrush technique and oil-glazed green serpentine trim. The *faux bois* moldings and entablature, RIGHT, were painted by Crowell for a New York City apartment.

PHOTO OPPOSITE PAGE GIL AMIAGA

PHOTO ERNST BEADLE

PHOTO DON GRAY

PHOTO DON GRAY

Stenciling is a means of creating intricate pattern and color that anyone can master, as Adele Bishop and Cile Lord demonstrate in their book *The Art of Decorative Stenciling* (Penguin, 1978). With this technique, ordinary floors, walls, doors, and furniture can become decorative features transforming space. The corner cabinet, TOP LEFT, was stenciled in a polka-dot pattern by Cile Lord, and the stylized floral design on the three-panel screen, TOP RIGHT, was executed by Adele Bishop. Cile Lord stenciled the dining room, ABOVE, with small diaper patterns and Chinoiserie in eighteenth-century French style, working in collaboration with interior designer Hariet Eckstein. The Moroccan patterned door and floor-cloth, OPPOSITE, were painted by Adele Bishop, using eleven stencils and four colors on the door and five stencils with two colors on the white cotton canvas cloth.

PHOTO OPPOSITE PAGE HORST, COURTESY HOUSE AND GARDEN

PHOTO ERNST BEADLE

Living room with floors and walls stenciled by Cile Lord in Early American patterns, using twelve stencils and two colors.

Painted finishes can transform a small room into the most elaborate of fantasies. This child's bedroom in New York City is artists Eric Appel and Richard Dimmler's version of the Doge's Palace in Venice, complete with clouds and fanciful skyline. The floor is a simple stencil pattern, and the "tower" shelf and storage unit were built by the artists to complete the theme. Describing this room, completed in 1978, Appel says, "We were trying to get away from the spare industrial look. . . . That whole attitude of 'form follows function' is too sterile." His collaborator on this project, Richard Dimmler, is now a partner with Suzanne Dimmler in Dimmler Studios, New York City.

PHOTO RICHARD DIMMLER

Alessandro Mendini's "Proust" chair, 1978, designed for Studio Alchymia, Milan, and Art et Industrie, New York. The chair is intended to "explode in the tranquil privacy of a bourgeois living room . . . suggesting ways of escaping from the dictatorship of design through the liberation of the individual imagination." Wood and fabric, hand-painted, 45 × 41 × 31 in.

FURNISHINGS & LIGHTING

The dynamic of Ornamentalism is nowhere more evident than in recent furniture and lighting design. It is here that the decorative impulses in architecture, the crafts, and fine arts converge. Although early Modernists like Marcel Breuer, Mies van der Rohe, and Le Corbusier were as well known to the public for their furniture as for their architecture, the following generation of architects in the United States concentrated most of its efforts on building design. Now, as they loosen the constraints of Modernism, American architects like Michael Graves (opposite), Rodolfo Machado (page 214), Richard Fernau, and Laura Hartman (page 236) are once more turning attention to the possibilities of furniture as an architectural element. On the other hand, the fact that much of the new wave of Italian furniture (pages 226–28) is being designed by architects reflects established practice in that country, which has led the field of Modern furniture design for the last twenty years.

In the United States, some highly original and decorative furniture is also being produced by craftspeople. Woodworkers like Judy McKie, Ed Zucca, Gary Bennett, and Wendel Castle (pages 216–23) are designing very sophisticated pieces in which the grain is concealed by paint or stain, where surfaces are carved, colored, and inlaid in a manner reminiscent of traditional styles and completely unrelated to the organic or "tree trunk" school of craft furniture. The imagery of these woodworkers is intensely personal, often based in nature as in McKie's animal forms or Bennett's cloud motif.

A different kind of natural imagery is seen in the furnishings of Tigerdale Studios (pages 233–35) or Pedro Friedeberg (page 237) where plant and animal forms explode into voluptuous fantasy; or in Fabio Alvim's "Forma" lamp (page 224) and Michele De Lucchi's "Sinerpica" lights (page 228) where nature is abstracted and synthesized with modern industrial materials and fabrication techniques. There are also many historical references, not only to past furniture styles as in Machado's "L. A. Borghese" lounge and Trent Whitington's "Chair No. 2" (page 215), but to architecture itself as in Graves's tables or Robert Haussmann and Trix Haussmann-Högl's "Colonna" storage unit (page 224). Indeed, the styles and sensibilities of Ornamentalist furniture range from the conventional decorativeness of Alessandro's "Lady Bombe" console (page 231) to the rakish humor of Howard Meister's "Nothing Continues to Happen" chair (page 224).

What is common to all of the work shown here is an emphasis on furniture design as an art form, on the importance of the individual piece as opposed to the harmony of style. It is difficult to imagine an entire living room, let alone an executive suite, furnished with the designs of James Evanson, Paola Navone, or Ettore Sottsass, Jr. (pages 225, 226). This is furniture meant to break "the dictatorship of design," as Italian architect Alessandro Mendini explains his "Proust" chair (page 211), to serve as the object of contemplation in much the same manner as one of artist Jane Kaufman's screens (pages 256, 257) or Joyce Kozloff's and Betty Woodman's pitchers (page 274). Indeed, it is difficult to distinguish, at least superficially, between the work of an artist like Jennifer Cecere whose medium is furnishings (pages 284, 285) and the furniture of Mendini (pages 211, 227). Some of Cecere's chairs can be sat in as, of course, can Mendini's, but that is not the point of either. Although much of the furniture shown here is quite comfortable and useful, it rejects utility as its sole or even primary purpose. This furniture is meant to be looked at, to be confronted visually on its own terms, to be admired for its unique personality and not for the ease with which it might be slipped, anonymously, into some larger scheme of things.

This furniture is not found today in department stores or even, for the most part, in contract showrooms. Many pieces are designed and produced on private commissions or in limited editions and sold directly out of the designer's studio or through small specialized galleries. Significantly, it is through fine-arts dealers that more and more of this work is being shown, and some of it is being bought by museums before it reaches the marketplace. By no means, however, is this furniture intended only for collectors. The shops and galleries that carry it do a brisk walk-in business, and the influence of this furniture on the public taste is spreading. Even at the corporate level it is finding acceptance—and this is important because, for the last twenty years, home and office furnishings have been virtually interchangeable. The fact that Sunar, a major manufacturer of office furniture, is producing one of Graves's tables suggests the impact that this kind of furniture is going to have on interior design over the next decade.

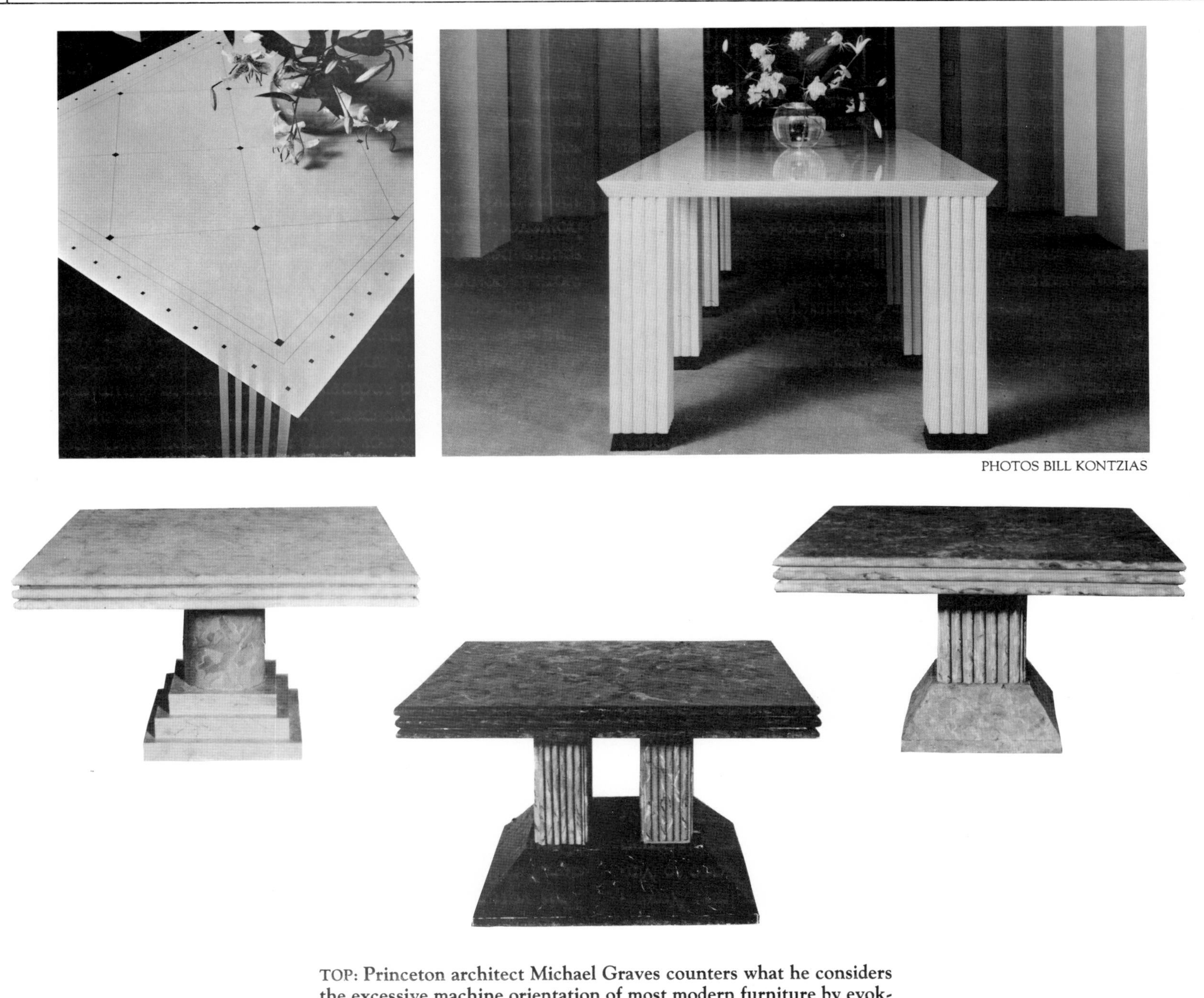

PHOTOS BILL KONTZIAS

TOP: Princeton architect Michael Graves counters what he considers the excessive machine orientation of most modern furniture by evoking craft techniques in this 1981 prototype table for Sunar, a manufacturer of office furniture. The legs carry architectural references in their similarity to fluted columns, and the *faux* inlay top, LEFT, recalls the painted tin-top tables of the 1930s and 1940s. Prototype version shown here is lacquered wood with silkscreened pattern, 29 × 105½ × 39½ in. Available from Sunar. BOTTOM: Michael Graves's study models of tables for Sunar, 1979, proposed marble or wood with painted *faux marbre* finish, 29 × 42 × 42 in.

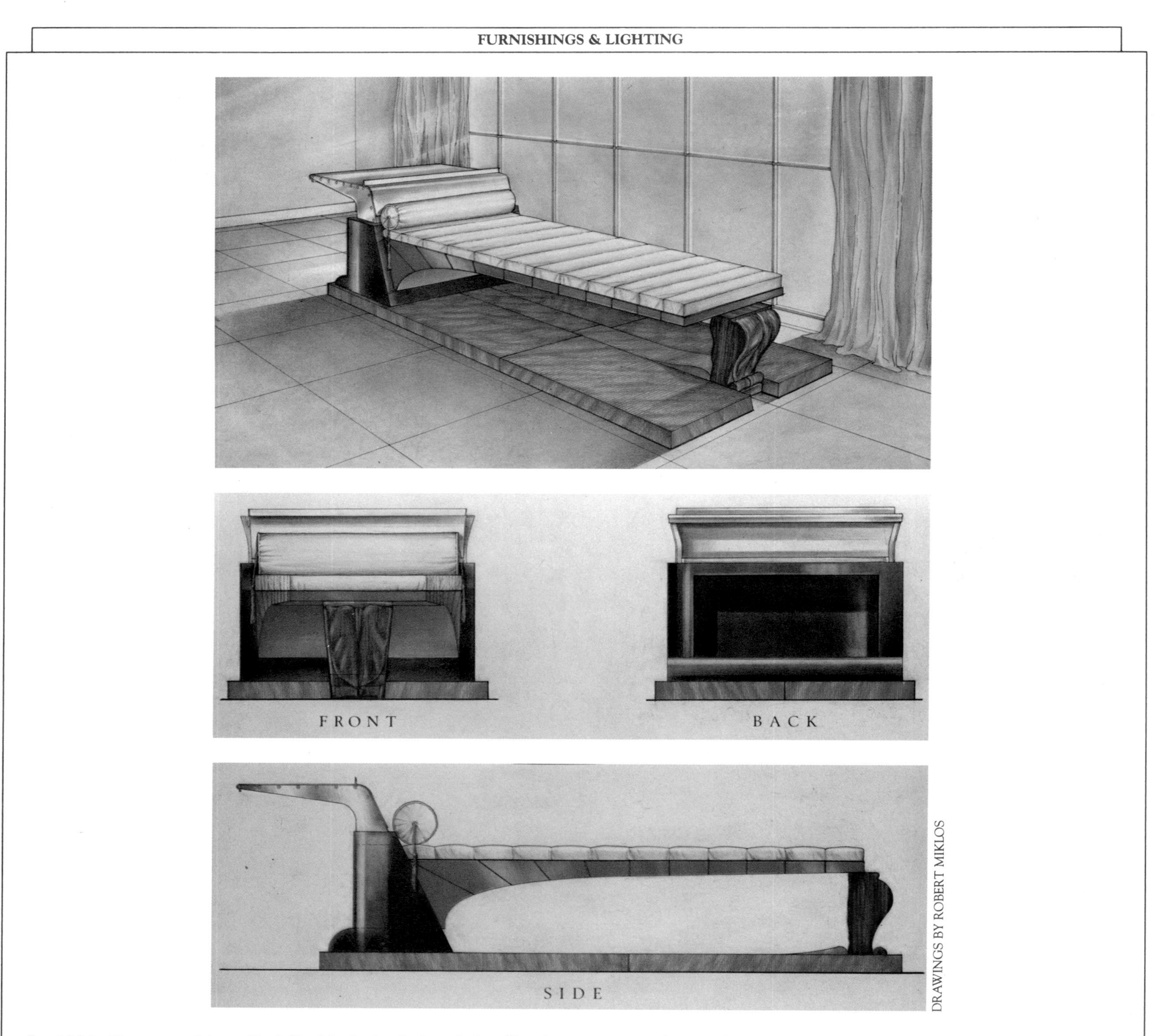

In 1981, Boston architect Rodolfo Machado designed the "L. A. Borghese" daybed or chaise longue as an ancient "trapezia," or three-legged Greek table transformed into a reclining couch with a cantilevered table added. Machado's intention is to create an important piece of furniture that is an antidote to what he views as the blandness of most modern architectural settings. The podium is solid sycamore with table base and couch leg of glossy black lacquer, arched elements of glossy red lacquer, scroll leg of rosewood with back side unfinished, tabletop and two supporting ribs of stainless steel, and silk or leather upholstered cushions. 30 × 90 × 42 in.

PHOTOS DAVID CARAS

TOP: "Two Chairs for a Tall Room with a Short Ceiling," 1981, were designed by California architect and cabinetmaker Trent Whitington as a "distortion on Charles Rennie Mackintosh," the turn-of-the-century Scottish designer noted for his furniture and sumptuously decorative Art Nouveau interiors. Where Mackintosh used furniture to define space, Whitington tries to "create space within space" in these chairs, stripping Mackintosh's ladder-back motif to its essence and introducing a checkerboard inlay pattern reminiscent of the Vienna Secessionists. Ebonized red oak, bent and painted Baltic birch, maple feet, mother of pearl inlay and gabardine cushions. 30 × 26 × 20 in. BOTTOM: Whitington's "Chair No. 2," 1981, is "intentionally symbol-laden to make a kaleidoscopic comment on furniture styles," with cabriole legs recalling the eighteenth century and a color palette that refers to Modern design. Painted Baltic birch with maple veneer back splat and chintz-covered cushion. 28 × 21 × 25 in. All available from the Workbench Gallery, New York.

PHOTOS GREG HEINS

Furniture maker Judy Kensley McKie of Cambridge, Massachusetts, transforms cats, dogs, birds, fish, and other natural forms into supports and articulations for her pieces, concealing joints and playing down wood-grain so that carved surface details are more freely expressed. Reacting against the highly technical approach to contemporary furniture, McKie uses a variety of decorative techniques such as carving, marquetry, laminating, and painting on wood to create pieces that convey warmth and animation through a very personal imagery. OPPOSITE: "Sly Rocker," 1980, carved poplar, painted, 37 × 24 × 35 in. Collection, Judy and Patrick Coady. ABOVE: "Table with Birds and Fish," 1979, carved mahogany, painted, 29½ × 66 × 36 in. Collection, Judy and Patrick Coady.

PHOTO OPPOSITE PAGE GREG HEINS

PHOTOS GREG HEINS

TOP LEFT: Judy Kensley McKie, "Bench with Horses," 1979, carved mahogany, 26 × 62 × 24 in. Collection, Museum of Fine Arts, Boston. TOP RIGHT: "Table with Cat," 1979, carved butternut with glass top, 30 × 30 × 12 in. Collection, Ainsley Donaldson, Massachusetts. BOTTOM LEFT: "Table with Dogs," 1978, carved laminated mahogany with glass top, 34 × 62 × 18 in. Available through the artist. BOTTOM RIGHT: "Couch with Dogs," 1978, carved poplar, 24 × 80 × 35 in. Collection, Stephen Clark, Boston. OPPOSITE: "Jewelry Cabinet with Dogs," 1976, marquetry in maple, walnut, cherry, and teak, 29 × 19 × 7 in. Collection, Florence Hazelton, Connecticut.

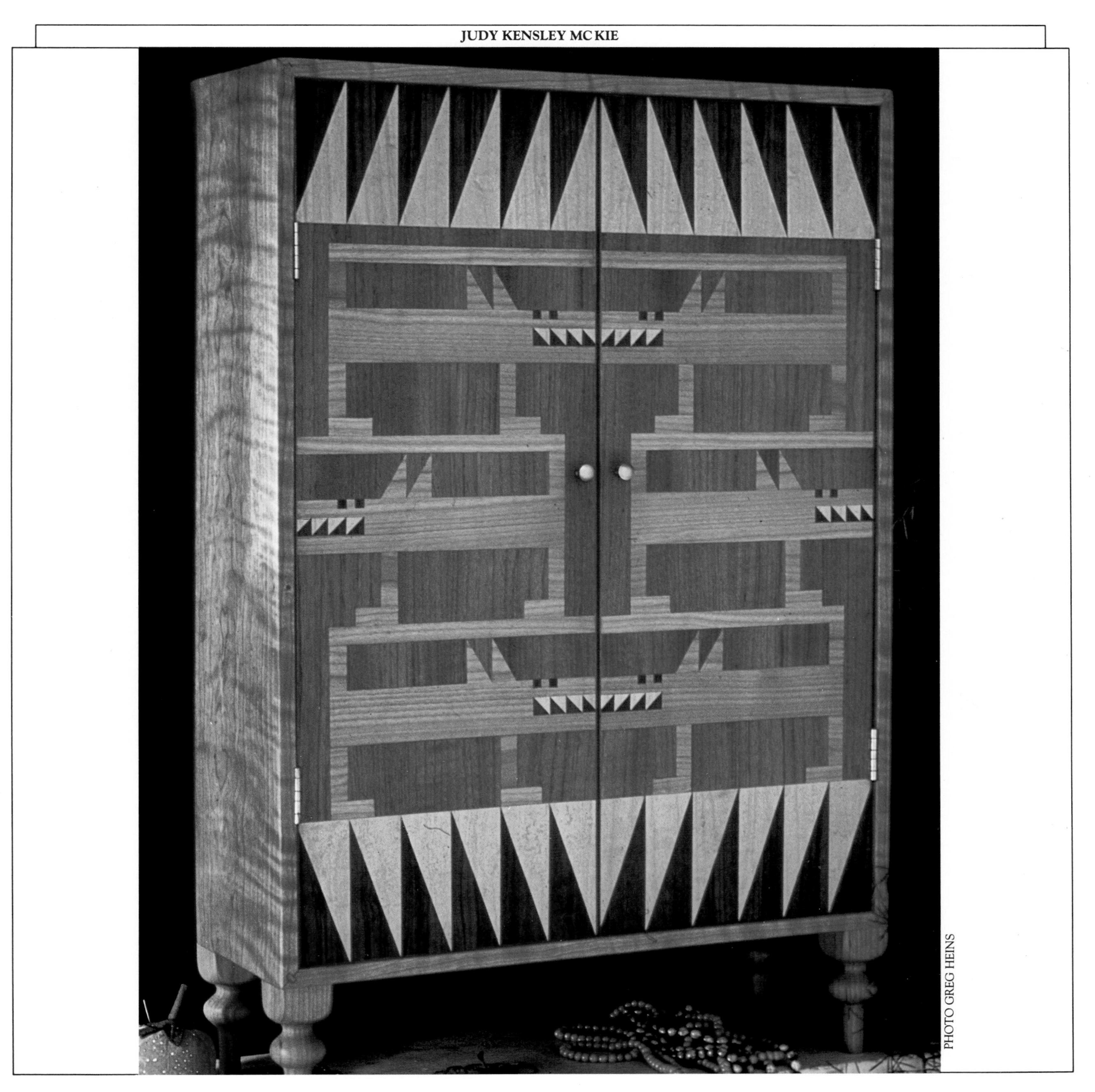

PHOTO GREG HEINS

Furniture maker Edward Zucca of Putnam, Connecticut, combines references to traditional furniture design with modern technology in his "Twelve-Legged Table," 1979, OPPOSITE, TOP. Worked over solid fine-grained cherry are inlays of primavera and ebony veneer, with two frosted acrylic panels set into the front and back-lit by fluorescent bulbs. 33 × 70 × 21 in. Available through the Workbench Gallery, New York.

Gary Knox Bennett, an Alemeda, California, furniture maker, uses a wide variety of materials and construction techniques in his pieces, most of which are individually commissioned or one-of-a-kind. OPPOSITE, BOTTOM: "Bow-Wow, Cluck-Cluck," bench, 1978, is natural and dyed redwood with cherry edging on the seat, 16½ × 70 × 14½ in. Collection, Judy and Patrick Coady. ABOVE, TOP: Table, 1980, shedua, Honduras mahogany, bubinga, ebony, and brushed aluminum with glass top, 30 × 54 in. diameter. BOTTOM: Desk, 1980, bubinga, ebony, Honduras mahogany, and brushed aluminum, 29 × 61 × 31 in. Both collection, Warren Rubin, New York.

PHOTOS STEVEN SLOMAN

COURTESY ALEXANDER F. MILLIKEN GALLERY

Scottsville, New York, designer Wendel Castle was trained as a sculptor and is well known for the wood-laminate furniture carved in curvilinear forms and emphasizing natural grains which he produced in the 1960s and 1970s. Recently he designed a series of illusionist or trompe l'oeil pieces, OPPOSITE, that fool the eye without any attempt to disguise the natural wood. Intended primarily as decorative sculptures, the utility of these casual still lifes is a secondary consideration.

CLOCKWISE FROM TOP LEFT: "Table with Gloves and Keys," 1980, mahogany, 33 × 4¾ × 16 in. radius. Private collection, New York. "Coat Rack with Hat and Scarf," 1979, mahogany, 72 × 20 in. diameter. Private collection. "Umbrella Stand with Umbrella," 1979, mahogany, 36½ × 13 in. diameter. Private collection, Rochester, New York. "Table with Cloth," 1980, mahogany, 30½ × 34 × 18 in. Private collection, New York. "Tail Coat on French Chair," 1980, ebonized mahogany, 39 × 24 × 29 in. Courtesy Alexander F. Milliken Gallery.

ABOVE: In Castle's most recent work, which takes the history of furniture and rearranges it at random, his characteristic emphasis on natural wood color and grain gives way to elaborate surface treatment and ornamental embellishment. "Desk and Chairs," 1981, English curly sycamore with light pink stain, fifteen coats of hand-rubbed lacquer, and 8,500 pieces of ebony inlay. Desk with amaranth interior, 40 × 41½ × 22¼ in. Chairs with silk-covered slip seats top and bottom, 36 × 22 × 23 in. Private collection, Switzerland.

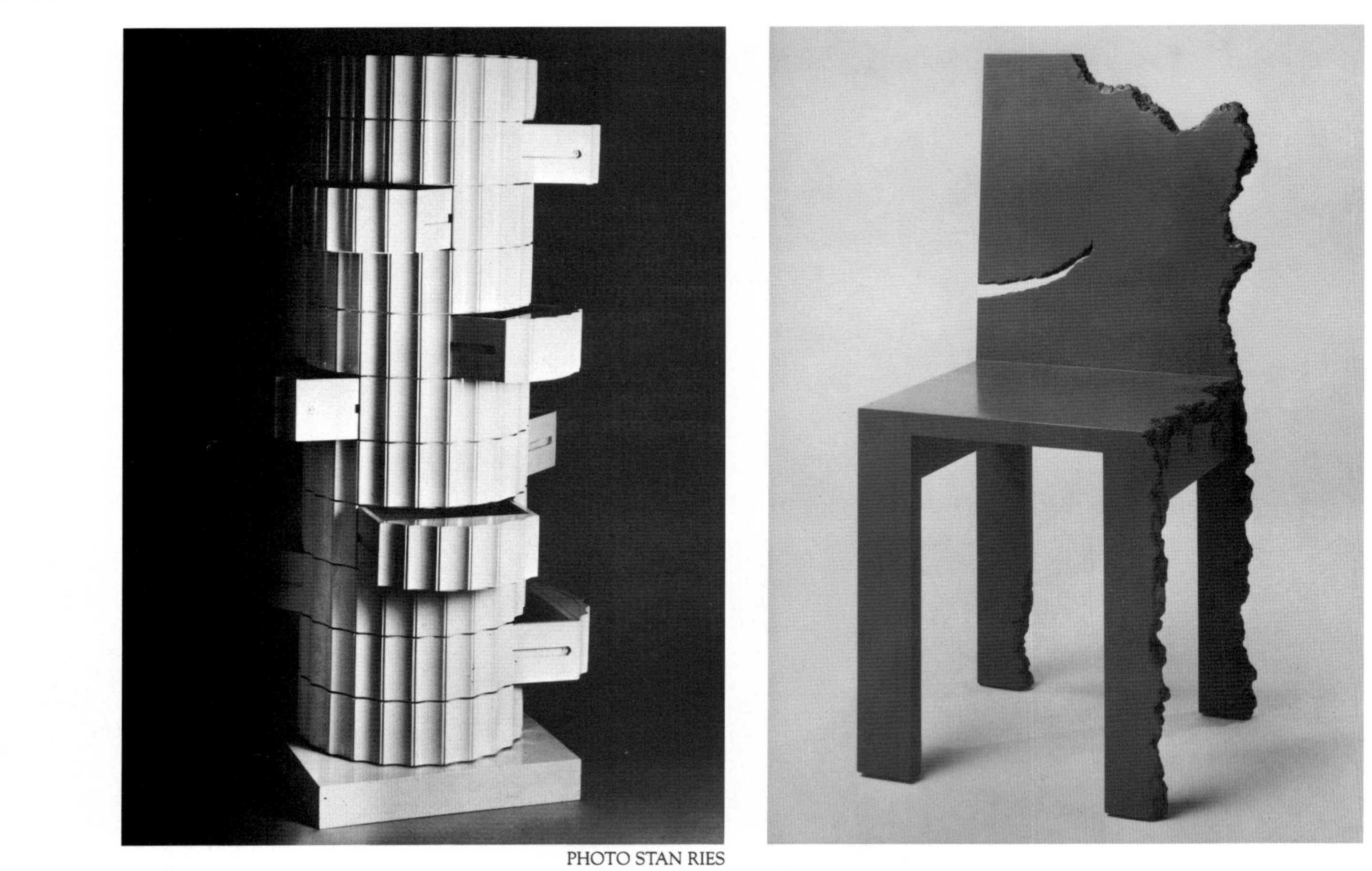

PHOTO STAN RIES

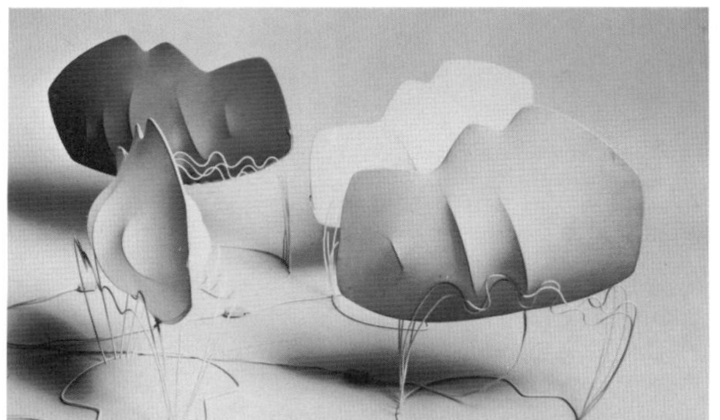

TOP LEFT: Swiss architects Robert Haussmann and Trix Haussmann-Högl designed the "Colonna" storage unit, 1980, for Studio Alchymia, Milan, and Art et Industrie, New York. Fluted column is lacquered wood with nine clear-bottomed drawers, 60 × 20 in. in diameter. TOP RIGHT: "Nothing Continues to Happen" chair, 1980, was designed by Howard Meister, an American, and executed by Arthur Robins for Art et Industrie. Painted Baltic hardwood, 37 × 16 × 18 in. BOTTOM: Fabio Alvim, a Brazilian artist and designer, created the "Forma" table or floor lamp, 1980, for Art et Industrie.

PHOTOS STAN RIES

All three pieces shown above were designed by American architect James Evanson. TOP: "Hedron" table, 1979, wood with hand-finished silkscreened lacquer, 17 × 42 × 42 in. Available from Art et Industrie, New York, or through the artist. BOTTOM LEFT: "Bi-Angle" chair, 1980, lacquered wood with colored plastic inserts and silk-screened fabric upholstery, 34 × 26 × 26 in. Available through the artist. BOTTOM RIGHT: "Primazoid" chair, 1980, plastic laminate over wood with laminated cotton-ribbed upholstery, 32 × 24 × 32 in. Designed for Art et Industrie.

PHOTO STAN RIES

LEFT: The "Gadames" chest, 1980, was designed for Studio Alchymia, Milan, and Art et Industrie, New York, by Italian architect and designer Paola Navone. Specially printed plastic laminate over wood with mirror-faced drawers, 64 × 32 × 20 in. RIGHT: Also for Studio Alchymia and Art et Industrie, Italian architect and designer Ettore Sottsass, Jr., created the "Trembling Structure" table, 1979. Plastic laminated wood base with enameled metal supports and glass top, 45 × 24 × 24 in.

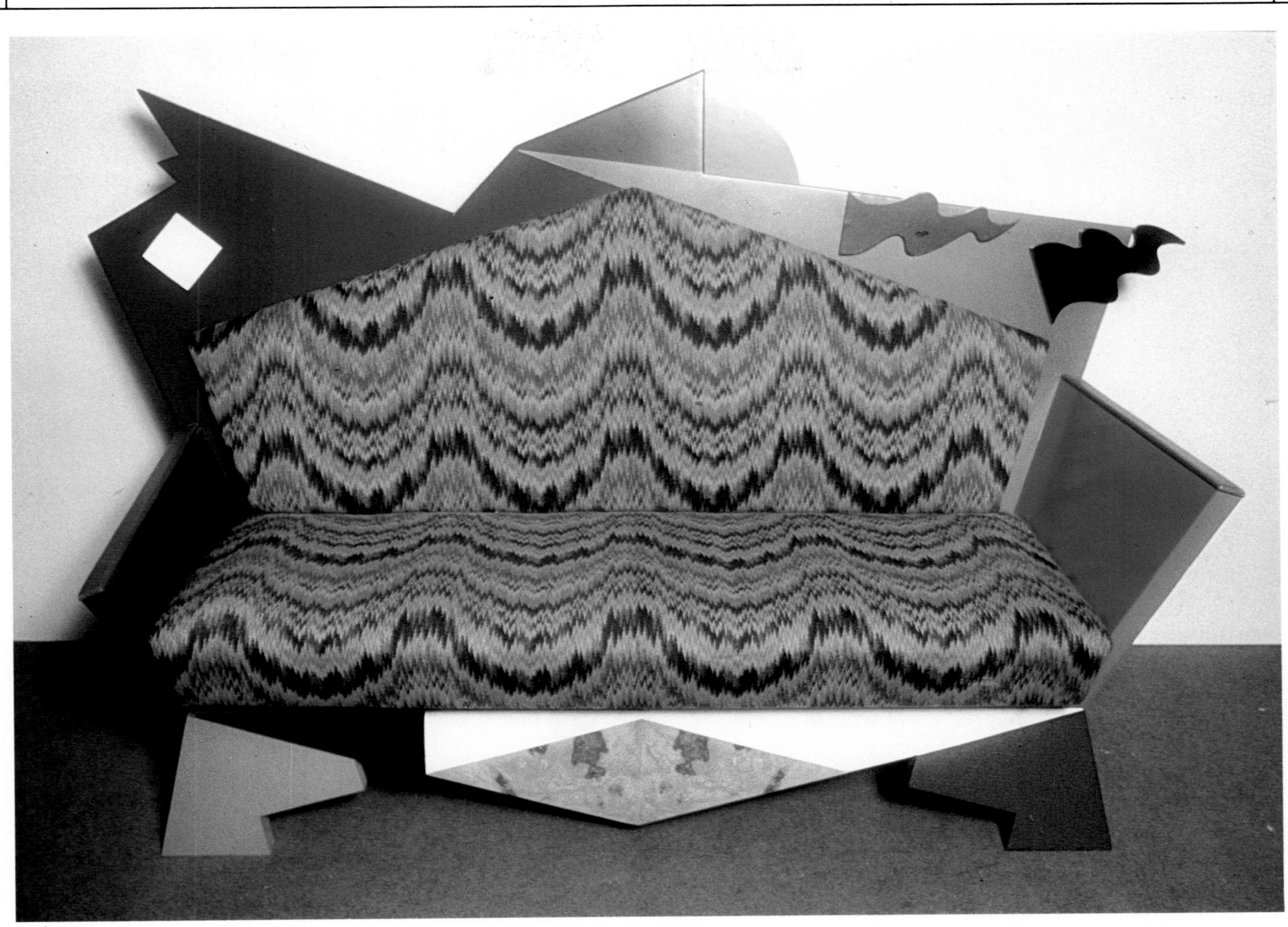

The "Kandissi" divan, designed for Studio Alchymia and Art et Industrie by Italian architect and design journalist Alessandro Mendini, 1978. Lacquered wood, briar, and tortoise shell with tapestry-weave upholstery, 45 × 41 × 31 in.

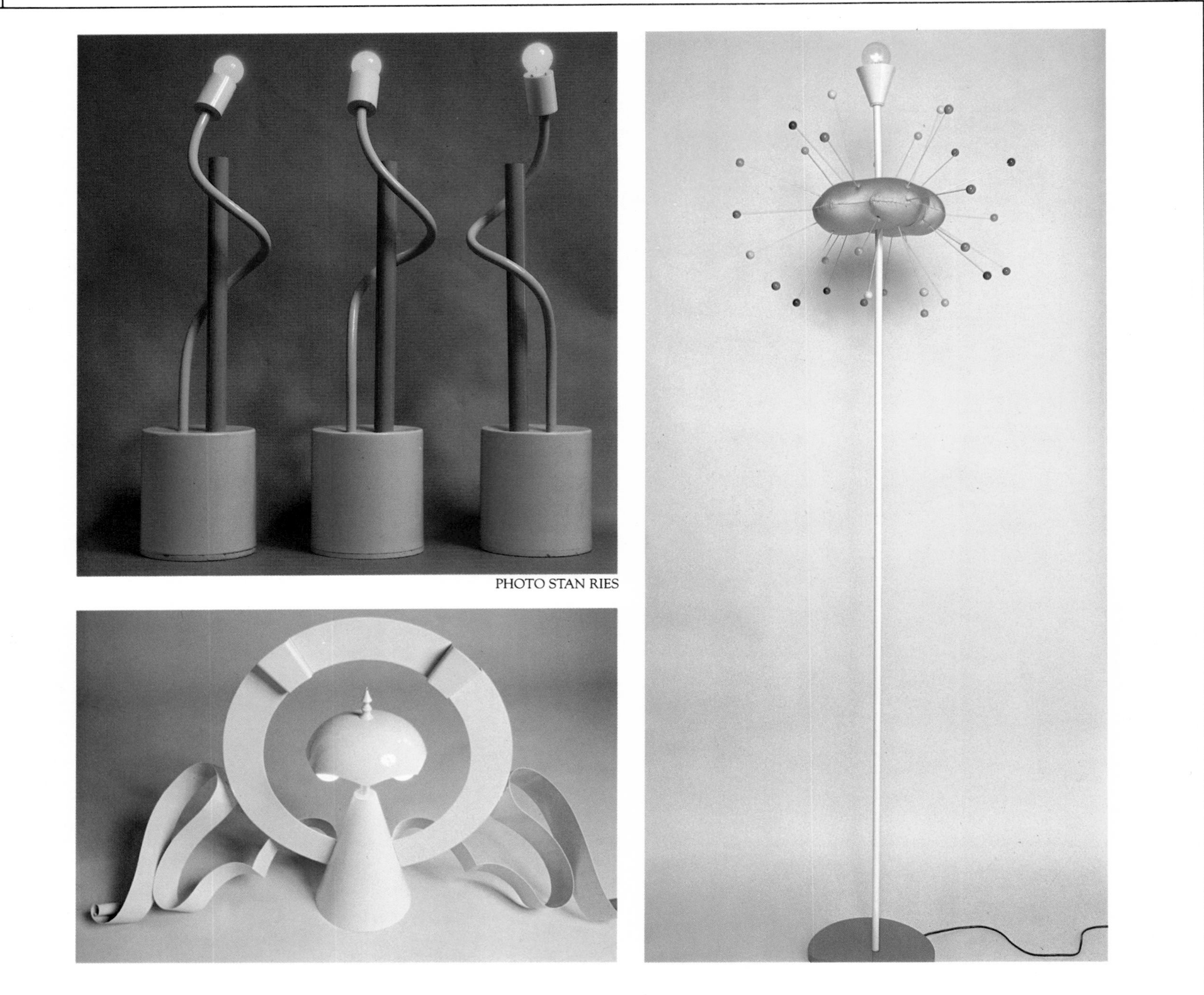

PHOTO STAN RIES

Italian designer Michele De Lucchi created these two lighting designs for Studio Alchymia, Milan, and Art et Industrie, New York. TOP LEFT: "Sinerpica" lamps, 1978, enameled metal, each 28 × 7 in. diameter. RIGHT: "Sinvola" floor lamp, 1980, enameled metal with cloth cushion and multicolored ceramic pins, 80 × 28 in. diameter with pins. BOTTOM LEFT: Also for Studio Alchymia and Art et Industrie, the "MGM" table lamp, 1979, lacquered metal, 21 × 37 × 7½ in. Designed by UFO, an Italian group.

PHOTO STAN RIES

"Homage to Bugatti" table-seat, 1979, solid hardwood with turned legs and lacquer finish, 15 × 28 × 28 in. American designers Steve Ditch and Molly Amsler for Art et Industrie.

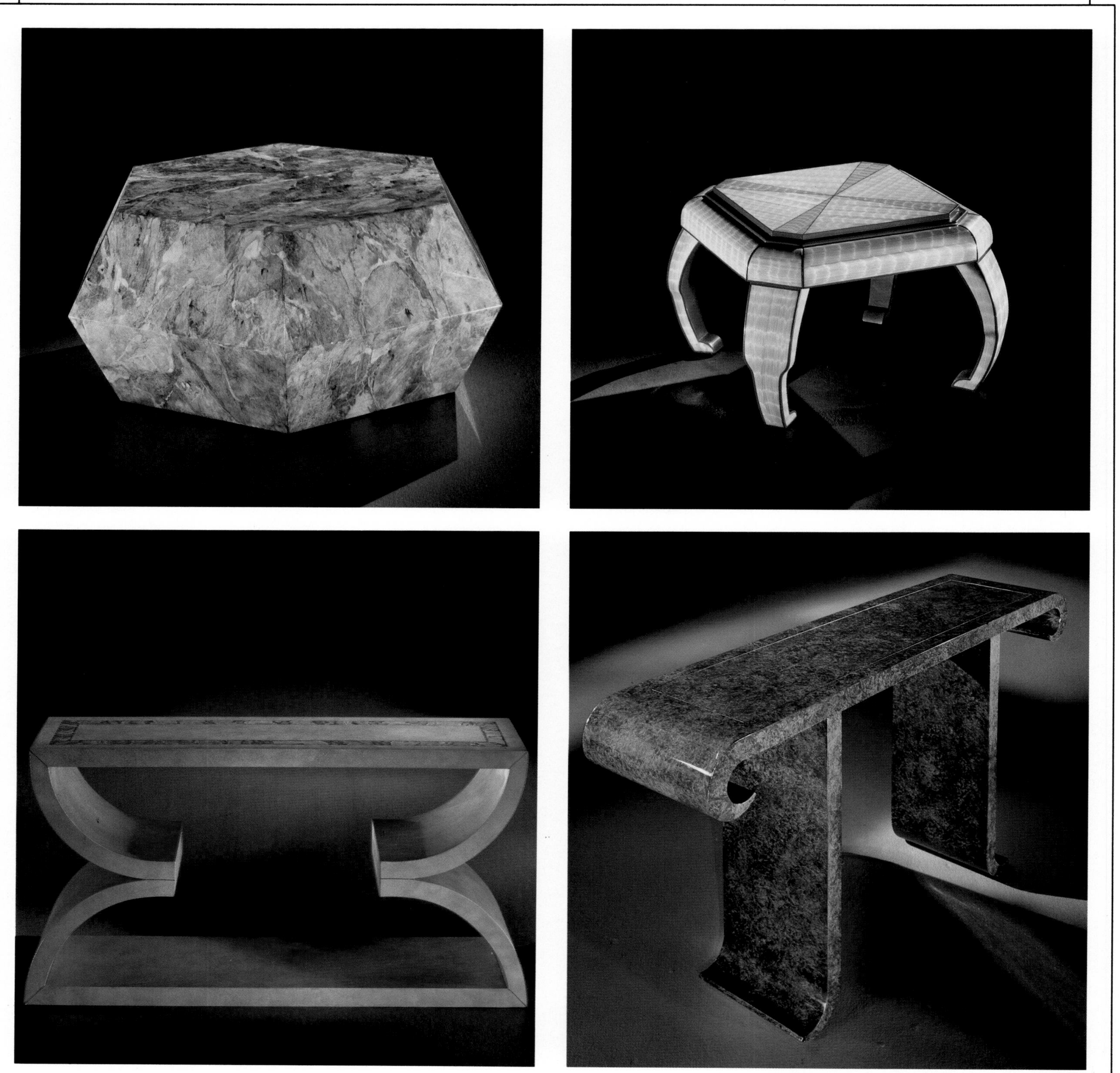

PHOTOS COURTESY BAKER FURNITURE COMPANY

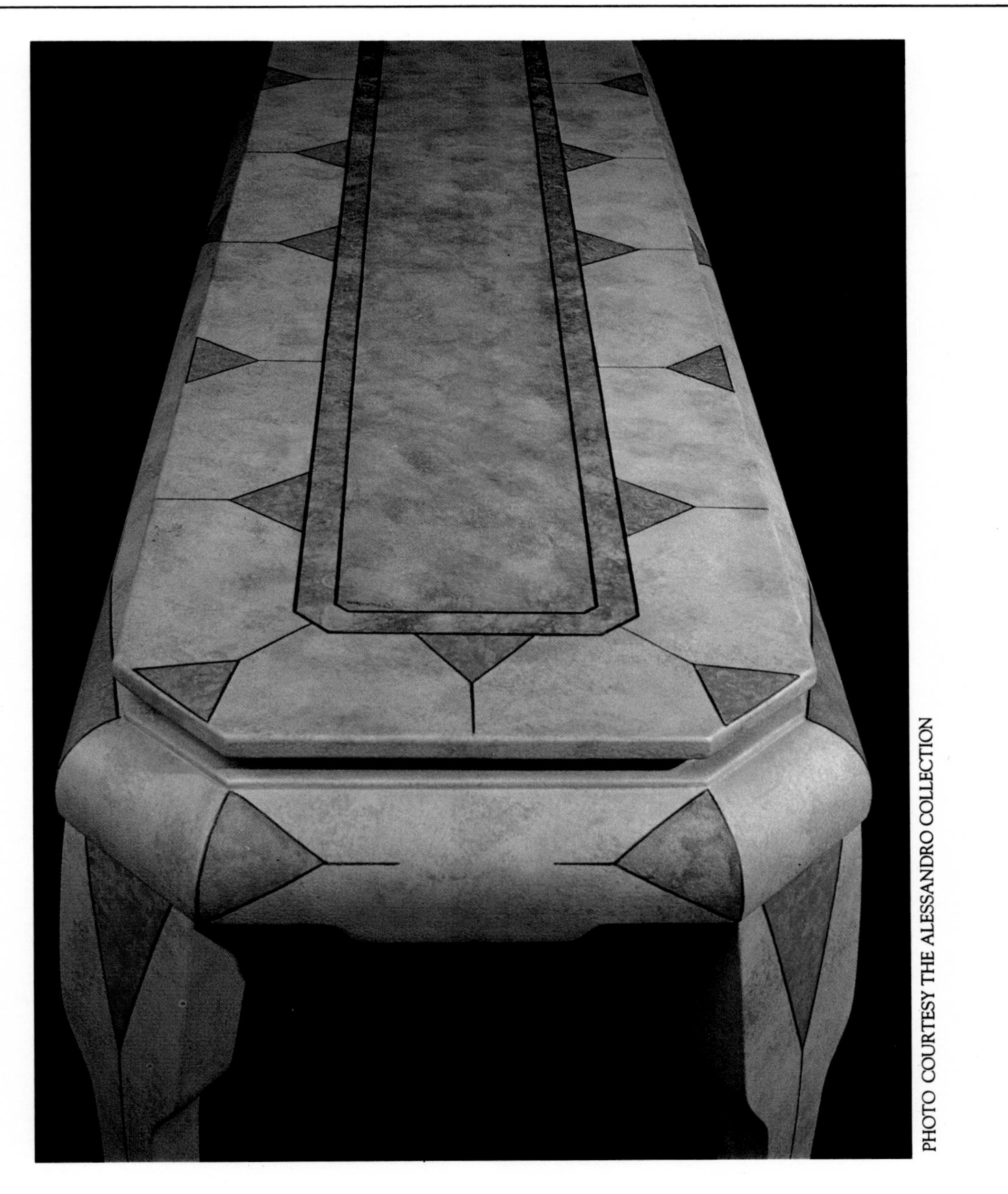

PHOTO COURTESY THE ALESSANDRO COLLECTION

The Italian-born Alessandro, schooled in fresco, sculpture, and restoration, has been designing hand-painted lacquer-finish furniture out of his New York City studio since he arrived in the United States twelve years ago. In 1979 the Baker Furniture Company, best known for its traditional and reproduction furniture, introduced a series of modern sculptural pieces with fantasy finishes for which Alessandro designed both the forms and the finishes. The finishes are executed by factory craftspeople whom Alessandro retrained for two years in the art of *faux* and trompe l'oeil painting.

OPPOSITE, CLOCKWISE FROM TOP LEFT: "Saturno" cocktail table, parrot wing agate lacquer finish, 18 × 46 in.; "Lady Bombe" chow table, trompe l'oeil Venetian stone lacquer finish, 16 × 22 × 22 in.; "Olympia" server, trompe l'oeil emerald jade lacquer finish, 34½ × 64 × 16 in.; "Reflecto" console, terra-cotta leather with *faux* onyx inlay lacquer finish, 28 × 54 × 16 in. All pieces available from the Baker Furniture Company, Holland, Michigan.

ABOVE: "Lady Bombe" console, private commission, 1978, *faux* textured lacquer with trompe l'oeil mosaic inlay, 30 × 83 × 20 in. Collection, Mr. and Mrs. Bob Hope, Palm Springs. Available with custom modifications from the Alessandro Signature Collection.

Sherle Wagner's decorative bathroom fixtures, most often used in private residences, are found increasingly in executive office suites and commercial installations. TOP LEFT: China washstand, hand-painted in "Ming Blossoms" pattern with matching fittings finished in antique pewter over brass, scaled for smaller spaces, 32 × 23 × 18½ in. TOP RIGHT: Self-rimming basin, platinum finish over china with genuine tiger's-eye fittings and antique pewter finish over brass, 19½ × 15½ in. BOTTOM LEFT: Self-rimming china wash basin, hand-painted in "Water Lilies" pattern with matching fittings finished in 24-carat gold plate over brass, 19½ × 15½ in. BOTTOM RIGHT: Shell-shaped washstand hand-carved from a solid block of brown onyx with matching fittings finished in 24-carat gold plate over brass, 32 × 26 × 23 in. All available from Sherle Wagner International, New York.

PHOTO DOMINIC MARSDEN

West Coast designers James Tigerman and Norman List create soft-sculpture fantasy furnishings in which animals and plants are the predominant imagery. ABOVE: "Iris Screen," 1980, stitched and bleached satin over wood frame with polyester fill, two panels 8 × 3 ft. overall. Available from Tigerdale Studios, Los Angeles.

PHOTO STAN RIES

PHOTO STAN RIES

TOP LEFT: Tigerdale Studios's "Elephant" lounge and ottoman, 1979, cotton velvet with canvas over wood frame and polyester fill. Lounge, 66 × 54 × 30 in. Ottoman, 24 × 24 × 24 in. Private collection, Los Angeles. TOP RIGHT: "Banana Bunch" floor lamp, 1977, quilted satin and cotton over wood and wire frame with polyester fill, 66 × 24 in. diameter. Available in various colors from Tigerdale Studios. BOTTOM LEFT: "Indian Paint Brush" floor lamp, 1978, partially quilted satin and cotton in basket with moss, 30 × 14 in. diameter. Available from Tigerdale Studios. BOTTOM RIGHT: "Teddy Bear" love seat, 1980, fake fur with satin over wood frame and polyester fill, 48 × 84 × 28 in. Collection of the artist.

OPPOSITE: "Ostrich" bar and "Ballerina" table, 1979. Bar is satin and canvas over metal frame and polyester fill with 3-inch-thick polished travertine table top, 84 × 36 × 30 in. diameter overall. Table has polished marble top with canvas legs and satin slippers over steel pipe frame and polyester fill, 29 × 24 in. diameter. Both available from Tigerdale Studios.

PHOTO ELYSE LEWIN

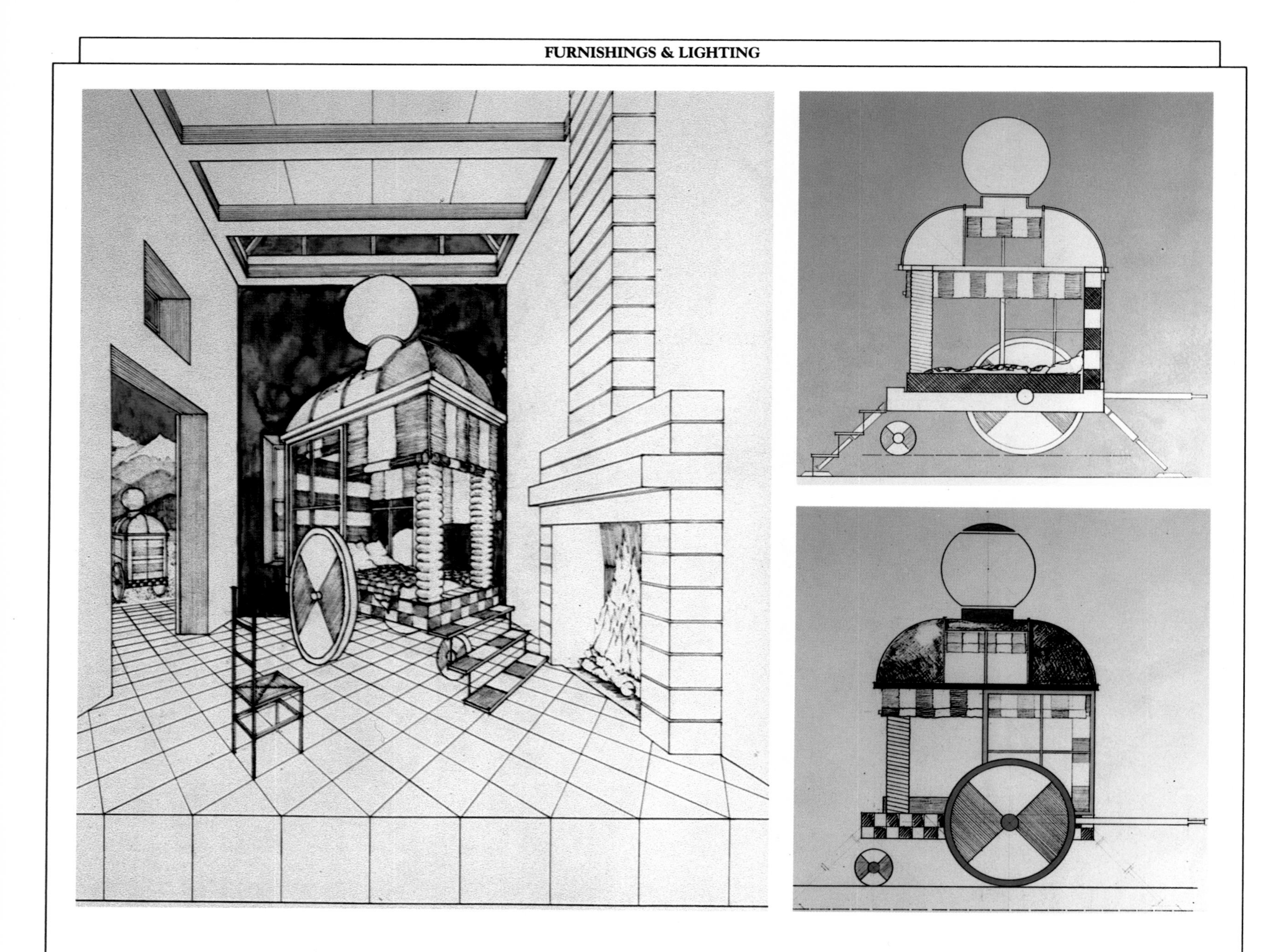

Berkeley, California, architects Richard Fernau and Laura Hartman designed the "BEDroom," 1981, as a "roomitized" sleeping unit which recognizes energy considerations by limiting the volume to be heated or cooled. Heralding a return to the "great bed," the "BEDroom" can be wheeled by day near a window, under a skylight, in front of a fireplace, or directly out into the sun. Heat is trapped in a glazed enclosure and stored in the thermal mass of the mattress, posts, and bedstead, then slowly released at night. During the summer, the "BEDroom" can be wheeled out of the sun or sponged down. Frame is aluminum and wood with a marble or water mattress, marble or steel and water posts, plastic canopy and glazing, canvas and down curtains, and painted tin wheels. With wheels, the "BEDroom" is 102 × 84 × 48 in. with an additional 24-inch height for the ventilator.

PHOTOS CRISPIN VASQUEZ

Italian-born Pedro Friedeberg, who studied at the Art Institute of Boston and has lived most of his life in Mexico City where he was trained as an architect at the American University, creates fantasy furniture that is completely antithetical to Bauhaus functionalism. His "Lepidopterical" chair, shown here in two variations, asks the question, can one sit on a butterfly? Why not? Hand-painted wood with gold leaf, 36 × 20 × 14 in. Available from David Barrett, Inc., New York, or the Phyllis Needlman Gallery, Chicago.

Miriam Shapiro, detail, "Bal Masque," 1980, acrylic and fabric on canvas, 6 panels, 84 × 168 in. overall.

PATTERNING, DECORATION & USABLE ART

PHOTO D. JAMES DEE, COURTESY BARBARA GLADSTONE GALLERY

The revolt against minimalism and the machine aesthetic in architecture has been paralleled, and in many ways surpassed, by a similiar reaction in painting and sculpture. In the early 1970s, a number of formerly abstract painters began to use pattern—floral, geometric, or representational—to cover surfaces in a manner that, contrasted to the perfect cubes and white-on-white paintings of mid-1960s minimalism, seemed startlingly colorful and sensuous. Sometimes the patterns were newly invented, but more often they were borrowed: from Mexican tiles, Moorish architecture, Moroccan ceramics, Early American quilts, and numerous other ethnic, folk art, and craft sources. As the decorative aspects of this kind of patterning came to be more specifically acknowledged, what began as Pattern Painting broadened to include sculpture and environmental art—this movement has been called the New Decorativeness, or simply "P & D" (pattern and decoration).

This movement coalesced in late 1974/early 1975 when a number of painters who had been independently pursuing pattern and decoration began meeting to discuss certain ideas at issue in their work. Among those present were several artists whose work is shown here, and the late critic Amy Goldin, whose influence on the movement was formative. Despite stylistic differences, these artists were all working in ways that challenged established hierarchies, i.e., the assumed superiority of fine (nonutilitarian) arts over the applied (useful) arts and crafts; Western European industrial culture over Third World and ethnic culture; art which refers only to itself (the Modern ideal of "art for art's sake") over art which refers to architecture, nature, or other art. These artists, both men and women, also came to challenge the long-held belief that women's arts (needlework, carpet making, basket weaving, quilting) are inherently inferior to the male-dominated "high" arts, a challenge that has linked the Patterning and Decorating Movement directly to the larger issues of feminism.

Just in the last year or two, another tendency has emerged out of the Patterning and Decorating Movement. It is called Usable Art and its emergence is perhaps inevitable, given that pattern and decoration traditionally have been used to enhance functional objects. However, the recent appearance of "usable" cups, saucers, vases, screens, and chairs in art galleries has disturbed some observers because "art," in Modern terms, has been defined as essentially nonutilitarian. Were this same work shown in craft galleries it would cause no controversy, but the specific intent of these artists has been just that: to break down the rigid, elitist distinction between fine arts and crafts.

Bored by the "invisible" art of the mid-sixties, many people have welcomed Patterning, Decorating, and Usable Art as a release from sensual deprivation. Not surprisingly, conservative critics are less enthusiastic. "Nonserious," "hedonistic," "trivial," and "pleasure-seeking" are some of the epithets hurled at this new art. Worst of all, it is accused of being "luxurious." According to some critics, "high" art may coexist with the luxurious surroundings of those who can afford to buy it, may even be "used" to decorate or confer status upon those surroundings; but art *itself* may not be luxurious. Nevertheless, Patterning, Decorating, and Usable Art seem to be quickly assimilating into the mainstream of contemporary art, and the importance of this movement—which is principally an American phenomenon—is affirmed by the numerous exhibitions it has had in major museums both here and in Europe.

That these tendencies constitute a movement, not a style, is apparent from the tremendous range of sensibilities manifest in this work and the variety of sources from which these artists draw their inspiration. One source, and a principal model for all things decorative in Modernism, is the French artist Henri Matisse (1869–1954), whose affinity with the decorative arts is evidenced by the frequent use of exotically patterned rugs, wall hangings, tablecloths, and screens as motifs in his paintings. Cynthia Carlson's "wallpaper" installations have obvious connections to Matisse's late cutouts, while the bright, lyrical shapes of Robert Kushner's paintings on fabric and Kim MacConnel's use of dazzling color are also reminiscent of Matisse.

Another important source for contemporary decorative art is Islamic geometric patterning, which contemporary decorative artists are using in much the same way that the Cubists used African sculpture: adopting its motifs and principles but manipulating them in new and clearly Western ways. For example, Miriam Shapiro's shaped canvases allude to Persian miniatures, but the patterns are collaged out of carefully layered bits of paper, calico, lace, gilded trimmings, and brocades—the detritus of domestic handiwork which Shapiro uses to establish connections with what she regards as the authentic traditions of women's arts. Valerie Jaudon's use of interlacing geometric forms refers to both Islamic and Celtic sources, but the extraordinarily complicated patterns which result are her own invention. In Cynthia Carlson's "wallpaper" installations, Islamic calligraphy becomes sculptural in thick pieces of tinted acrylic gel squeezed out of pastry tubes and glued directly on the wall. Ned Smyth's nonsupporting columns have a foliated, mosaic-encrusted look that suggests Islamic architecture, yet at the same time can be read as trees.

Folk art, decorative crafts, and the vernacular (i.e., ordinary "popular" style) are other important sources in Patterning and Decorating. The flowers that Robert Zakanitch paints do not come directly from nature but, rather, from wallpaper patterns, 1950s linoleum sample books, woodcuts, prints, and Czechoslovakian embroidery. Rodney Ripps's leaves, formed of fabric and wire, then loaded with pigment in a wax medium and fixed to the canvas from which they appear to grow, are reminiscent of five-and-dime store artificial corsages. Jane Kaufman also uses vernacular materials, but hers is the vernacular of luxury: gold, silver, copper wire, glass beads, pearls, semiprecious stones, and iridescent feathers constructed into opulent screens and curtains. Contrast the luxuriant sensibility of Thomas Lanigan-Schmidt, who uses the vernacular of the immigrant working classes (florist's foil, glitter, and paste jewels) to construct altars, tabernacles, and ecclesiastical icons that parody the kitsch of cheap religious articles yet are, in feeling, genuinely devotional; or the scaled-down façades of Donna Dennis's subway stations, hotels, and rooming houses that mutate the forms of vernacular architecture into mysterious, erotic shrines.

Unlike those painters who have arrived at decorative art through patterning, Richard Kalina and Brad Davis have succumbed to the ornamental impulse via realism. In Kalina's paintings, two or three figurative images are repeated, symmetrically, within ornately patterned borders, while Davis's paintings depict plants and animals in a colorful manner reminiscent of Persian, Indian, and medieval European stylizations. Among Arlene Slavin's favorite motifs are birds, which she paints in vividly colored compositions directly on walls or on screens.

The "utility" of Slavin's screens places her work in the still evolving category of Usable Art: art that, like Jane Kaufman's screens, can divide a room; or like Kim MacConnel's "found" and painted furniture and Jennifer Cecere's acrylic-on-lace chairs can be sat upon. Similarly, some of Robert Kushner's painted fabrics can be worn as robes, and Patsy Norvell's *Glass Garden* can be both a piece of sculpture and a functioning greenhouse. By defying the notion that art must be purely contemplative, must be removed from use and therefore from life, Usable Art seeks environmental extensions for the decorative impulse. In moving off their canvases and onto walls, floors, and furnishings—often using tiles, unstretched fabrics, and other "nonart" materials—these artists are clearly penetrating the boundaries not only of craft but of architecture.

Whether architecture, notwithstanding its own currently Ornamentalist tendencies, is ready to accommodate this incursion remains to be seen. Since the clean sweep of Modernism, the true integration of art and architecture rarely has been achieved, last appearing in the Art Deco and Moderne monuments of the 1930s. In an attempt to rekindle the collaborative spirit that permeated pre-Modern building, the Architectural League of New York celebrated its centennial in 1981 with an exhibition entitled "Artists & Architects: Collaboration." Eleven artist-architect teams were commissioned to design visionary projects, but the generally disappointing results proved only how forced and uneasy such academic efforts can be. Nevertheless, a number of artists whose work is shown here are actively seeking participation in real building projects. Joyce Kozloff, for example, is now working on two public commissions, both in tile and both with architects Skidmore, Owings & Merrill. One is for a very Modern renovation of the Harvard Square subway station in Cambridge, Massachusetts, and the other for a restoration of the Wilmington, Delaware, train station designed in 1908 by architect Frank Furness who, himself, used decorative tilework in many of his buildings. The persistence of artists like Kozloff in pursuing a dialogue with architects gives rise to the possibility that the decorative sensibilities of both architecture and the fine arts—supported by the rejuvenated building crafts—may yet lead to a true artistic reintegration in which the full potential of the Ornamentalist Movement will be realized.

PHOTOS D. JAMES DEE, COURTESY HOLLY SOLOMON GALLERY

TOP: Robert Kushner, "Antelope Gate," 1979, acrylic on cotton, 114 × 173 in. Private collection, New York City. BOTTOM: "Pink Leaves," 1979, acrylic on mixed fabric, 80 × 130 in. Collection, Dr. Peter Ludwig, Aachen, West Germany.

OPPOSITE: Robert Kushner, "Same Outfit," 1979, mixed media and acrylic on mixed fabric, 122 × 97 in. overall. Collection of the artist.

PHOTOS D. JAMES DEE, COURTESY HOLLY SOLOMON GALLERY

PHOTO D. JAMES DEE, COURTESY HOLLY SOLOMON GALLERY

ABOVE: Robert Kushner, "Fish Gate," 1979, acrylic on fabric, 99 × 71 in. Private collection, Paris.

OPPOSITE, TOP LEFT: Robert Kushner, "Geometric Gate," 1979, acrylic on fabric, 110 × 101 in. Private collection, London. TOP RIGHT: "Bird of Paradise," 1978, acrylic on fabric, 98 × 68 in. Collection, Morton G. Neumann family, Chicago. BOTTOM: "Cincinnati A," 1978, acrylic and glitter on fabric, 108 in. high. Collection, Dr. Peter Ludwig, Museum für Moderne Kunst, Vienna.

PHOTOS D. JAMES DEE, COURTESY HOLLY SOLOMON GALLERY

PHOTOS D. JAMES DEE, COURTESY HOLLY SOLOMON GALLERY

TOP, LEFT TO RIGHT: Valerie Jaudon, "Mineral Wells," 1980, oil on canvas, 120 × 108 in. Collection, Thomas B. Solomon, New York. "Leflore," 1981, oil and metallic pigment on canvas, 120 × 90 in. "Crossroads Station," 1980, oil and metallic pigment on canvas, 84 × 72 in. Collection, I. Gablinger, Zurich.

BOTTOM, LEFT TO RIGHT: Valerie Jaudon, "Bastesville," 1980, oil on canvas, 100 × 84 in. "Tupelo," 1980, oil on canvas, 72 × 72 in. "Natchez," 1979, oil on canvas, 75 × 66 in. Collection, Dr. Peter Ludwig, Aachen, West Germany.

OPPOSITE: Valerie Jaudon, "Canton," 1979, oil on canvas, 72 × 72 in. Private collection, Sweden.

PHOTO D. JAMES DEE, COURTESY HOLLY SOLOMON GALLERY AND JAMES CORCORAN GALLERY, LOS ANGELES

COURTESY HOLLY SOLOMON GALLERY

PHOTO BEVAN DAVIS, COURTESY HOLLY SOLOMON GALLERY

TOP: Donna Dennis, "Hotels," 1973, mixed media with sound, West Broadway Gallery installation view.

BOTTOM: Donna Dennis, "Hotels and Subway Stations," 1976, mixed media, Holly Solomon Gallery installation view.

OPPOSITE: Donna Dennis, "Two Stories with Porch (for Robert Cobuzio)," 1977–79, mixed media, 126 × 120½ × 85 in.

PHOTO D. JAMES DEE, COURTESY HOLLY SOLOMON GALLERY

PHOTOS D. JAMES DEE, COURTESY HOLLY SOLOMON GALLERY

PHOTOS COURTESY HOLLY SOLOMON GALLERY

OPPOSITE, TOP: Ned Smyth, "Yin Fish," 1979, cast and molded concrete with pigment, 87 × 80 × 11 in. Collection, Morton G. Neumann family, Chicago.

OPPOSITE, BOTTOM: Ned Smyth, "Adoration/Adornment," 1980, cast and molded concrete with pigment, and silkscreen on fabric, Main Gallery installation view.

ABOVE: Ned Smyth and Brad Davis collaboration, "The Garden," 1977, poured concrete, cut aluminum, and acrylic on unstretched canvas, Holly Solomon Gallery installation view and details.

OVER: Ned Smyth and Brad Davis collaboration, "The Garden," installation view. Courtesy Holly Solomon Gallery.

OVERLEAF: PHOTO COURTESY HOLLY SOLOMON GALLERY

PHOTOS COURTESY HOLLY SOLOMON GALLERY

TOP: Thomas Lanigan-Schmidt, "Two Seconds Before the End of the World," 1979, mixed media, Neuberger Museum installation view. BOTTOM: Centerpiece of "Two Seconds Before the End of the World."

PHOTO LARRY FUCHSMAN

PHOTOS COURTESY HOLLY SOLOMON GALLERY

TOP LEFT: Thomas Lanigan-Schmidt, "The Bread of Life and the Fruit of the Fall: Sexism, Racism, Marxism, Capitalism, and the Portrait of Dorian Gray," 1981, mixed media, Pratt Manhattan Gallery installation view. TOP RIGHT: "Daytime Nite Light (A Solitary Drinker)," 1975, mixed media, 40½ × 24½ × 15 in. BOTTOM LEFT: ". . . from a hot summer's day . . . ," 1979–80, mixed media, 21½ × 17 in. Collection, M. Rittenberry, Tulsa. RIGHT: "Float for a Brat Day Parade," 1974–75/79, mixed media, 32 × 34 × 24 in.

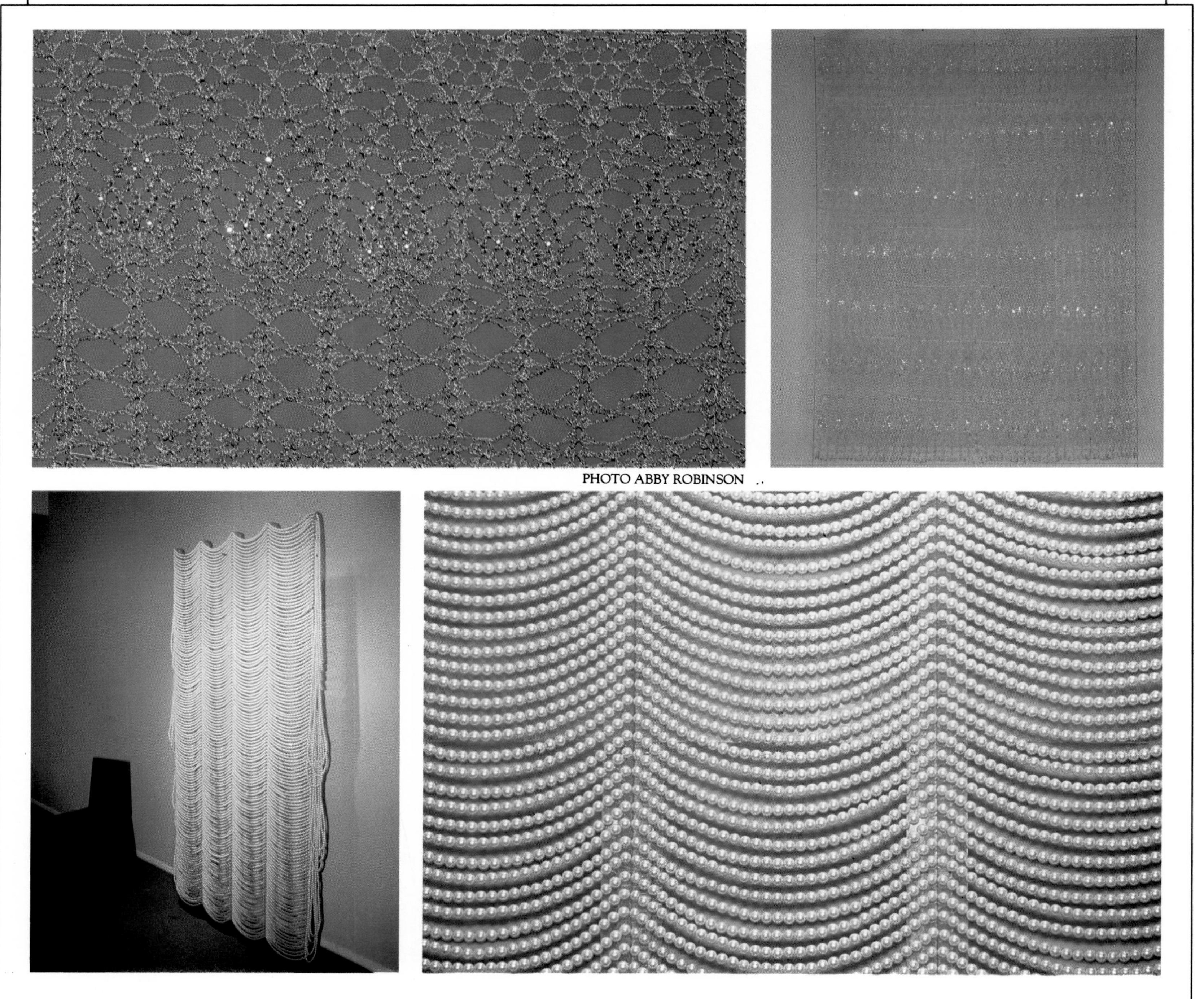

PHOTO ABBY ROBINSON

TOP LEFT: Jane Kaufman, detail of "Gold Curtain," RIGHT, 1979, crocheted gold filament, 8½ × 5½ ft. BOTTOM LEFT: "Pearl Screen," 1980, glass pearls, 8 × 4 ft. RIGHT: Detail of "Pearl Screen."

OPPOSITE: Jane Kaufman, detail of "Pheasant Feather Screen," 1980, pheasant feathers and bugle beads on satin, three panels 67½ × 33 in. each. Collection, William and Norma Roth.

PHOTO OPPOSITE PAGE ABBY ROBINSON

ARTSCHWAGER
CARLSON
HAAS

PHOTOS COURTESY PAM ADLER GALLERY

OPPOSITE: Cynthia Carlson, "Rooms," 1981, acrylic, latex, and watercolor, MIT Hayden Gallery installation view.

TOP LEFT: Cynthia Carlson, "Homage to the Academy Building," 1979, latex and acrylic on Masonite, and latex and acrylic on walls with acrylic, pencil, and watercolor drawings, Pennsylvania Academy of the Fine Arts installation view.
BOTTOM LEFT: Cynthia Carlson, "Inside Out-Oberlin," 1980, watercolor, charcoal on Masonite, acrylic on canvas, and ceramic, Allen Memorial Art Museum installation view.
RIGHT: Cynthia Carlson, "Richmond, Va., Circa 1980," acrylic, latex, watercolor, and potted geraniums, Institute of Contemporary Art installation view.

PHOTO OPPOSITE PAGE COURTESY PAM ADLER GALLERY

PHOTOS COURTESY PAM ADLER GALLERY

PHOTO COURTESY PAM ADLER GALLERY

OPPOSITE: Cynthia Carlson, "Installation: A Medley," 1981, acrylic, latex, and watercolor, Pam Adler Gallery installation view and details.

ABOVE: Cynthia Carlson, "Gingerbread House, Restored Version," 1977, acrylic paint, polyurethane foam, and fiberglass on plywood and 2 × 4 in. support with urethane and colored lights, 13 × 6½ × 13 ft.

PHOTO COURTESY HOLLY SOLOMON GALLERY

PHOTO D. JAMES DEE, COURTESY HOLLY SOLOMON GALLERY

PHOTO D. JAMES DEE, COURTESY HOLLY SOLOMON GALLERY

OPPOSITE, TOP: Kim MacConnel, Holly Solomon Gallery show, 1980, acrylic on cotton with metallic paint and acrylic on cardboard and puffed paper, installation view. BOTTOM LEFT: "Decorum," 1980, acrylic on cotton with metallic paint, 101 × 117 in. Collection Mr. and Mrs. Robert Grimes, New York. BOTTOM RIGHT: "Gymnasium," 1980, acrylic on cotton with metallic paint, 94 × 126 in.

TOP LEFT: Kim MacConnel, "Collapsible Table and Plastic Vase," 1980, mixed media, table 16½ × 23¾ × 16 in., vase 13½ × 4½ in. Collection of the artist. TOP RIGHT: "Lamp," 1978, acrylic on porcelain with nylon shade, 37½ × 13½ in. BOTTOM: "Furnishings," 1977, acrylic on fabric and furniture, Holly Solomon Gallery installation view.

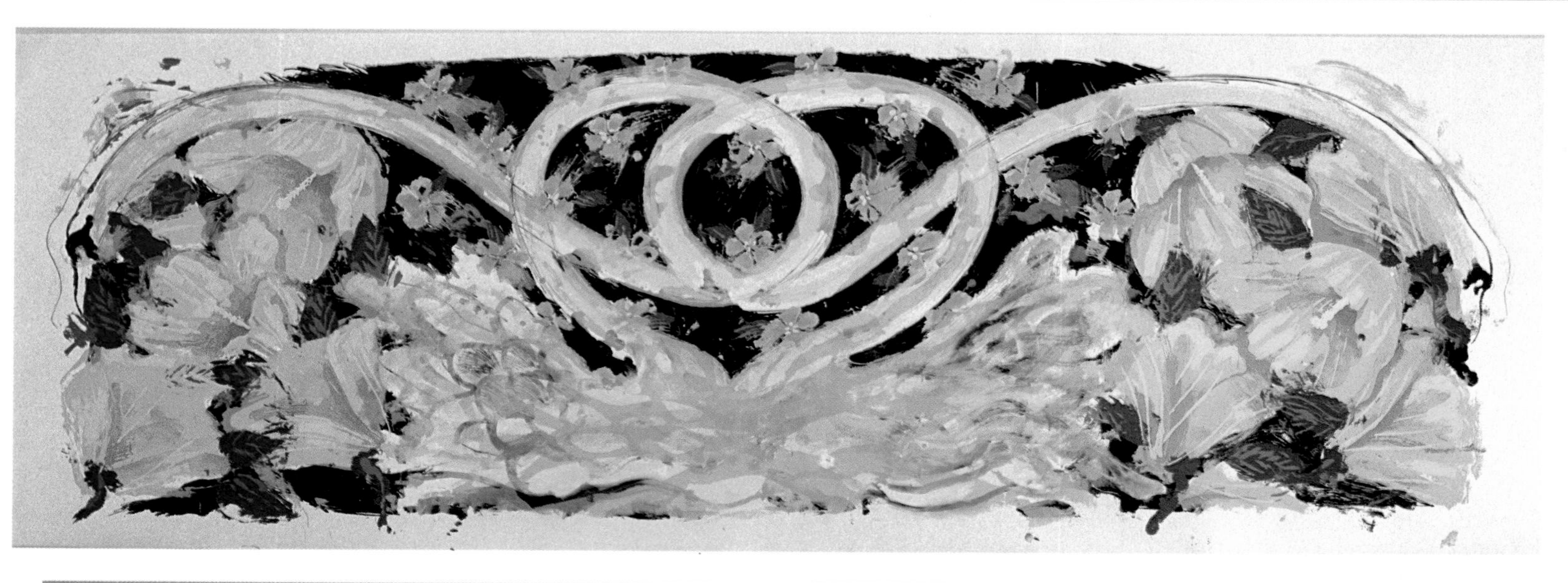

PHOTOS COURTESY ROBERT MILLER GALLERY AND TYLER GRAPHICS LTD

PHOTO COURTESY ROBERT MILLER GALLERY

OPPOSITE, TOP: Robert S. Zakanitch, "How I Love Ya, How I Love Ya," 1981, 21-color lithograph and silkscreen print with pochoir, 3½ × 10 in. BOTTOM LEFT: "Straight Backed Swans I," 1980, colored and pressed paper pulp, 86 × 71 in. Private collection, New York. BOTTOM RIGHT: "Veranda," 1981, colored and pressed paper pulp, 64 × 48 in. Collection Tyler Graphics Ltd.

ABOVE: Robert S. Zakanitch, "Pluming Trumpets," 1980, acrylic on paper, 85 × 50 in.

OVER: Robert S. Zakanitch, "Golden Gossip," 1979, acrylic on canvas, triptych 7 × 13½ ft. overall. Private collection, The Netherlands.

OVERLEAF: PHOTO COURTESY ROBERT MILLER GALLERY

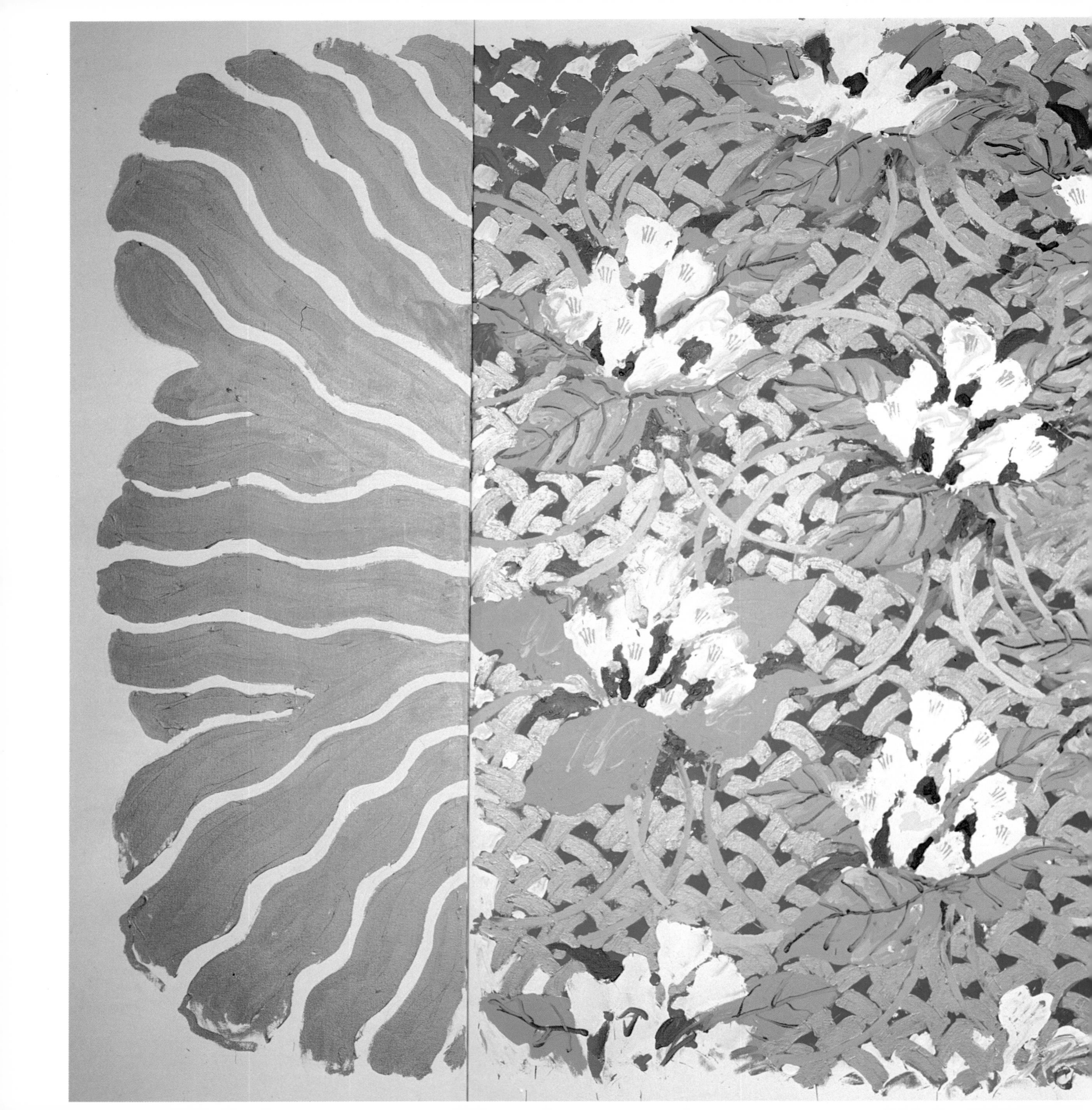

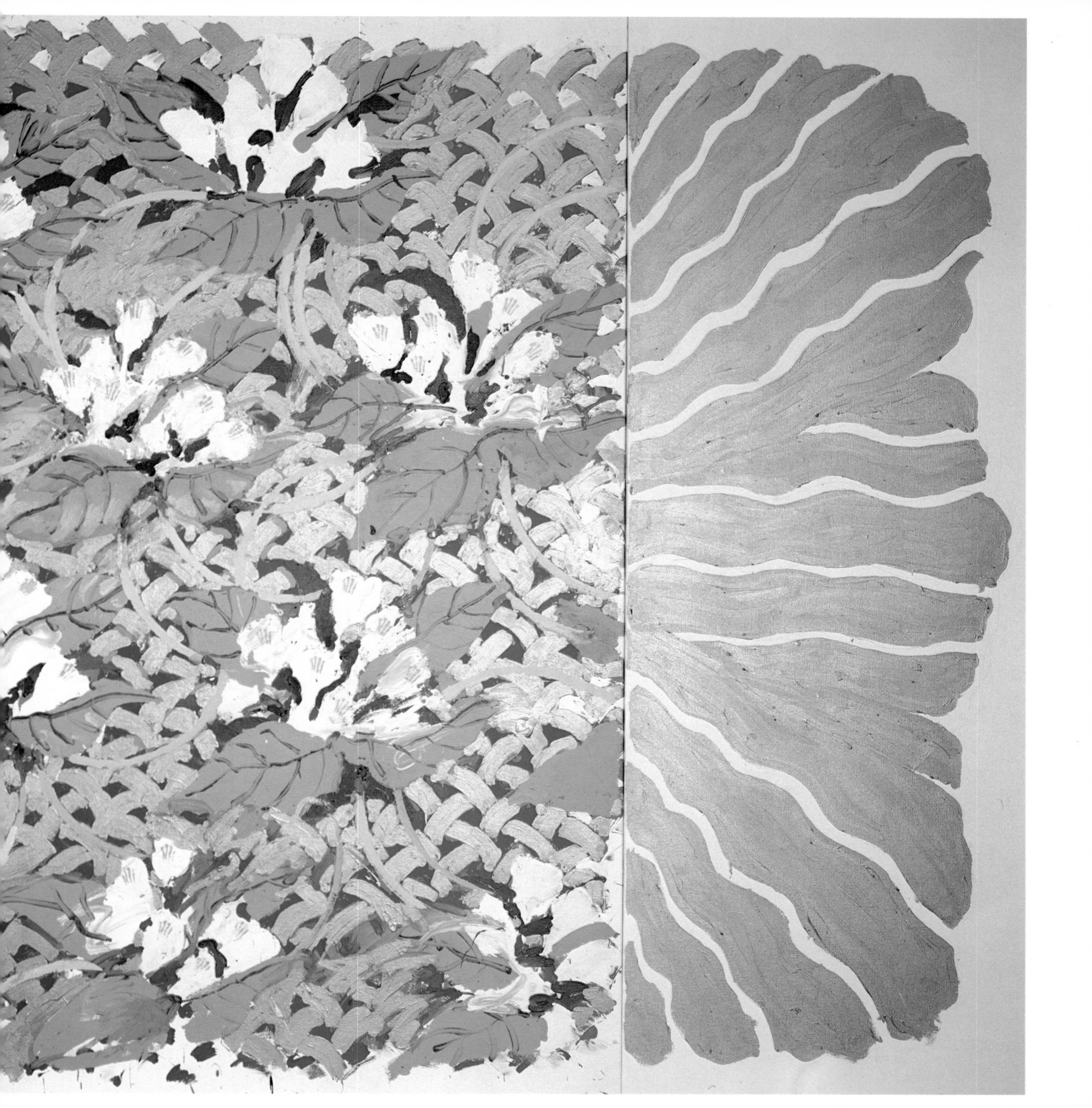

PHOTO COURTESY HOLLY SOLOMON GALLERY

ABOVE: Rodney Ripps, "Stargazing with Helene in the Spring," 1980, oil, cloth, and wax on wood, 122 × 88 × 10 in. Private collection, New York.

OPPOSITE: Rodney Ripps, pieces excerpted from "Spring's Chapel" installation, 1980, oil, cloth, and wax on wood, each piece 100 × 42 in. TOP, LEFT TO RIGHT: "Lilly Pond," collection of the artist; "The Storm," collection of the artist; "The Meadow," private collection; "Wild Flowers," private collection. BOTTOM, LEFT TO RIGHT: "Lilacs"; "Twilight," private collection, New York; "Cherry Blossoms," collection, C. Esswein, Karlsruhe, West Germany; "Tempest," private collection.

PHOTOS COURTESY HOLLY SOLOMON GALLERY

PHOTOS EEVA-INKERI, COURTESY A.I.R. GALLERY

TOP LEFT: Patsy Norvell, "Glass Garden" (foreground) and "Henrietta's Amethyst" (background), 1978–80, A.I.R. Gallery installation view. "Glass Garden," Woodlife painted frame, etched glass, plants and flowers, 102 × 90 × 94 in. "Henrietta's Amethyst," painted wood base, Plexiglas, mineral oil and dye, column heights 6½ ft. to 7½ ft. TOP RIGHT: "Closed Tulip," etched glass panel detail from "Glass Garden." BOTTOM AND OPPOSITE: Details from "Glass Garden."

PHOTO OPPOSITE PAGE EEVA-INKERI, COURTESY A.I.R. GALLERY

PHOTO JANE COURTNEY FRISSE

ABOVE: Joyce Kozloff, "An Interior Decorated," 1979, tile and grout on plywood, silk-screen on silk, and lithographs on silk backed with rice paper, Everson Museum installation view. Painting on rear wall: "Striped Cathedral," 1976–77, acrylic on canvas, 6 × 15 ft. Collection of the artist.

OPPOSITE, LEFT SIDE: Joyce Kozloff, "Pilaster," 1979, tile, grout, and plywood, 8 ft. × 8 in. Collection Tibor de Nagy. RIGHT SIDE: "Pilaster," 1979, tile, grout, and plywood, 8 ft. × 8 in. Collection, Dr. Peter Ludwig, Aachen, West Germany.

OPPOSITE, CENTER, CLOCKWISE FROM UPPER LEFT: Joyce Kozloff, "Spinning Off," 1980, ceramics, tile, grout, and plywood, 18½ × 19½ in. Collection, Mr. and Mrs. George J. York. "Tile Multiple," 1980, tile, grout, and plywood, 24 × 24 in. "If I Were an Astronomer, p. 3," "p. 5," and "p. 7," 1977, collage, markers, and colored pencil, each 15 × 11½ in. "If I Were a Botanist, p. 8," 1977, collage, markers, and colored pencil, 15 × 11½ in. Collection, Max Kozloff.

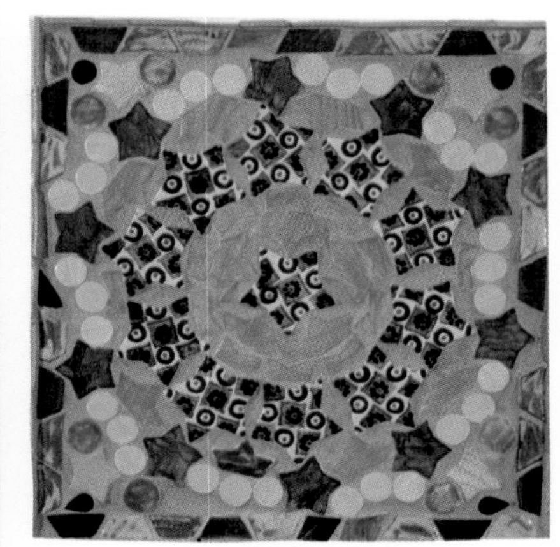

PHOTO THOMAS W. ROSE

PHOTO COURTESY BARBARA GLADSTONE GALLERY

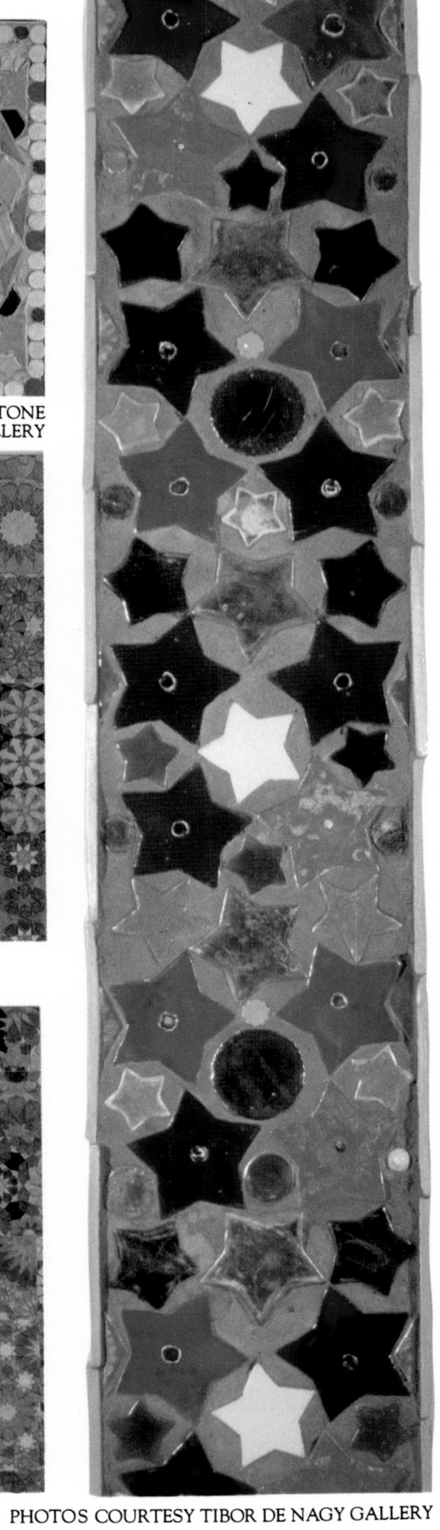

PHOTOS COURTESY TIBOR DE NAGY GALLERY

PHOTOS THOMAS W. ROSE, COURTESY TIBOR DE NAGY GALLERY

ABOVE LEFT: Joyce Kozloff and Betty Woodman collaboration, "Purple Toucan Pitcher," 1981, glazed earthenware, 17 × 16 × 8½ in. Collection, Betty Woodman. RIGHT: "Chrysanthemum Vase," 1981, glazed earthenware, 14 in. high. Collection, Robert Kushner.

OPPOSITE: Joyce Kozloff and Arlene Slavin collaboration, "Slavin-Bregman Fireplace," 1980, tile, grout, board, and latex wall mural.

PHOTO OPPOSITE PAGE EEVA-INKERI, COURTESY TIBOR DE NAGY GALLERY

PHOTOS COURTESY ALEXANDER F. MILLIKEN GALLERY

PHOTO COURTESY ALEXANDER F. MILLIKEN GALLERY

OPPOSITE, TOP LEFT: Arlene Slavin, "Heron Mural," 1978, latex paint on walls. Barbara and Eugene Schwartz apartment. TOP RIGHT: "Waterbird Mural," 1979, acrylic paint on walls, Alexander F. Milliken Gallery installation view. BOTTOM: "Dancing Cranes Screen, Side I," 1980, acrylic on plywood, 8 × 6 ft.

ABOVE: Arlene Slavin, "Waterbird Mural," 1979, acrylic paint on walls, Alexander F. Milliken Gallery installation view.

PHOTO D. JAMES DEE, COURTESY BARBARA GLADSTONE GALLERY

ABOVE: Miriam Shapiro, "Bird in Paradise," 1981, acrylic and fabric on canvas, 36 × 36 in. Private collection, Scottsdale, Arizona.

OPPOSITE, TOP: Miriam Shapiro, "Baby Block Bouquet," 1981, acrylic and fabric on canvas, 69 × 63 in. Collection, Louis Hornick & Company, New York City. BOTTOM: "Medusa," 1981, acrylic and fabric on canvas, six panels 84 × 168 in. overall. Collection, Mr. and Mrs. Robert W. Schneebeck, Cincinnati, Ohio.

OVER: Miriam Shapiro, "Black Bolero," 1980, acrylic, fabric, and glitter on canvas, 72 × 144 in.

PHOTOS D. JAMES DEE, COURTESY BARBARA GLADSTONE GALLERY

OVERLEAF: PHOTO D. JAMES DEE, COURTESY BARBARA GLADSTONE GALLERY

LEFT: Richard Kalina, "Mandalay," 1980, oil on canvas, 70 × 40 in. Collection, Louis Hornick & Company, New York. RIGHT: "Kansas," 1980, oil on canvas, 70 × 40 in. Private collection, Sweden.

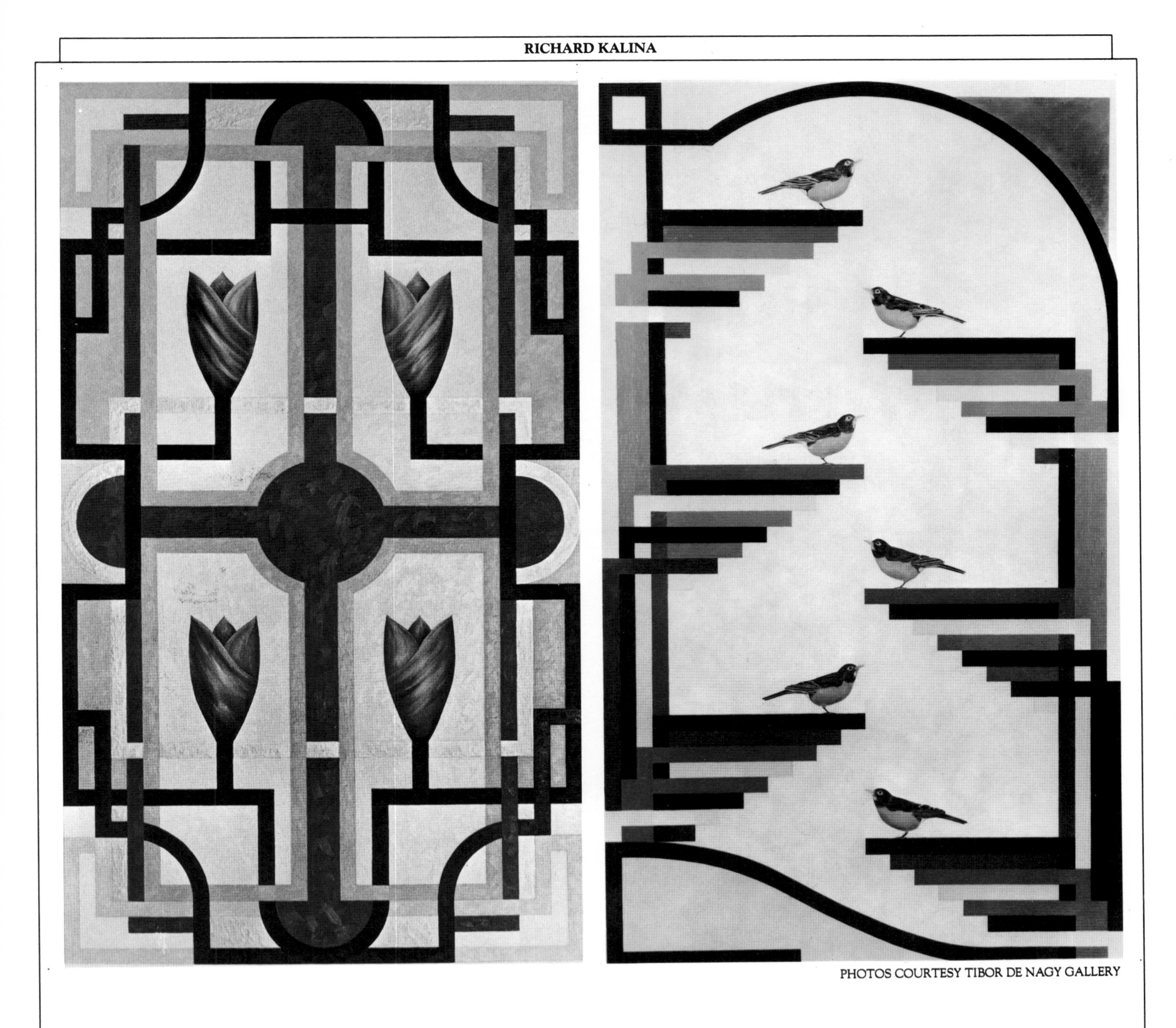

PHOTOS COURTESY TIBOR DE NAGY GALLERY

LEFT: Richard Kalina, "Philidor," 1979, oil on canvas, 84 × 48 in. Private collection, New York. RIGHT: "Equinox," 1979, oil on canvas, 70 × 40 in. Collection, Morton G. Neumann family, Chicago.

PHOTOS COURTESY ROBERT FREIDUS GALLERY

TOP LEFT: Jennifer Cecere, "Bed Model," 1981, acrylic on lace with sequins and cardboard base with fiberfill, 9½ × 13½ × 7 in. TOP RIGHT: "Chair," 1980, acrylic on lace with wood frame and fiberfill, 33 × 16 × 17 in. BOTTOM LEFT: "Faux Bed," 1981, acrylic on lace with sequins, wood, and Styrofoam base with fiberfill, 52 × 66 × 48 in. BOTTOM RIGHT: "Sofa," 1979, acrylic on lace, collaged doilies and antimacassars, and cotton duck with fiberfill stuffing and Styrofoam frame, 26 × 63 × 32 in. Collection, Don and Mera Rubell, New York.

OPPOSITE: Jennifer Cecere, "Cat Throne," 1980, acrylic on lace with wood frame, 25 × 26 × 18 in.

PHOTO COURTESY ROBERT FREIDUS GALLERY

A Directory of Crafts & Furnishings

This directory lists certain craft and furnishing designers who have come to the authors' attention during the writing of *Ornamentalism*. It also includes an abbreviated list of craft organizations within the United States and the location of galleries and showrooms where Ornamentalist furniture and lighting can be found. This directory is not meant to be representative of the vast number of craft and furnishing designers now working in the United States. For anyone interested in such an overview, two current source books might be useful: Brent C. Brolin and Jean Richards, *Sourcebook of Architectural Ornament: Designers, Craftsmen, Manufacturers and Distributors of Custom and Ready-made Exterior Ornament*, Van Nostrand Reinhold Co. (New York, 1982), and Lynne Lapin, ed., *Craftworker's Market*, Writer's Digest Publishers (Cincinnati, 1982). Lapin's book is revised and reissued each year.

Glasswork

Valerie Arber
P.O. Box 10121
Alameda, NM 87184

Bedford/Downing Glass
202 E. 83rd Street
New York, NY 10028
Contact: Ingo Williams (**p. 174**)

Ed Carpenter
3125 Van Waters
Milwaukie, OR 97222

James Carpenter Associates
47 West Street
New York, NY 10006
Contact: James Carpenter (**pp. 170, 171**)

Dale Chihuly (pp. 170, 171)
115 Williams Street
Providence, RI 02906

Dufour Glass Studios
P.O. Box 336
Baton Rouge, LA 70821
Contact:
Paul Dufour (**p. 169**),
Charles Devillier (**pp. 168, 169**),
Samuel Corso (**pp. 168, 169**)

Fire Island Hot Glass Studio
Chestnut and Main Streets
Bastrop, TX 78602
Contact: Richard Burns, Mathew LaBarbera

Glasssearch
Creative Arts Center
122 E. 5th Street
Dallas, TX 75203
Contact: Jim Bowman, Roal Enix

James Harmon
Art Department, Glass
2535 Mall Manoa
Honolulu, HI 96822

Steve Hecht
1949 Welch Street
Houston, TX 77109

Gene Hester
2704 Sackett Street
Houston, TX 77098

Kazanjian Stained Glass
423 Pier Avenue
Hermosa, CA 90254

Ray King (pp. 176–78)
603 S. 10th Street
Philadelphia, PA 19147

Peter Mollica
10033 Broadway Terrace
Oakland, CA 94611

William Morris
P.O. Box 3966
Carmel, CA 93921

Brigitte Pasternak
301 River Road
Grandview, NY 10960

Drew Patterson
2012 E. 6th Street
Austin, TX 78702

Flo Perkins
Route 5, P.O. Box 322F
Sante Fe, NM 87501

K. M. Phillips Studio
5423 Walnut Street
Pittsburgh, PA 15232
Contact: Ken Phillips **(pp. 172, 173)**

Phoenix Studios
374 Fore Street
Portland, ME 04101
Contact: Malcomb Mailloux, Arthur Davis, John Laberge, D. William Johnson

Narcissus Quagliata
1550 Bryant Street
San Francisco, CA 94103

Renaissance Glass Co.
1013C W. 34th Street
Austin, TX 78705
Contact: Susan Stinsmuehlen, **(pp. 164–167)**, Rodney Smith

Jeff Smith
2416 McKinney Avenue
Studio 8
Dallas, TX 75201

Robert Sowers (p. 174)
303 Degraw Street
Brooklyn, NY 11231

David Traub
P.O. Box 360
Brownsboro, TX 75756

Kenneth vonRoenn (p. 175)
17 Bradley Avenue
Branford, CT 06405

Patrick Wadley
19131 Cliff Street
Austin, TX 78705

Claire Wing
1520 W. 9th Street
Dallas, TX 75208

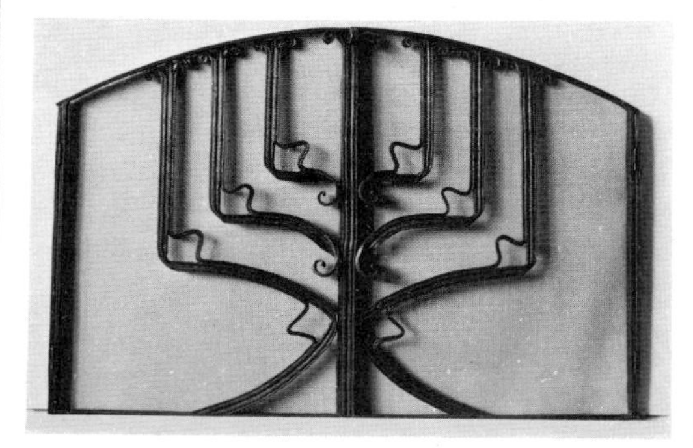

Metalwork

Antares Forge and Metalworks
501 11th Street
Brooklyn, NY 11215
Contact: David Zatz **(pp. 179–81)**

Ivan Bailey Studio
1260 Foster Street N.W., Bldg. 4
Atlanta, GA 30318
Contact: Ivan Bailey

Blue Goose Forge
1190 Main Street
Plain, WI 53577
Contact: Eric Moebius

Bondi Metals
4360 East Shore Highway
Emeryville, CA 94608
Contact: Stephen and Michael Bondi

Tom Bredlow, Metalworker
1827 E. Limberlost Street
Tucson, AZ 85719

Cedar Creek Forge
North 70 West 6340 Bridge Road
Cedarberg, WI 53012
Contact: Leon Piwoni, Jim English

Creative Metal Crafts, Inc.
1708 Berkley Street
Santa Monica, CA 90404
Contact: George Martin

De Leon Ornamental Iron
Route 2, P.O. Box 216B
Santa Fe, NM 87501
Contact: Rolando De Leon

Fire-fly Forge
Black Hall Road, RFD 1
Epsom, NH 03234
Contact: Jennifer Sayre, Kathleen Daigle

Dimitri Gerakaris (p. 189)
Upper Gates Road, RFD 2
North Canaan, NH 03741

Gregory Litsios
198 Oxford Street
Rochester, NY 14607

Robert Owings Metal Design
615 2nd Street
Petaluma, CA 94952
Contact: Robert Owings

Albert Paley, (pp. 182–85)
335 Aberdeen Street
Rochester, NY 14619

Christopher Ray (pp. 186, 187)
315 E. Wister Street
Philadelphia, PA 19144

Steven Rosenberg
148 Old Long Ridge Road
Stamford, CT 06903

Schwartz's Forge and Metalworks
P.O. Box 205, Forge Hollow Road
Deansboro, NY 13328
Contact: Joel Schwartz **(p. 188)**

Richard Sextone
Peter's Valley Craft Center
Peter's Valley
Layton, NJ 07851

Upper Bank Forge
Valleybrook Road
Wawa, PA 19063
Contact: Gregg Leavitt **(pp. 190–91)**

Brushwork

Arno Grelack Interiors
1 Ridgerock Lane
East Norwich, NY 11732
Contact: Arno Grelack

David Barrett
131 E. 71st Street
New York, NY 10021

Neel Bate
337 W. 22nd Street
New York, NY 10011

William Bell (pp. 196, 197)
18 Marshall Street
Norwalk, CT 06854

Adele Bishop (pp. 206, 207)
P.O. Box 64
Dorset, VT 05251

Eloi Bordelon (pp. 202, 203)
308 E. 79th Street
New York, NY 10021

Craftsmen Decorators
2611 Ocean Avenue
Brooklyn, NY 11229
Contact: Howard Zucker

Creative Painted Finishes
175 Stuyvesant Avenue
Rye, NY 10580
Contact: Alice Beringer,
Sarah W. Vorder Bruegge

Cricket Cage
Route 10
Denville, NJ 07834
Contact: June Meier

Nicholas Crowell (p. 205)
248 E. 90th Street
New York, NY 10028

Decorative Painted Finishes
13 Walden Place
West Caldwell, NJ 07006
Contact: Harriet Pomerance

Dimmler Studios
330 Lafayette Street
New York, NY 10012
Contact: Richard Dimmler **(p. 209)**,
Suzanne Dimmler

Kakia Livanos (pp. 198, 199)
116 E. 63rd Street
New York, NY 10021

Cile Lord (pp. 206, 208)
42 E. 12th Street
New York, NY 10003

Hight Moore
33 Stuyvesant Street
New York, NY 10003

Richard Lowell Neas (p. 204)
157 E. 71st Street
New York, NY 10021

Isabel O'Neil Studio Workshop
177 E. 87th Street
New York, NY 10028
Contact: Kakia Livanos

Painted Finish, Ltd.
Mead Street
Waccabuc, NY 10597
Contact: Joan Kane

Megan Parry, (pp. 192–95)
1727 Spruce Street
Boulder, CO 80302

Philip Standish Read, (pp. 200, 201)
P.O. Box 204
Brookhaven, NY 11719

Conrad Schmitt Studios
2405 S. 162nd Street
New Berlin, WI 53151
Contact: Conrad Schmitt

David Scott-Melville
P.O. Box 2889
Taos, NM 87571

Dorothy Slover
9460 River Road
Potomac, MD 20854

Nat Weinstein
489 27th Street
San Francisco, CA 94131

Craft Organizations

Allied Arts of Seattle
107 S. Main Street
Seattle, WA 98104
Contact: Mary Owen

American Craft Council
22 W. 55th Street
New York, NY 10019
Contact: Joanne Polster

American Craft Museum and Library
44 W. 53rd Street
New York, NY 10019
Contact: Joanne Polster

Artist-Blacksmiths Association of North America
5029 Montcrest Drive
Chattanooga, TN 37416
Contact: Joe Humble

Baycrafters
28795 Lake Road
Huntington Metropark, OH 44140
Contact: Sally Price

California Blacksmith Association
737 Dwight Way
Berkeley, CA 94710
Contact: Raffi Bedayn

Connecticut Guild of Craftsmen, Inc.
P.O. Box 155
New Britain, CT 06050
Contact: Joseph Mehan

Contemporary Crafts Association
3934 S.W. Corbett Avenue
Portland, OR 97201
Contact: Marlene Gabel

Craft Guild of Dallas
6923 Snider Plaza
Dallas, TX 75080
Contact: Catherine Claman

Empire State Crafts Alliance
9 Vassar Street
Poughkeepsie, NY 12601
Contact: Mary Fiad

Florida Craftsmen
Route 1, P.O. Box 327K
Melrose, FL 32666
Contact: Raymond C. Ferguson

Glass Art Society, Inc.
122 Market Street
Amesbury, MA 01913
Contact: Dan Dailey

Indiana Artist-Craftsmen, Inc.
5254 Moonlight Drive
Indianapolis, IN 46226
Contact: Cecelia D. Barron

Long Island Craftsmen's Guild
P.O. Box 221
Sea Cliff, NY 11579

Louisiana Crafts Council
139 Broadway
New Orleans, LA 70118
Contact: Mary Lynn Eckert

National Wood Carvers Association
7424 Miami Avenue
Cincinnati, OH 45243
Contact: Edward Gallenstein

Nebraska Crafts Council
Department of Art
Kearney State College
Kearney, NB 68847
Contact: Ray Schultz

Ohio Arts & Crafts Guild
9 N. Main Street
Mt. Vernon, OH 43050
Contact: Duke Wagoner

Oregon School of Arts and Crafts
8245 S.W. Barnes Road
Portland, OR 97225
Contact: Nan Tupper-Malone

Pennsylvania Guild of Craftsmen, Inc.
P.O. Box 618
Bedford, PA 15522
Contact: Lyn Jackson

Wisconsin Designer Craftsmen
2742 N. 95th Street
Milwaukee, WI 53222
Contact: Brian Sullivan

Furniture & Lighting Designers

The Alessandro Collection (pp. 230, 231)
315 E. 62nd Street
New York, NY 10021
Contact: Sal Lanza

Fabio Alvim (p. 224)
Art et Industrie
464 West Broadway
New York, NY 10012

Gary Knox Bennett (pp. 221, 222)
1011 Grand Street
Alameda, CA 94501

Wendel Castle (pp.222, 223)
18 Maple Street
Scottville, NY 14546

Michele De Lucchi (p. 228)
Art et Industrie
464 West Broadway
New York, NY 10012

Steve Ditch and Molly Amsler (p. 229)
113 W. 28th Street
New York, NY 10001

James Evenson Associates (p. 225)
1 Bond Street
New York, NY 10012
Contact: James Evenson

Pedro Friedeberg (p. 237)
Apartado Postal 6-613
Mexico City, 6DF, Mexico

Robert Haussmann and Trix Haussmann-Högl (p. 224)
Mittelstrasse 47
8008 Zurich, Switzerland

Rory McCarthy
3147 E. Ft. Lowell Road
Tucson, AZ 85716

Judy Kensley McKie (pp. 216–19)
462 Putnam Avenue
Cambridge, MA 02139

Laura and Terrence Main
224 Eighth Avenue
New York, NY 10011

Wendy Maruyama
Appalachian Center for Craft
P.O. Box 347, A-1
Smithville, TN 37166

Howard Meister (p. 224)
191 State Street
Brooklyn, NY 11201

Alessandro Mendini (pp. 210, 227)
Editoriale Domus
Viale Del Ghisallo 20
20151 Milan, Italy

Paola Navone (p. 226)
Art et Industrie
464 West Broadway
New York, NY 10012

Richard Scott Newman
66 Frost Avenue
Rochester, NY 14608

Dana Simmons
East Main Road
Little Compton, RI 02837

Sherle Wagner International (p. 232)
60 E. 57th Street
New York, NY 10022
Contact: Vince Geoffroy

Ettore Sottsass, Jr. (p. 226)
Barbara Radice
11 Via S. Caldino
Milan, Italy

Tigerdale Studios, Inc. (pp. 233–35)
1931 Bay Street
Los Angeles, CA 90021
Contact: Jim Tigerman, Norman List

UFO (p. 228)
Art et Industrie
464 West Broadway
New York, NY 10012

Trent Whitington (p. 215)
441 Whiskey Hill Road
Woodside, CA 94062

Joy Wulke
333 Central Park West
New York, NY 10025

Edward Zucca (p. 220)
Route 1
Park Street
Putnam, CT 06260

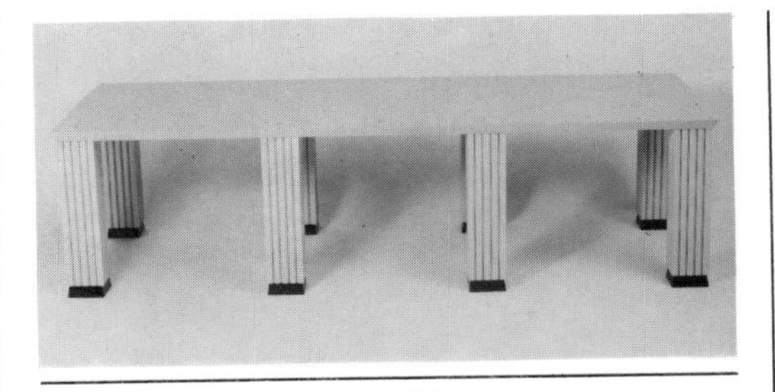

Galleries & Showrooms

American Art Inc.
56 E. Andrews Drive N.W.
Andrews Square
Atlanta, GA 30305
Contact: Robert W. Farrar

Art et Industrie
464 West Broadway
New York, NY 10012
Contact: Rick Kaufman

Richard Kagen Gallery
326 South Street
Philadelphia, PA 19147
Contact: Richard Kagen or Steve Johnson

Knoll International

Pacific Design Center
8687 Melrose Avenue
Los Angeles, CA 90069
Contact: George Kordaris

1111 Merchandise Mart
Chicago, IL 60654
Contact: Bob Hinmann

655 Madison Avenue
New York, NY 10021
Contact: Jana Goldin

676 World Trade Center
Dallas, TX 75207
Contact: Steve Duinick

Light Inc.
1162 Second Avenue
New York, NY 10021
Contact: Ralph Jacobowitz

Alexander F. Milliken, Inc.
98 Prince Street
New York, NY 10012
Contact: Alexander F. Milliken

Pritan and Eames
29 Race Lane
East Hampton, NY 11937
Contact: Bebe or Warren Johnson

Los Robles
167 Hamilton Avenue
Palo Alto, CA 94301
Contact: Milton Seick

Signature: A Gallery of Furnishings
55 Pacific Avenue
San Francisco, CA 94133
Contact: Dan or Cynthia Gordon

Sunar

Suite 206
Pacific Design Center
8687 Melrose Avenue
Los Angeles, CA 94133
Contact: John Franzese

Suite 988
Merchandise Mart
Chicago, IL 60654
Contact: David Betanski

730 Fifth Avenue, Room 612
New York, NY 10019
Contact: Roy Lamendola

Suite 100
Pace Tower
3700 Buffalo Speedway
Houston, TX 77098
Contact: Bob McGregor

Workbench Gallery
470 Park Avenue South
New York, NY 10016
Contact: Judy Coady

The Works Gallery
319 South Street
Philadelphia, PA 19147
Contact: Ruth or Rick Snyderman

Index

Numbers in italic refer to names or terms in captions.

Photography Sources

The text of this book was set in Goudy Old Style, designed by Frederic William Goudy, who died in 1947 at the age of eighty-two. He designed more than a hundred different typefaces. His Goudy Old Style has had a strong influence on type style in American periodicals and advertising. He began his career as a bookkeeper in the Midwest. At the sight of some newly published works of the Kelmscott Press he was determined to bring understanding of the new movement of William Morris to printers in the United States. Goudy Old Style has the smoothness and evenness of color and generous width of curves that are found in most of the designer's best typefaces. The book was composed by Publishers Phototype Inc. in Carlstadt, New Jersey, and printed and bound by Toppan Printing Co. (America), Inc., in Japan.

Edited by Carol Southern
Editorial assistance by Kathy Powell
Editorial production by Virginia Wentworth
Production supervision by Jane Treuhaft
Production assistance by Lynne Arany
Design by Hermann Strohbach